THE

GUIDE TO NORTH AMERICA'S THEME PARKS

SECOND EDITION

THE

GUIDE TO
NORTH AMERICA'S
THEME PARKS

SECOND EDITION

American Automobile Association

Revised and Updated by Doreen Russo

Collier Books
Macmillan Publishing Company
New York

Maxwell Macmillan Canada
Toronto

Maxwell Macmillan International
New York   Oxford   Singapore   Sydney

Collier Books   Maxwell Macmillan Canada, Inc.
Macmillan Publishing Company   1200 Eglinton Avenue East
866 Third Avenue   Suite 200
New York, NY 10022   Don Mills, Ontario M3C 3N1

Macmillan Publishing Company is part of the Maxwell Communication Group of Companies.

Library of Congress Cataloging-in-Publication Data

The AAA guide to North America's theme parks / American Automobile
  Association.—2nd ed., rev. and updated / by Doreen Russo.
      p.   cm.
  "First Collier Books edition."
  Includes index.
  ISBN 0-02-030251-7
  1. Amusement parks—United States—Directories.   2. Amusement
parks—Canada—Directories.   I. Russo, Doreen.   II. American
Automobile Association.
  GV1853.2.A33   1992
  791.06′8′0257—dc20   91-33196
                      CIP

Macmillan books are available at special discounts for bulk purchases for sales promotions, premiums, fund-raising, or educational use. For details, contact:

Special Sales Director
Macmillan Publishing Company
866 Third Avenue
New York, NY 10022

First Collier Books Edition 1992

10 9 8 7 6 5 4 3 2 1

Printed in the United States of America

CONTENTS

EDITOR'S NOTE

All operating seasons and hours, admission fees, rides, events, and shows listed in this book are subject to change—and in fact do change frequently. We suggest you check with the park before arriving to get the latest information.

HELPFUL TIPS ON MAKING YOUR VISIT MORE ENJOYABLE

Since the parks are at their most crowded during July and August, plan your visit, if possible for before or after those months. No matter what time of year you visit, the parks are always less crowded on weekdays than weekends, the earlier in the week the better. Try to arrive as early in the day as possible, by the posted opening time at the latest, and make sure you allow yourself enough time to see all that you want to see.

As soon as you arrive at the park, pick up a map and show schedule and decide which rides, attractions, and shows you want to be sure to see. Then plot your course. Try to pace yourself—it may be a good idea to schedule a show every couple of hours as a break. Remember that shows tend to fill up quickly, so get there at least 15 minutes before showtime to be sure to get a seat (even earlier to get a good seat). Keep in mind that the best way to beat the crowds is to try to do the opposite of what everyone else is doing. Some tips: Start in the back of the park and work your way to the front; visit the most popular rides and attractions first; eat your meals at off hours—before noon or after 2 P.M.; and do your souvenir shopping as you go along since most people shop at the end of the day.

Remember that you'll be spending a *full* day walking, standing, and moving around, so dress appropriately: Wear loose-fitting clothes, comfortable walking shoes, and if you're visiting a park with water-related rides, clothes that dry easily since you will get wet. Bear in mind that in most cases you will be out in the bright sunshine all day, so be sure to bring sunscreen, sunglasses, and a hat.

If you're visiting a water park, don't forget your swimsuit and a towel. And note that most water parks do not allow cutoffs or swimwear with exposed metal fasteners.

HELPFUL TIPS ON MAKING YOUR VISIT MORE ENJOYABLE

PREFACE

Wild roller coasters and handfuls of tickets. Hot dogs and ice cream and places for picnics. Carousel horses in colors of spring . . . These are a few of the favorite things lyricist Oscar Hammerstein might add if he were writing "My Favorite Things" for *The Sound of Music* today. For millions of tourists each year, these things mean theme parks.

Few experiences are as unique to North American travel. From Walt Disney World in Florida to Knott's Berry Farm in California to Canada's Wonderland in Ontario, theme parks provide a variety of activities in a single colorful, consolidated package. Most states and many Canadian provinces have at least one theme park, and the themes vary as much as the tourists they attract.

Some parks transport visitors to future worlds of imagination. Others take them to old worlds of tradition. Many offer musical revues or petting zoos or craft fairs. And *all* have rides.

To help visitors decipher which park has what, how much a full day will cost, and where to find the best parks, the travel experts at the American Automobile Association have compiled the AAA *Guide to North America's Theme Parks.*

AAA began publishing travel guides in the 1920s and today distributes more than 35 million travel publications annually. As the world's largest travel and motoring services organization, AAA is dedicated to making travel safe, comfortable, and enjoyable for the association's 32 million members and the general public.

The AAA *Guide to North America's Theme Parks* is another opportunity for the association to provide a needed travel service. Describing more than 100 parks in the United States and Canada, the guide includes complete, up-to-date listings of rides and attractions, restaurants and snack bars, admission fees and schedules, directions and accommodations.

So, with guide in hand, have fun exploring some of the favorite things North America has to offer—its theme parks.

Alex Gamble
DIRECTOR OF CONSUMER PUBLICATIONS
AMERICAN AUTOMOBILE ASSOCIATION
APRIL, 1992

NORTHEAST

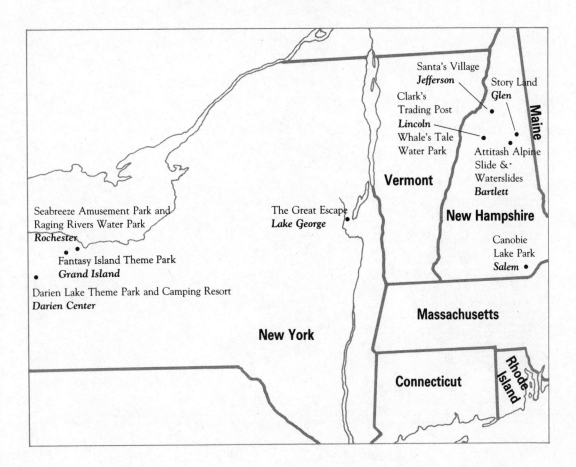

Santa's Village
Jefferson

Story Land
Glen

Clark's
Trading Post
Lincoln
Whale's Tale
Water Park

Attitash Alpine
Slide &
Waterslides
Bartlett

Maine

Vermont

New Hampshire

Seabreeze Amusement Park and
Raging Rivers Water Park
Rochester

Fantasy Island Theme Park
Grand Island

Darien Lake Theme Park and Camping Resort
Darien Center

The Great Escape
Lake George

Canobie
Lake Park
Salem

Massachusetts

New York

Connecticut

Rhode
Island

NEW HAMPSHIRE

ATTITASH ALPINE SLIDE & WATERSLIDES

Half a million guests each year take in the family-oriented activities of Attitash Alpine Slide & Waterslides. The Alpine Slide combines a scenic ride aboard the Attitash skylift and a thrilling ¾-mile slide down and across mountain meadows and woods. Visitors can also try the refreshing water slides and the all new Scenic Chairlift Ride.

ADDRESS AND TELEPHONE

Attitash Alpine Slide & Waterslides
U. S. Route 302
Bartlett, NH 03812

(603) 374-2368

LOCATION

Attitash Alpine Slide is located east of Bartlett on Route 302.

OPERATING SEASONS AND HOURS

Alpine Slide is open weekends from the end of May to June and in September and October. Hours: 10 A.M. to 5 P.M.

All slides are open daily from the end of June to September. Hours: 10 A.M. to 6 P.M.

ADMISSION FEES

For one ride on the Alpine Slide and 30 minutes on the water slides: Adults: $5. Children ages 5 to 12: $4. Children under 4: free. Seniors 70 and over: free.

For unlimited use of the Alpine Slide and one hour on the waterslides: Adults: $14. Children under 4: free. Seniors 70 and over: free.

TRANSPORTATION AND ACCOMMODATIONS WITHIN THE PARK

None.

GUEST SERVICES

Restrooms, telephones, first aid, day lockers. Visa, MasterCard, American Express, and Discover cards accepted.

RIDES

Alpine Slide: combines scenic ride up the Attitash skylift and ¾-mile slide down. You control the speed.

Aquaboggan Waterslides: swoosh down these speedy, splashing slides.

Scenic Chairlift Rides: view the breathtaking White Mountains as you travel to the Observation Tower.

SPECIAL ANNUAL EVENT

Half-price Father's Day special in June.

RESTAURANTS

None.

SNACK BARS

Cafeteria: sandwiches, burgers, hot dogs, pizza, tacos, drinks.
Ice Cream Shop

CATERING

Not available.

SOUVENIR SHOP

T-shirts, candy, film, sunglasses, Attitash mementos.

CANOBIE LAKE PARK

Canobie Lake Park ranks as one of the most beautiful amusement parks in the country and is among New England's most popular entertainment centers. Opened in 1902, the 80-acre park features rides, attractions, and games for the entire family, including four thrilling roller coasters, an antique carousel, a 24-gauge steam train, an authentic paddlewheel riverboat, an exhilarating log flume, a swinging pirate ship, and a dramatic haunted mine. Other delights include spectacular fireworks displays, costumed characters and specialty acts, tree-lined promenades, flower gardens, and a tranquil lake setting.

ADDRESS AND TELEPHONE

Canobie Lake Park
P. O. Box 190
Salem, NH 03079

(603) 893-3506

LOCATION

Canobie Lake Park is in Salem, just across the Massachusetts border, in southeastern New Hampshire. From Boston take I-93 north to exit 2 in Salem.

OPERATING SEASONS AND HOURS

Open weekends from mid-April to mid-May. Hours: 12 P.M. to 6 P.M.

Open daily from Memorial Day to Labor Day. Hours: noon to 10 P.M. Opening and closing times vary, so check with the park before arriving.

ADMISSION FEES

Adults: $13. Children under 4 feet tall: $8. Seniors 60 and over: $8.

TRANSPORTATION AND ACCOMMODATIONS WITHIN THE PARK

None.

GUEST SERVICES

Restrooms, telephones, information booth, first aid, lost and found, lockers, stroller and wheelchair rental. Visa and MasterCard cards accepted.

RIDES

Antique Carousel: ride on handcarved horses.
Antique Cars: drive your own old-time auto.
Canobie Corkscrew: corkscrew roller coaster.
Canobie 500: race your own car on a junior track.
Canobie Queen Paddlewheel Riverboat: cruise on an authentic southern-style paddleboat and watch the magic of the old Mississippi come alive.
Caterpillar: circular ride with covered caterpillar top.
Crazy Cups: whirl about in colorful cups.
Dodgem: bumper cars.
Galaxy: smaller roller coaster with its share of thrills.
Giant Skywheel: award-winning Ferris wheel.
Haunted Mine: get set to be spooked on this dark ride.
Kosmo Jets: control your own spaceship and take part in a laser battle.
Log Flume: speed down a turn-of-the-century sawmill log flume.
Matterhorn: bobsled-style ride that speeds you around.
Mirror Maze: glass house with mirrors.
Missile: get ready to blast off in a giant rocket that tilts upward.
Moon Orbiter: board a spaceship that circles the moon.
Paratrooper: ride a tilted Ferris wheel and watch the bottom drop out.
Pirate Ship: experience the thrills of pirating on this replica of a Spanish galleon.
Psychodrome: ride an indoor scrambler with fog and strobe lights.
Round Up: centrifugal force holds you in place.
Rowdy Roosters: large roosters swing in a circle.
Sky Ride: get a sky-high view of the park.
Steam Train: journey on this 24-gauge train.
Tilt-a-Whirl: spin around, then tilt.
Turkish Twist: spin in a circle while standing up.
Vertigo Theatre: a dizzying experience.
Yankee Cannonball: built in 1936, this giant coaster is one of the few vintage ones still in operation today.

KIDDIE RIDES

Autobahn: a small sports car track especially for kids.
Fire Engines: fire engines go around a track.
Helicopter: minicopters.
Jr. Carousel: mini merry-go-round.
Jr. Tanks and Boats: float in a circle.
Jr. Turnpike: junior-sized sports car.
Kiddie Canoes: a gentle canoe ride in the water.
Kiddie Jeeps: minijeeps move in a circle.
Land-Sea Rescue: helicopters, planes, and boats move in a circle.
Mini-Bumpers: little bumper cars.
Pony Carts: circular ride in a pony cart.
Sky Fighter: flights into the air.

ATTRACTIONS AND GAMES

Costumed Characters: Boris the Bear, Winslow Farnsworthy III, Ollie the Skunk, and Pinky the Blue Elephant roam the park daily, greeting kids and adults alike.
Games: Over 30 games of skill are located throughout the park.

SHOWS

Fireworks: see the sky ablaze in color with fireworks displays every Saturday night in July and August.
High-tech musical extravaganzas and specialty acts entertain visitors. Shows and schedules vary, so check the park before arriving.

SPECIAL ANNUAL EVENTS

Annual Corvette Show: in late May.
Annual Antique and Street Rod Show: in July.

RESTAURANT

Portofino Restaurant: lakeside restaurant that features pasta, pizza, and other Italian specialties.

SNACK BARS

Food stands located throughout the park serve hot dogs, burgers, ice cream, candy, soft drinks.

CATERING

Contact Marriott Corporation at (603) 893-6443.

SOUVENIR SHOPS

Three shops offer T-shirts, sweatshirts, cups, and other Canobie Lake Park memorabilia.

Other gift stands located throughout the park sell T-shirts, hats, balloons, artificial flowers, and more.

CLARK'S TRADING POST

Located in New England's scenic White Mountains, Clark's Trading Post offers visitors a touch of New England Americana. Florence M. and Edward P. Clark founded the park in 1928, and since then it has become one of the area's most popular vacation-time attractions. The premier feature is the park's family of native New Hampshire black bears. Visitors can see the bears perform and feed them as well. Other park attractions include an excursion on the White Mountain Central Railroad and visits to the fire station, old-time gas station, Merlin's Mystical Mansion, and the Haunted House.

ADDRESS AND TELEPHONE

Clark's Trading Post
Box 1, Route 3
Lincoln, NH 03251

(603) 745-8913

LOCATION

Clark's Trading Post is located on Route 3 north of Woodstock. From I-93 take exit 33 onto Route 3 and head south for one mile.

OPERATING SEASONS AND HOURS

Weekends from Memorial Day through June and from Labor Day to mid-October. Open daily July and August. Hours: 10 A.M. to 5 P.M. Grounds close at 6 P.M. Bear shows start July 1.

ADMISSION FEES

Preseason: Adults: $5. Children ages 6 to 11: $3. Children under 6: free.

Regular season: Adults: $6. Children ages 6 to 11: $4. Children under 6: free.

TRANSPORTATION AND ACCOMMODATIONS WITHIN THE PARK

None.

GUEST SERVICES

Restrooms, telephones, baby strollers, lost and found, RV parking, dump station. Visa and MasterCard ($25 minimum) accepted.

RIDES

Merlin's Mystical Mansion: a topsy-turvy adventure through Merlin's Mansion.
Mill Pond Bumper Boats: drive your own water bumper boat on the pond.
White Mountain Central Railroad: 2½-mile excursion on a standard-gauge, wood-burning steam locomotive that takes you through a quaint covered bridge and along the Pemigewasset River.

ATTRACTIONS

Pemigewasset Hook & Ladder Fire House: an 1884 replica of a fire station, complete with authentic horse-drawn fire equipment.

Americana Building: home of past electrical, advertising, and mechanical treasures.

Clark Museum: displays of early cameras, typewriters, guns, swords, children's toys, and hotel china.

Avery's Garage: location of three antique autos on display with a variety of motoring memorabilia.

Tuttle's Rustic House: a humorous guided tour through an old-time tilted house.

Kilburn's Photo Parlour: have your old-time photo taken in antique-style costumes.

SHOWS

Native Black Bear Show: 30-minute show featuring native black bears that perform unmuzzled and unleashed. Bears perform three times daily: noon, 2 P.M. and 4 P.M., from July 1 to Labor Day. Weekends only in the fall to mid-October.

SNACK BARS

Clark's Dairy Bar: burgers, hot dogs, soft ice cream, cold drinks.

Peppermint Saloon: make-your-own sundaes, cones, cold drinks, frappes, floats.

Old-Time Popcorn Wagon

Candy Counter: fudge, old-fashioned candies.

Pullman's: pizza, hot subs, sandwiches, soups, cold drinks.

SOUVENIR SHOPS

Clark's Trading Post: one of the largest gift shops in the White Mountains; offers a unique selection of country-style gifts and Clark's mementos.

Maple Cabin: country-style gifts, maple products.

J. B. Nimble Candle Shop: a wide selection of candles, including some you dip yourself.

HINT FOR TRAVELING WITH CHILDREN, ELDERLY, HANDICAPPED

Clark's Trading Post, railroad station, and restrooms are wheelchair accessible.

SANTA'S VILLAGE

Santa's Village, a fun park with a Christmas theme, is located in New Hampshire's White Mountains. Kids can meet with Santa, say hello to Rudolph, and pet the other friendly reindeer. Rides include Rudy's Rapid Transit coaster, the Yule Log Flume, and the Jinglebell Junction train ride around the park. There's also a gift shop filled with Christmas ornaments, and several snack shops for hungry visitors.

ADDRESS AND TELEPHONE

Santa's Village
Route 2
Jefferson, NH 03583

(603) 586-4445

LOCATION

Santa's Village is located between Gorham and Lancaster, on Route 2 just north of Jefferson.

OPERATING SEASONS AND HOURS

Open weekends from Labor Day to Columbus Day. Hours: 9:30 A.M. to 5 P.M. Open daily from Father's Day to Labor Day. Hours: 9:30 A.M. to 7 P.M.

ADMISSION FEES

General: $10. Children under 4: free. Purchase a ticket after 3 P.M. and be admitted free the next day.

TRANSPORTATION AND ACCOMMODATIONS WITHIN THE PARK

None.

GUEST SERVICES

Restrooms, strollers, camera loans, diaper-changing facilities, lost and found, kennels.

RIDES

Christmas Ferris Wheel: a park classic, with Christmas trimmings.
Himalaya Ride: a speed-filled circular ride.
Jinglebell Junction: take a train ride around the park.
Nutcracker Soldier Slide: slide down a giant toy soldier–shaped nutcracker.
Old-Time Travel: ride in an antique car.
Rudolph-Go-Round: ride a reindeer on this Christmas carousel.
Rudy's Rapid Transit: soar around and down this holiday-spirited coaster.
Santa's Smackers: bumper cars.
Sleigh Ride: take a sleigh ride through the air, gliding up and down and around.
Yule Log Flume: ride in a yule log around, up, and down to a final splashdown.

ATTRACTIONS AND GAMES

Rudolph the Talking Reindeer: Rudolph greets you and yours.
Santa's Home: meet old St. Nick himself.
Reindeer Ranch: pet real reindeer.
Village Gameroom: pinball, arcade, and video games.

SHOWS

Jingle Jamboree: an animated musical show featuring such characters as "Elfis."
Twelve Days of Christmas: an animated Christmas pageant.
Live Tropical Bird Show: trained macaws perform.

RESTAURANTS

None.

SNACK BARS

Sugarplum Corner Snack Bar: burgers, fries, chicken burgers, peanut butter and jelly sandwiches, tuna fish sandwiches, ice cream, frozen yogurt.
Frosty's Freezer Ice Cream
Nick's Pizza Emporium
Gingerbread Man Bake Shop
Candy Cane Store: fudge, penny candy.

CATERING

Not available.

SOUVENIR SHOPS

Snowball Mall: T-shirts, hats, pencils, park mementos.
Stocking Stuffer Shop: Christmas ornaments and decorations.

STORY LAND

Spread over 20 acres of New Hampshire's White Mountains, Story Land's storybook theme is played out in a life-sized theatrical setting with animated and live performances. Children can ride a pumpkin coach to Cinderella's Castle and walk through exhibits that feature Little Red Riding Hood, Peter Pumpkin Eater, and Humpty Dumpty, among others. They can meet their favorite storybook characters, such as the Old Woman in the Shoe and Heidi's grandfather, and mingle with farm animals at the petting zoo. The park also offers rides for adult visitors who can walk through 300 years of New Hampshire history.

ADDRESS AND TELEPHONE

Story Land
P. O. Box 1776
Glen, NH 03838

(603) 383-4293

LOCATION

Story Land is located on Route 16, five miles north of North Conway.

OPERATING SEASONS AND HOURS

Open weekends from Labor Day to Columbus Day. Hours: 10 A.M. to 5 P.M. Open daily from Father's Day to Labor Day. Hours: 9 A.M. to 6 P.M.

ADMISSION FEES

General: $13. Children under 4: free.

TRANSPORTATION AND ACCOMMODATIONS WITHIN THE PARK

None.

GUEST SERVICES

Restrooms, telephones, first aid, kennels, lockers, lost and found, message centers, baby strollers, wheelchairs, loaner cameras. Visa and MasterCard accepted.

RIDES

Antique Cars: drive your own gas-propelled minicar on a track.
Carousel: German turn-of-the-century carousel with 36 horses.
Dr. Geyser's Remarkable Raft Ride: raft down a 700-foot serpentine path on this spectacular Victorian-style ride that begins at a Victorian mansion. Rounding the bends you'll encounter a rainmaker, firemen, windmills, and geysers, and even go through a mystical foggy cave.
Great Balloon Chase: ride in a balloon in this Ferris-wheel-style attraction.
Pirate Ship: you help propel this 32-foot boat for a pirate's journey.
Polar Coaster: a smaller-scale coaster ride.
Safari Ride: ride in four wagons pulled by a tractor; kids ride in "safari cages."
Story Land Queen Boat: cruise on a 32-foot swan boat.
Teacup Ride: spin around and around.
Train: board a Huntington train for a ride around the park.
Voyage to the Moon: journey through outer space on this animated dark ride.

KIDDIE RIDES

Dutch Shoe Ride: little tykes ride in circles in Dutch shoes.
Pumpkin Coach: kids ride a real pumpkin-shaped coach to Cinderella's Castle.
Swan Boat: tots navigate their own mini swan-shaped boats in a pond.

ATTRACTIONS AND GAMES

Storybook Characters: meet the Old Woman in the Shoe, Cinderella, a living scarecrow, and Heidi's grandfather in person.
Petting and Feeding Zoo: meet, pet, and feed Baa Baa Black Sheep, Billy Goats Gruff, Three Little Pigs, Peter Rabbit, and Goosey Goosey Gander.
Fairy Tale Section: walk-through exhibits that feature the Three Bears' house, Little Red Riding Hood, Peter Pumpkin Eater, Humpty Dumpty, and more.
A Child's Visit to Other Lands: a visit to an African Safari, the Moroccan Pavilion, the Dutch Area, and a silver mine South of the Border.
Shooting Gallery: practice your shot.

SHOWS

Farm Follies: See talking vegetables and more in a musical animated show that illustrates how a garden grows. Shown daily every 20 minutes.

Circle of Friends Theater: outdoor theater that features shows on a rotating schedule.

RESTAURANTS

None.

SNACK BARS

Mexican Cantina: tacos, nachos.
Moroccan Food Oasis: pizza, sandwiches.
Guard House: cotton candy, snacks.
Pixie Kitchen: hot dogs, burgers, fries.
Fudge & Candy Shop

CATERING

Not available.

SOUVENIR SHOPS

General Store: games, toys, books, candy.
Main Gift Shop: T-shirts, park mementos.
South of the Border: straw hats, jewelry.
The Little Dutch Village: raincoats, park mementos.

HELPFUL TIPS ON MAKING YOUR VISIT MORE ENJOYABLE

Allow five to six hours to see all the park sights and attractions.

WHALE'S TALE WATER PARK

Approximately 100,000 guests visit the Whale's Tale Water Park each year. The park, located in the scenic White Mountains, features a variety of water rides, including two Serpentine Flume Slides, two Blue Lightning Speed Slides, a giant Wave Pool, Whale Harbor (a kiddie pool), and a 1,200-foot-long Lazy River. The park also offers picnic areas, a volleyball court, a horseshoe pit, an arcade, a sandbox, and assorted playground equipment for the entire family.

ADDRESS AND TELEPHONE

Whale's Tale Water Park
P. O. Box 67
Lincoln, NH 03251

(603) 745-8810

LOCATION

The park is north of Lincoln. From I-93 take exit 33 (North Lincoln) to Route 3 north. Continue north ½ mile; the park will be on your left.

OPERATING SEASONS AND HOURS

Open mid-June (Father's Day weekend) to Labor Day. Hours: 10 A.M. to 6 P.M.

ADMISSION FEES

Adults: $14; after 1 P.M., $11; after 3 P.M., $8. Children under 42 inches tall and seniors 70 and over: free.

TRANSPORTATION AND ACCOMMODATIONS WITHIN THE PARK

None.

GUEST SERVICES

Restrooms, telephones, showers, changing facilities, basket rental, locker rental, tube rental, first aid, free life jackets, free parking, paging system. Visa, MasterCard, and Discover cards accepted.

RIDES

Blue Lightning Speed Slides (2): feel as if you're free-falling off a mountaintop as you plunge down these speed slides.
Lazy River: grab a float and unwind as you float gently through a canyon of White Mountain boulders.
Serpentine Flume Slides (2): snake through the turns of these slippery slides.

ATTRACTIONS AND GAMES

Whale Harbor: youngsters can drop anchor at this activity pool with water guns and more for the little ones.
White Mountain Waves: a giant wave pool that brings the thrill of the surf to the White Mountains.
Arcade

RESTAURANTS

None.

SNACK BARS

Harbor Side Cafe: burgers, hot dogs, fries, onion rings, beer, soft drinks, cotton candy, pretzels, ice cream, popcorn.
Leonardo's: pizza, sandwiches, dairy bar, beer, soft drinks.

CATERING

Contact Bruce Engler or Jan Downing at (603) 745-8810.

SOUVENIR SHOP

Swimsuits, T-shirts, hats, park mementos, White Mountain souvenirs, games, toys, stuffed animals.

HELPFUL TIPS ON MAKING YOUR VISIT MORE ENJOYABLE

To beat the crowds, visit on days other than Tuesdays and Wednesdays.

NEW YORK

DARIEN LAKE THEME PARK AND CAMPING RESORT

Darien Lake Theme Park and Camping Resort, located in the hills of upstate Genesee County, is one of the largest amusement centers in the Empire State. Each year the park plays host to approximately 1.3 million visitors from Memorial Day to Labor Day. They come to enjoy rides that include the Grizzly Run white water adventure, the Predator, New York State's tallest wooden roller coaster, Country Carousel, and tube and speed slides in Barracuda Bay Water Park, as well as shows and other attractions. The camping resort offers over 2,000 sites suitable for RVs and tents.

ADDRESS AND TELEPHONE

Darien Lake Theme Park and Camping
  Resort
Darien Center, NY 14040

(716) 599-4641

LOCATION

The park is located at exit 48A on the New York State Thruway (I-90).

OPERATING SEASONS AND HOURS

Open daily from Memorial Day to Labor Day. Hours: 10 A.M. to 10 P.M. June hours may vary, so check with the park upon arrival.

ADMISSION FEES

General: $15.95. Children 2 and under: free. Seniors 62 and over: $9.95.

TRANSPORTATION AND ACCOMMODATIONS WITHIN THE PARK

Darien Lake Camping Resort: 2,000 sites suitable for RVs and tents. RV rentals also available.

GUEST SERVICES

Restrooms, telephones, information booth, message center, lost and found, stroller and wheelchair rental, locker rental. Visa, MasterCard, American Express, and Discover cards accepted.

RIDES

Antique Cars: motor around in your own vintage auto.
Boat Docks: ride a paddleboat.
Boat Docks II: try these pelican paddleboats.
Bumper Cars: everyone's favorite.
Corn Popper: hold on as you swing around.
Country Carousel: lovely carousel for youngsters and adults.
Enterprise: spin at top speeds.
Getty Grand Prix Speedway: drive a racing car at speeds over 20 miles per hour.
The Giant Wheel: reportedly the highest Ferris wheel in North America, it is spectacular at night when the ride is lit with 15,000 colored light bulbs.
Grizzly Run: twist, turn, and wind through three acres of wooded and open terrain as your craft meets raging rapids and torrential waterfalls.
Haymaker: twist and turn.
Lasso: swing up, down, and around.
Petersberg: take a fast and furious sleigh ride.
Pirate: get all shook up in this thrill ride.
The Predator: New York State's tallest wooden roller coaster.
Rainbow Mountain: splash through a whole complex of water slides.
Thunder Rapids: splash and zoom down this log flume ride.
The Viper: this snake of a coaster reaches speeds of 50 miles per hour and features five upside-down turns and a 360-degree loop.

KIDDIE RIDES

Amazon Adventure: a gentle flume.
BMX Motorcross: a mini motorcycle ride.
Earth Orbiter: kiddie Ferris wheel.
Junior Bumper Cars
Nessie the Dreamy Dragon: a love-bug coaster, downsized for kids.
The Pirate's Cove: junior boats.
The Red Baron: kids can pilot their own miniplane as they fly up, down, and around.

ATTRACTIONS AND GAMES

Treasure Island Golf: an 18-hole mini golf course with a water theme.
Video Arcade: more than 300 video games.

Games of skill and amusement, including darts, roll-a-ball, and Kentucky Derby, are located throughout the park.

SHOWS

The park offers five different live shows, from music to comedy, daily. Check with the park for its performance schedule and show times.

SPECIAL ANNUAL EVENTS

Fourth of July: fireworks display.
International Festival: a variety of ethnic foods and entertainment on Labor Day weekend.

RESTAURANTS

Maria's Spaghetti House: spaghetti, breaded veal, lasagna, stuffed shells, drinks.
Ann's Country Chicken: southern-style chicken dinners, Buffalo chicken wings.
Station House: burgers, hot dogs, drinks.

SNACK BARS

Sausage Haus: sausage, peppers, onions, fries, drinks.
Perry's Ice Cream Parlor
Pizza Corral
Other stands located around the park serve ice cream, chips, and other snacks.

CATERING

Contact Mike Botticelli at (716) 599-4641.

SOUVENIR SHOPS

The following souvenir shops sell T-shirts, sweatshirts, and park souvenirs:
Darien Square
The Emporium
Lakeview Gift Shop
TI Trading
Treasure Chest

FANTASY ISLAND THEME PARK

The 78-acre Fantasy Island Theme Park is located on an island in the Niagara River between Buffalo and Niagara Falls. The park features four theme areas including Fantasyland, with rides and shows geared for young children; Western Town, a mining town set in the 1880s; the Midway, featuring a mix of thrill rides, family rides, and live shows; and Water World, with an array of water-oriented attractions. There are also more than ten different live shows, each performed several times a day, so visitors can always find a fun place to take a break.

ADDRESS AND TELEPHONE

Fantasy Island
2400 Grand Island Boulevard
Grand Island, NY 14072

(716) 773-7591

LOCATION

To get to Fantasy Island take the New York State Thruway (I-190) north toward Niagara Falls. The park is located at Exit N19 on Whitehaven Road.

OPERATING SEASONS AND HOURS

Open weekends from Memorial Day to mid-June. Open daily from mid-June through Labor Day. Hours: 11:30 A.M. To 8:30 P.M.

ADMISSION FEES

Adults: $15.95. Children ages 3 to 11: $11.95. Children under 3: free.

TRANSPORTATION AND ACCOMMODATIONS WITHIN THE PARK

None.

GUEST SERVICES

Restrooms, telephones, lost children center, camera rental, wheelchairs, strollers, locker rental, changing rooms, showers, picnic area. Visa and MasterCard accepted.

RIDES

Antique Car Ride: replica gasoline-powered antique cars that adults and children can drive.
Balloon Race: up, up, and away in a hot air balloon look-alike that tilts and spins.
Bumper Cars: crash and bash.
Devil's Hole: you stick to the wall when the floor drops.
1848 Train: take the trip over the trestle from Fantasyland to the Midway on the Fan Ta Se Express.
Ferris Wheel: up and over in Fantasyland.
Flying Bobs: a musical bobsled ride.
Giant Slide: a family favorite.
Old Mill Scream: a log flume ride with two wet splashdowns.
Paratrooper: like a Ferris wheel with a new twist.
Raging Rapids Water Slides: wet and wild fun in Water World.
Scrambler: a mixed-up family fun ride.
Sky Diver: a twisting, turning thrill ride that dives toward the ground.
Space Shuttle: blast off as the shuttle swings to and fro.
Splash Creek River Ride: a tube ride with lots of surprises.
Splash-N-Bash Bumper Boats: like bumper cars only with water.

Super Spiral: turning, centrifugal force thrills.
Tilt-a-Whirl: twirling fun.
Tip Top: twisting teacups.
Trabant: you will rotate on two axes at the same time.
Wild Cat Roller Coaster: a great family coaster.
Yo Yo: swirling swings.

KIDDIE RIDES

Children's Boat Ride: boats geared for the little ones.
Children's Bumper Cars: pint-sized cars for pint-sized people.
Circus Menagerie Ride: a carousel with assorted animals.
Coronation Coach: children ride with the princess around the Fantasy Castle in a coach pulled by matched ponies.
Little Dippler Roller Coaster: a pint-sized coaster with lots of action.
Magic Ring: children pick their vehicles on this carousel-type ride.
Red Baron: little ones control the altitude of their own airplane.
Roto-Whip: a whip ride.
Surf Hill: a waterslide complex.

ATTRACTIONS AND GAMES

Playport: a creative children's play area.
Petting Zoo: in Fantasyland.
Games of Skill: ring toss, basketball, dart games, and video arcade games are in the Midway section of the park.

SHOWS

All-American High Diving Show: skilled divers perform competitive diving routines, comedy diving, and a climactic high-dive from 80 feet.
Coke Theater Show: a fast-paced musical and dance revue.

Cyrus McCormick Magnetic Mine Show: join Cyrus McCormick as he provides a tour through his magnetic mine.
Fantasyland Puppet Show: an array of hand puppets and full-sized puppets make up this show for children.
Golden Nugget Music Show: a hand-clapping, toe tapping, Western musical.
Rainmaker: it's old-fashioned fun when the Rainmaker comes to Western Town.
Story Acting: everyone has the opportunity to dress up in costume and act out a story as it is told by a professional storyteller.
Western Stunt Show: shoot-out and stunt show in Western Town.
Zone Out: a game show for children where they compete for fun and prizes.

RESTAURANTS

Barbecue Barn: barbecue beef ribs, barbecue sandwiches, burgers.
Boppers: '50s theme, hamburgers, hot dogs, fries, drinks.
Laughing Giraffe: grilled foods, sandwiches, salads, desserts, cafeteria style.
Pizza Rocket: pizza, beer.

SNACK BARS

Snack stands located throughout the park sell soft ice cream, cotton candy, popcorn, sugar waffles, homemade fudge.

CATERING

Contact the Group Sales director at (716) 773-7591.

SOUVENIR SHOPS

Emporium: souvenirs, gift items.
Hat Shop: hats, clothing.
Western Shop: Western goods.

HINTS FOR TRAVELING WITH CHILDREN, ELDERLY, HANDICAPPED

Call in advance to reserve wheelchairs and strollers. The park offers handicapped parking. Bring swimsuits for the kids if they want to enjoy the water rides. Large groups can reserve special picnic pavilions.

THE GREAT ESCAPE

The Great Escape, one of the oldest theme parks in the United States, is located in Lake George, a popular vacation spot in New York State. The 140-acre park contains such special attractions as Ghost Town and the Circus, as well as high divers, animal acts, puppet and magic shows, and a petting zoo. The park also offers many thrill rides, including the 112-foot-high spinning Condor ride, Raging River raft ride, Ferris wheel, super roller coaster, bumper cars, and a wide assortment of games.

ADDRESS AND TELEPHONE

The Great Escape
P. O. Box 511
Lake George, NY 12845

(518) 792-6568

LOCATION

To get to The Great Escape take the Adirondack Northway (Route 87), south of Lake George, to exit 19 or 20, then Route 9 to the park (north from exit 19, south from exit 20).

OPERATING SEASONS AND HOURS

Open from Memorial Day to Labor Day. Hours: 9:30 A.M. To 6 P.M.

ADMISSION FEES

Adults: $16.45. Children ages 3 to 11: $14.50. Children under 3: free. Seniors 65 and over: $12.75.

TRANSPORTATION AND ACCOMMODATIONS WITHIN THE PARK

None.

GUEST SERVICES

Restrooms, telephones, lost children center, camera rental, wheelchairs, strollers, post office, picnic facilities. Visa, MasterCard, and American Express cards accepted.

RIDES

Astro Wheel: soar 70 feet in the air.
Ballon Ferris Wheel: ride in a simulated balloon as you go up and away.
Balloon Race: hot air balloon look-alikes that tilt and spin.
Bumper Cars: crash to your heart's content.
Cannonball Express: a train of cars that circle and speed up and down hills.
Carousel: ride this park classic.
Condor: spin 112 feet in the air on this thrill ride.
Desperado Plunge: splash down on this log flume ride.
Ghost Town Train: a train ride around the Ghost Town mountain and through a mine tunnel with special effects.
Giant Wheel: see the park from a 95-foot-high Ferris wheel.
Magical Mystery Tour: a sight and sound experience with a dome-covered scrambler.
Raging River: experience the sensation of white water rafting.
Rainbow Ride: swing back and forth in a 360-degree circle.
Rotor: you're held aloft by centrifugal force.
Sea Dragon: a swinging pirate ship.
Skylab: Ferris-wheel-style ride with cages that ascend and spin.

Sky Ride: this aerial gondola ride offers sky-high views of the park.

Spider: a great thrill ride.

Streamin' Demon: this speeding roller coaster loops you up, down, around, and back.

Swan Boat: a gentle cruise through the park canal.

Tip Top: a spinning cup ride.

Tornado: a family ride through an animated tornado.

Turnpike Cars: ride a mini race car.

KIDDIE RIDES

Cinderella Coach: a pumpkin coach with horses.

Convoy: pint-sized 18-wheelers.

C. P. Huntington Train: a minitrain journeys through the park.

Jumbo: fly with Jumbo the elephant.

Kiddie Bumper Cars: pint-sized autos.

Little Dragons: dragon-shaped cars go around, then up.

Mouse Train: mouse cars circle a track.

Noah's Lark: a swinging boat just for kids.

Old '99: little train engines circle a track.

Pony Carts: just for kids.

Turtles: children ride the turtles.

ATTRACTIONS AND GAMES

Playport: a kiddie play area complete with a bubble room that has rubber balls and tubes to crawl through.

Games of Skill: games of skill, including ring toss, baseball pitching, and Fascination, and a selection of video games, are located throughout the park.

SHOWS

Circus: live circus acts, including high-wire performers, animal acts, and motorcyclists. Performed three times daily.

All-American High Diving Show: skilled athletes show off their high-diving skills. Performed five times daily.

Magic Show: fascinating magic tricks especially geared for children. Performed four times daily.

Ghost Town Street Action: kid-oriented shoot-'em-up. Performed live four times daily.

Red Garter Saloon Show: music and ventriloquism.

Cinema 180: a 180-degree-theater film that features roller coasters and planes.

RESTAURANTS

Bavarian Beer Garden: German delicacies, including knockwurst and bratwurst, and kielbasa, potato salad, hot dogs, burgers, beer, soft drinks.

Coco Loco: chicken, fish, burgers, hot dogs, salads, ice cream, beer, soft drinks.

Gingerbread House: sandwiches, salads, ice cream, desserts.

Mang & Wongs: Chinese food including sweet and sour chicken, spicy beef and broccoli, shrimp and egg rolls, fried mushrooms, chicken wings, and soft drinks.

Pizzeria: pizza, beer, soft drinks.

Rib Pit: barbecue, burgers, chicken.

SNACK BARS

Snack stands located throughout the park sell funnel cakes, ice cream, cotton candy, popcorn, candy, fruit drinks.

CATERING

Contact Terry Grabois, director of group sales, at (518) 792-6568.

SOUVENIR SHOPS

International Village: a village with numerous shops that feature an array of merchandise from around the world. Includes the Toy Shop, the upscale Tiffany Shop, the Village Clothier, Emporium, Candy Shop, Craft Shop, Donut Shop, and more.

Joe's Treasure Chest: souvenirs with a safari theme.

Western Shop

Mad Hatter: hats and other wearables.

Several other stands located throughout the park sell jewelry, toys, clothing, souvenirs, arts and crafts.

HINTS FOR TRAVELING WITH CHILDREN, ELDERLY, HANDICAPPED

Call in advance to reserve wheelchairs and strollers. The park offers handicapped parking and a special handicapped entrance.

HELPFUL TIPS ON MAKING YOUR VISIT MORE ENJOYABLE

Feel free to bring your own food and drinks for lunch in the picnic area. Large groups can reserve special picnic pavilions.

SEABREEZE AMUSEMENT PARK AND RAGING RIVERS WATER PARK

Nestled along the scenic shores of Lake Ontario, Seabreeze Amusement Park offers a blend of modern thrills and old-fashioned charm. Visitors can enjoy shady walkways and a vintage carousel that evoke memories of traditional amusement parks. Or choose from among the many high-speed rides, such as the Jack Rabbit roller coaster. Cool off at Raging Rivers, the water park area with water slides, a log flume, and more. Games and music presented on the center lawn complete this family park's offerings.

ADDRESS AND TELEPHONE

Seabreeze Amusement Park
4600 Culver Road
Rochester, NY 14622

(716) 323-1900

LOCATION

Seabreeze Amusement Park is north of Rochester on Route 590.

OPERATING SEASONS AND HOURS

Weekends from May to mid-June. Open daily from mid-June to Labor Day. Hours: noon to 10 P.M.

ADMISSION FEES

General: $5 (includes 2 ride tickets). Children 2 and under: free. Rides pass (unlimited rides): Adults: $10.95. Children under 44 inches: $7.95. Night riders: $7.95.

TRANSPORTATION AND ACCOMMODATIONS WITHIN THE PARK

None.

GUEST SERVICES

Restrooms, telephones, information center, first aid, lockers, lost and found. Visa and MasterCard accepted.

RIDES

Adventure River: float along a lazy river filled with geysers and waterfalls.
Bobsled Coaster: twist and turn at top speeds.
Bonzai Speed Slide: speed down an enormous, twisting water slide.
Bumper Cars: crash on this park classic.
Giant Inner Tube: ride down a water slide in a giant inner tube.
Gyrosphere: ride inside a dome and enjoy a sight-and-sound show.
Jack Rabbit: reach "hare-raising" speeds on this giant roller coaster.
1915 Carousel: classic carousel with colorful steeds.

Scenic Train: take in the view from this scaled-down train.

Teacups: spin as fast as you can.

Tilt-a-Whirl: another park favorite.

Wildwater Log Flume: swoosh through a log flume ride that ends in a splashdown pool.

Yo-Yo: try this swing ride.

KIDDIE RIDES

Boats: kids can be the captain of a miniboat.

Jets: little ones pilot their own jet.

Mini River Waterslide and Activity Pool: pint-sized water fun.

Swing Ride: kids spin round and round through the air.

T Birds: self-driven little T Birds.

ATTRACTIONS AND GAMES

Kids' Kingdom: activity area with ball crawl and more.

Video Arcade

Games of Skill: located throughout the park.

SHOWS

Music Show: Dixieland band performs on weekends.

SPECIAL ANNUAL EVENT

Country Jamboree: country music and fun on Labor Day.

RESTAURANTS

None.

SNACK BARS

Stands located throughout the park serve burgers, hot dogs, ice cream, waffles, pizza, popcorn.

CATERING

Contact Jim Cardella at (716) 323-1900.

SOUVENIR SHOPS

Water Park Souvenirs: T-shirts, towels, swimsuits.

Main Gift Shop: park mementos, mugs, balloons, T-shirts.

MID-ATLANTIC

Pennsylvania

Shawnee Place Play
& Water Park
Shawnee on Delaware

Action Park
Vernon

Dorney Park and
Wildwater Kingdom
Allentown

Six Flags
Great
Adventure
Jackson

Kennywood Park
West Mifflin

Hersheypark
Hershey

Sesame Place
Langhorne

Dutch Wonderland
East Lancaster

Idlewild Park
Ligonier

Maryland

**New
Jersey**

Delaware

West Virginia

Kings Dominion
Doswell

Frontier Town
Western Theme Park
Berlin

Virginia

Busch Gardens,
The Old Country
Williamsburg
Water Country
USA

Ocean Breeze
Fun Park
Virginia Beach

MARYLAND

FRONTIER TOWN WESTERN THEME PARK

Set on 38 acres of woodlands west of Ocean City, Frontier Town Western Theme Park is just far enough away from town to ensure the feeling of actually being in the Old West. Visitors actually live a day in the life of a gunfighter, sheriff, or dance hall girl by participating in reenacted activities of the Old West such as riding a stagecoach, panning for gold, and even joining in a gunfight. Also featured at the park is the Indian Village of Red Bird where guests can shoot arrows, put on war paint, see authentic ritual dances, and learn about Indian culture.

ADDRESS AND TELEPHONE

Frontier Town Western Theme Park
8410 Raccoon Lane
Berlin, MD 21811

(301) 289-7877

LOCATION

Frontier Town is about six miles from Ocean City, Maryland, on Stephen Decatur Highway.

OPERATING SEASONS AND HOURS

Open mid-June until Labor Day. Hours: 10 A.M. to 6 P.M.

ADMISSION FEES

Adults: $7. Children ages 4 to 13: $6. Children 3 and under: free.

TRANSPORTATION AND ACCOMMODATIONS WITHIN THE PARK

None.

GUEST SERVICES

Restrooms, telephones, first aid, lost and found, picnic grounds.

RIDES

Steam Train
Paddle Boats
Pony Rides
Stage Coach
Adult Trail Ride

ATTRACTIONS AND GAMES

Pan for Gold: look for gold like the old miners used to.

Authentic Western Town: includes a church, barbershop, hotel, saloon, post office, bank, train station, jail, and schoolhouse.

Indian Village of Red Bird: face painting, bow-and-arrow shooting.

Old Mine

Boot Hill

Petting Zoo: get up close to the animals.

Play Area: for the kids.

SHOWS

Charlie Driver's Bar "D" Rodeo: see cowboys and champion riders on wild bucking horses and Brahman bulls, roping events, and even rodeo clowns. Twice a day.

Can Can Shows: three times a day.

Indian Ceremonial Dancing: three times a day.

Bank Holdups and Gunfights: three times a day plus the trial of an outlaw.

RESTAURANT

Golden Nugget Saloon: burgers, hot dogs, sandwiches, fries.

SNACK BARS

Long Horn Saloon: sodas.

Aunt Mary's Sweet Shop: candy, ice cream.

CATERING

Not available.

SOUVENIR SHOPS

Nelson Kennedy's Leather Shop: hats, gun belts, and handmade leather-crafted items.

General Store and Trading Post: T-shirts, moccasins, souvenirs.

NEW JERSEY

ACTION PARK

Action Park at the Great Gorge Resort is located on 200 acres of beautiful, mountainous, wooded terrain in northern New Jersey. It features an exclusive selection of completely self-operating action-packed rides and attractions, including more than 40 water rides in which guests control their own level of fun. A popular new addition to the park is The Whipper Snapper, in which riders experience the thrill of bungee jumping and rappeling from a 70-foot-high sports tower. Other popular rides are Wild River, Colorado River, and the Alpine Slides. There are also unique pool games, children's play areas, and plenty of shows and food.

ADDRESS AND TELEPHONE

Action Park
Route 94
Vernon, NJ 07462

(201) 827-2000

LOCATION

Action Park is located on Route 94. Take Route 80 west to Route 23 north to Route 515 north and get off at the Vernon exit. Turn left at the traffic light onto Route 94. Action Park is 1½ miles down the road.

OPERATING SEASONS AND HOURS

Open Thursday to Sunday from mid-May to mid-June. Open daily from mid-June through Labor Day. Opens at 10 A.M. Closing times vary, so check with the park upon arrival.

ADMISSION FEES

Adult: $24.95. Children under 48 inches tall: $17.95.

TRANSPORTATION AND ACCOMMODATIONS WITHIN THE PARK

Get around with Transmobile, a unique transportation system that allows easy access to the upper and lower regions of the park. Shuttles run regularly to bring guests from the parking lots to the park. Overnight lodging is available at the Great Gorge Village; call (201) 827-2222.

GUEST SERVICES

Restrooms, telephones, lockers, strollers, changing rooms, showers. Visa, MasterCard, and American Express cards accepted.

RIDES

Alpine Slides: six different and challenging slides that go from slow to super fast.

Alpine Tunnel: tunnels make this water slide even more exciting.

Bumper Boats: colliding bumper boats create a splash sensation.

Cannonball: riders emerge from a tunnel into a fresh mountain spring–fed lake.

Colorado River: a raft holding up to five people plunges and splashes through a roaring riverlike course.

Geronimo Slides: plummet down 100 feet at almost 60 miles per hour on this daring water slide.

Grand Prix I: take control of a scaled-down Grand Prix race car and streak around hairpin turns on this professionally designed race track.

Kamakazi: only the brave attempt this one that rises seven stories above a four-foot-deep pool.

Pacer Racers: zippy little go-carts that bring out your racing blood.

Paddle Boats: for a leisurely float around the park's natural lake.

Speed Boats: streak around a competitive boating race course in high-powered speed boats.

Super Go-Karts: take charge of these fully powered machines on a challenging raceway.

Surf Hill: ten separate chutes that range from mild to wild and are over 400 feet long.

Triple Aqua Skoot: soar down one of three 60-foot drops on a plastic sled before skimming along the surface of the landing pool.

Water Slides: three water slides send riders around a series of winding curves before an unbelievable splashdown.

The Whipper Snapper: experience bungee jumping and rappeling from a 70-foot-high sports tower, an all new thrill and the only one of its kind.

Wild River I: hop into a colorful inner tube and maneuver down 600 feet of winding white water rapids.

Wild River II: wilder and more elaborate than the original with more white water, splashes, and surprises in a 600-foot man-made river.

KIDDIE RIDES

Flying Turtles: a big hit with the kids and fascinating for parents to watch.

Kid's Rapids Ride: white water rides designed for the little ones.

Mini Cannonball: a tot-sized version of the adult ride.

Mini Surf Hill: a miniature version of the popular adult chutes.

ATTRACTIONS AND GAMES

Roaring Springs: eight acres of cascading pools, water slides, high-diving areas, waterfalls, and even a swirling hot spa.

Tarzan Swing Swimming Hole: go ape as you swing and splash from any of the three jungle vines.

Tidal Wave Pool: creates hundreds of sensational tidal waves continuously.

Rock Pools: two family-sized swimming pools allow hours of relaxing fun for all.

The Dance Shack: dance contests, sing-alongs, and Mr. and Mrs. Action Park contests can be found at this spot.

Battle Action Tanks: take control of a tank and win by zonking your buddies with an air-powered tennis ball gun.

Old Mill Putting Green: an elaborate 18-hole miniature golf course, complete with waterfalls, tunnels, caverns, and caves.

Upper Children's Play Park: a special area designed for kids 3 to 10 years old, including an obstacle course, a rope climb, a ball crawl, a bouncy foam swamp, and a Water World with water guns, slides, pools, sprinklers, and swings.

Lower Children's Park: a second play area located in the lower half of the park includes bumper boats, Big Wheel Race

Track, an obstacle course, and a ladder climb.

SHOWS

Rock 'n' Roll Action: a music and dance revue.
The park also features a selection of live shows.

SPECIAL ANNUAL EVENTS

Fourth of July: fireworks spectacular.
Polka Party: Memorial Day weekend.
Polish Fest: Labor Day weekend.
German and Irish Festivals: held during the summer in the 5,000-seat Fest Haus Tent.

RESTAURANTS

Surf City: hamburgers, hot dogs, fries, drinks.
Last Lap Cafe: hamburgers, hot dogs, fries, drinks.
Club Sandwich: hoagie sandwiches.
Cafeteria: hot and cold meals, soup, sandwiches.
Bermuda Triangle: beer, cocktails.
Hexagon: beer, cocktails.

SNACK BARS

Baskin-Robbins Ice Cream
Snack carts are located throughout the park.

CATERING

Contact Corporate Sales at (201) 827-4357.

SOUVENIR SHOPS

Main Gift Shop: souvenirs, clothing, accessories, sunblock.
Cobble Club: sportswear.
Sock It To Me: socks, gifts.
There are also gift areas throughout the park.

SIX FLAGS GREAT ADVENTURE

Six Flags Great Adventure is the northeast flagship of Six Flags' international network of family entertainment centers. It is spread over 2,000 acres, and nearly 3 million guests per season enjoy the park's many rides, shows, shops, and eateries. Major attractions include the Safari, a 350-acre drive-through wildlife preserve where more than 1,200 wild animals live; the Great American Scream Machine, a looping steel roller coaster; Shockwave, the only stand-up looping roller coaster in the Northeast; and Adventure Rivers, an all new 15-acre section of the park that features massive water raft rides that send riders down steep drops, over hills, and through tunnels.

ADDRESS AND TELEPHONE

Six Flags Great Adventure
P. O. Box 120
Jackson, NJ 08527

(908) 928-2000

LOCATION

Six Flags Great Adventure can be reached by taking the New Jersey Turnpike to exit 7A, then Interstate 195 east 12 miles to exit 16, Mt. Holly–Freehold. Or take the Garden State Parkway exit 98 to Interstate 195 west to exit 16, Mt. Holly–Freehold.

OPERATING SEASONS AND HOURS

Open daily from mid-May to Labor Day and selected weekends in March, April, and October. Hours: 10 A.M. to 10 P.M. Closing times may vary, so check with the park upon arrival.

ADMISSION FEES

For Theme Park and Safari: Adults: $26.
Children 54 inches and under: $17.
Children under 3: free. Seniors 55 and over: $13.

For Theme Park only: Adults: $24. Children 54 inches and under: $15. Children under 3: free. Seniors 55 and over: $12.

For Safari only: $9.

TRANSPORTATION AND ACCOMMODATIONS WITHIN THE PARK

None.

GUEST SERVICES

Restrooms, telephones, guest relations, wheelchairs, stroller rental, first aid, camera loan, check cashing, lockers, message center, kennels, baby care and lost parents center, picnic area. Visa, MasterCard, and American Express cards accepted.

RIDES

Big Wheel: soar high on this 150-foot Ferris wheel.

Buccaneer: swing back and forth through a 180-degree arc for a weightless feeling.

Carousel: a nineteenth-century classic.

Enterprise: spin and turn upside down.

FreeFall: experience an unrestricted drop from the edge of a 13-story building, attaining speeds of 55 miles per hour.

Great American Scream Machine: ride up high, then plummet down a 155-foot drop before curling into a 360-degree loop, all at top speeds.

Joustabout: ride in a rotating boat.

Lightnin' Loops: ride a 360-degree vertical loop roller coaster.

Little Wheel: an 80-foot-high Ferris wheel.

Log Flume: wind through the trees, then drop 40 feet to the water below.

Looping Starship: turn upside down in a large spaceship.

Musik Express: revolve clockwise to rock music.

Parachuter's Perch: climb 250 feet into the sky, then float back to earth.

Rolling Thunder: glide over 20 action-packed hills at top speeds in this dual-track coaster.

Round-Up: stand on the circumference of this ride that spins until you're pinned to the wall.

Runaway Mine Train: see how it feels to ride on a runaway train.

Shockwave: the only stand-up looping roller coaster in the Northeast.

Sky Ride: get a bird's-eye view of the park.

Splashwater Falls: a boat ride up 80 feet and around a 20-degree curve leading to a refreshing splashdown.

Swiss Bob: speed around sharply banked curves on this bobsled-style attraction.

Traffic Jam: operate your own bumper car.

Typhoon: spin around inside a barrel until the rotation pins you to the wall and the floor drops away.

Wave Swing: swing around while suspended in the air.

At Adventure Rivers:

Colorado Cooler: this air raft ride gives you a wild, swift sensation as it speeds you along at 45 miles per hour.

Congo Rapids: four sets of rapids in boats that hold up to 12 people at a time.

Irrawaddy Riptide: a water flume experience over hills and down steep drops.

Kiso Cascade: roar along this flume that makes 10 directional changes.

Limpopo Plunge: named after a river in Mozambique, this ride sends you through a 100-foot-long tunnel.

Mekong Pipeline: ride on one of the world's tallest water raft rides.

Oranje Falls: lets you experience a vertical curve midway down for an exciting twist.

Ruiki Rush: you'll make a straight, smooth plunge.

Salween Surge: change direction 10 times as you move in water flowing at 800 gallons per minute.

Snake Chute: 275 feet of high-speed vertical curves and fun.

Yangtze Chute: an air raft ride with 10 directional changes.

Zambezi Zoom: experience the thrill of traveling through a 100-foot tunnel.

KIDDIE RIDES

At Bugs Bunny Land:

Beep Beep Buggies: six pint-sized vehicles, each with its own steering wheel and buzzer.

Bugs Bunny Barnstormers: kids pilot their own planes.

Bugs Bunny Great Western Railroad: a five-car train rides along a 560-foot track.

Daffy Duck Magic Motorcade: eight different vehicles, each with its own steering wheel and buzzer.

Elmer Fudd Fun Factory: play area with ball crawl, ball climbs, net climbs, bopping bags, and slide.

Elmer Fudd Traffic Jam: tiny bumper cars.

Foghorn Leghorn Chicken Coop: ball crawl with 48,000 balls.

Marvin the Martian's Space Chase: 19-foot-high Ferris wheel.

Pepe Le Pew Pleasure Cruise: these boats have their own ringing bells.

Petunia Pig Loves Bugs: colorful cars rotate clockwise.

Porky Pig Pipeline: play unit with a maze of tunnels and pipelines to crawl through.

Speedy Gonzales Tijuana Taxi: three arms containing four seats that rotate around each other.

Tasmanian Devil Tornado: swings that ride clockwise.

Tweety Round-Up: carousel with 20 horses.

Wile E. Coyote Wild Wild Web: a climb up an inclined net to a platform with bopping bags and two slides.

Yosemite Sam Desert Diggers: cranelike diggers in a sandbox.

ATTRACTIONS AND GAMES

Safari: a 350-acre drive-through wildlife preserve that is home to more than 1,200 wild animals. Natural habitats simulate 11 regions of the world from six continents.

Koala Canyon: a winding river walk, splashy wading pool, play fountains, water cannons, a water-spraying crocodile, and soft play areas just for kids. At Adventure Rivers.

Arcade: the hottest video games.

Goodtime Games Square: win prizes playing games of skill, including basketball, ring toss, and bull's eye.

Hernando's: games for the park's youngest guests.

Remote Control: cars and boats located throughout the park.

Shooting Galleries: set your sights and fire away.

Skee Ball Barn: over 50 machines.

SHOWS

Blockbuster: a 12-minute film that will keep you amazed and swaying during its dizzying and hair-raising adventures.

Fireworks: weekends in June and July at the Great Lake Grandstand.

Concerts: top talent at the Great Arena.

Water Ski Spectacular: skiing, long-distance jumping, and more.

The Bugs Bunny Magic World of Kids: kids' favorite Looney Tune characters perform circus stunts.

The Great American High-Dive Show: high dives and aquatic comedy.

The Dynamic Dolphin Show: dolphins perform marine mammal maneuvers.

Fun Factory Show: using magic, storytelling, and more, this show encourages children to interact with their parents and peers.

The Spotlights: musical trio.

SPECIAL ANNUAL EVENTS

Kidsfest: a two-week celebration just for kids up to 12 years old, featuring extra shows, entertainers, and activities; at the end of July and early August.

Oktoberfest: celebrate with foods and festivities in October.

Halloweekends: a festival in October that offers families a safe way to celebrate Halloween with storytelling and costume contests.

RESTAURANTS

Gingerbread Fancy: fried chicken.

Yum Yum Palace: burgers, ice cream.

Best of the West: chicken, ribs, barbecue beef sandwiches.

SNACK BARS

Bandstanza Cafe: burgers, roast beef sandwiches, fries.

Casa de Taco: tacos, nachos, soft drinks.

Conestoga Wagon: hot dogs, fries.

Foghorn Leghorn Chicken: chicken sandwiches, fries, cold drinks.

Food Fair: burgers, hot dogs, pizza.

Front Gate Soft Serve: ice cream, funnel cakes.

Great American Hamburger: burgers, fries, drinks.

Kiddie Waffle Cone: ice cream sundaes in a waffle cone.

La Cantina: Mexican specialties such as tacos, and hot dogs.

La Pizzeria: individual pizzas.

Lightnin' Loops Cafe: burgers, hot dogs, pizza.

Mustard's Last Stand: hot dogs.

Parachute Soft Serve: ice cream.

Pizza Parlor

Rapids Funnel Cake

Safari Hut: burgers, hot dogs, fries, cold drinks.

Safari Soft Serve

Seafood House: fried fish, shrimp, clams, chowder.

Ski Show: hot dogs, cold drinks.

CATERING

•Contact the Sales Department at (908) 928-2000.

SOUVENIR SHOPS

Emporium: ceramics, gifts, T-shirts.

Declaration of Gifts: collectible dolls, figures, gifts.

Hang Ups: Looney Tunes character merchandise.

Village Clothier: beach-and sportswear, sunglasses.

Tweety Twadin' Post: children's Looney Tunes merchandise.

Souvenirs and Crazies: apparel, posters, jewelry, novelties.

Fairy Tales: stuffed animals.

Tee-Rific: T-shirts.

Super Teepee: Western and Indian fashions, jewelry, gifts.

River's Edge Trading Post: suntan lotion, swimwear, T-shirts, gifts.

HELPFUL TIPS ON MAKING YOUR VISIT MORE ENJOYABLE

To avoid the heaviest crowds, come early, drive through the Safari first, then visit the theme park. The park is less crowded on Monday and Tuesday.

PENNSYLVANIA

DORNEY PARK AND WILDWATER KINGDOM

Dorney Park and Wildwater Kingdom is one of the oldest family-owned-and-operated amusement centers in the nation with an annual attendance of more than 1.8 million. Situated on 163 acres, Dorney Park features a variety of "landlubber" rides and attractions, including Hercules, a wooden roller coaster, and Totspot, a mecca of children's rides and attractions. Wildwater Kingdom is an award-winning 38-acre water theme park highlighted by such attractions as the brand-new Wildwater River, an inner tube river ride filled with special effects; Runaway River, an inner tube adventure; speed slides; and a wave pool that is as big as a football field. Dorney Park and Wildwater Kingdom also offers live shows, kiddie play areas, over 25 picnic groves, and an assortment of souvenir and gift shops.

ADDRESS AND TELEPHONE

Dorney Park and Wildwater Kingdom
3830 Dorney Park Road
Allentown, PA 18104

(215) 395-3724

LOCATION

Dorney Park and Wildwater Kingdom is just west of Allentown and south of I-78 on State Route 309.

OPERATING SEASONS AND HOURS

Open selected weekends in April, May, and September. Open daily from June to Labor Day. Hours: 10 A.M. to 10 P.M. Closing times vary before July, so check with the park upon arrival.

ADMISSION FEES

Combo Dorney Park and Wildwater Kingdom: Adult: $20.95. Children ages 3 to 6 and seniors over 61 or handicapped: $12. Children 2 and under: free. Evening (after 5 P.M.) admission for all ages: $9.95.

Dorney Park only: Adults: $17.95. Children ages 3 to 6 and seniors over 61 or handicapped: $9.50. Evening: $9.95.

Wildwater Kingdom only: Adults: $17.95. Children ages 3 to 6 and seniors over 61 or handicapped: $9.50. Evening: $9.95.

Two-day combo: Adults: $26.95. Children ages 3 to 6 and seniors over 61 or handicapped: $17.95.

TRANSPORTATION AND ACCOMMODATIONS WITHIN THE PARK

None.

GUEST SERVICES

Restrooms, telephones, guest relations office, lost and found, lockers, changing areas, diaper-changing facilities, wheelchairs, strollers, first aid. Visa, MasterCard, and American Express cards accepted.

RIDES

At Dorney Park:

Apollo 2000: swirls, twirls, and sweeps you and your chariotlike car in a circle.

Balloon Race: rise 25 feet up and swing around at an angle while experiencing a hot air balloon flight.

The Enterprise: looks like a Ferris wheel but spins and circles at a superhigh rate of speed.

Hercules: prepare for banked curves of 55 degrees and a cruise over a lake at more than 65 miles per hour in this wooden roller coaster.

The Joker: reach a height of 65 feet, then drop quickly.

The Lazer: try this 90-foot-high, double-looping steel coaster and experience a breathless sensation.

The Magnificent Carousel: enjoy the charm of a menagerie of horses, sea dragons, and other handcarved figures.

Skyscraper: a beautiful 90-foot-high Ferris wheel—the perfect family ride.

Thunder Creek Mountain: hollow log-style boats ride through a maze of trees, then plunge 210 feet down into a "white water wipeout."

Thunderhawk: this 69-year-old wooden coaster, a legend at Dorney Park, surprises guests with sudden drops at high speeds.

Tomcat: feel what it's like to be in an airborne dogfight.

Wave Swinger: swirls in a huge circle while moving up and down.

At Wildwater Kingdom:

Activity Pools: enjoy fast-moving slides, rope walks, and more.

Pepsi Aquablast: this new high, long-winding water slide that features rafts big enough to fit six people at a time is the longest elevated water slide in the world.

Riptide Run: a thrilling inner tube ride over rapids and through curves.

Runaway River: float 1,400 feet in an inner tube through whirlpools, waterfalls, mist-filled caves, fountains, and more.

Serpentine Slides: journey up to 465 feet in two curved, intertwining slides and one straight slide.

Spaghetti Slides: start 60 feet in the air and slide down three intertwining and twisting spaghetti speed slides to a splashdown finish.

Speed Slides: two high-speed slides lead you to a fast and furious plunge.

Torpedo Tubes: slip down four slides, each designed for speedy adventure.

Wildwater River: huge sheets of water speed you over rocks, under waterfalls and fountains, and through blowholes, waves, and rapids.

KIDDIE RIDES

At Dorney Park, in Totspot:

Antique Cars: kids can beep the horn and blink the lights of their own little cars.

Clown Ride: a ride in a circle with happy clowns.

Convoy: kids can ride in a circle in their own vehicle.

Dragon Coaster: a scaled-down coaster for the whole family.

Helicopters: copters piloted in a circle.

Jet Fighters: kids control the ups and downs of this circular air ride.

Kiddie Carousel: a mini merry-go-round.

The Manhattan Tour: children fly in helicopters that hover around the Empire State Building.

The Red Baron: sends kids soaring on airplanes.

Train Ride: a circular journey.

At *Wildwater Kingdom:*

Auto Kids Wash: complete with sprays of water, soft brushes, and blow-drying air, kids enjoy a trip through a human car wash.

ATTRACTIONS AND GAMES

Chester Cheetah's Playland: an all new kiddie area offering the latest in interactive play equipment specially designed to challenge children by allowing them to use their imagination. Included are a giant river boat and tug boat, special features for climbing and exploring, a living maze, giant sandbox attractions, and more.

Thrills Unlimited: try your skills at race cars, monster trucks, speedboats, and bumper boats in this participatory play area, or play on one of two 18-hole courses in Fantasy Land Miniature Golf where you'll be surrounded by castles, a mill with a working waterwheel, a lighthouse, and more. (Separate admission.)

Wave Pool: ride the waves in this Wildwater Kingdom pool that's as big as a football field.

Playport: ball crawl, ladders, fences, and other pint-sized activities for younger guests. At Dorney Park.

Lollipop Lagoon: filled with water guns, slides, swings, showering elephants and mushrooms, and more for the little ones. At Wildwater Kingdom.

Tank Tag and Boat Tag: in miniature tanks and boats, self-operated by a driver and with a seat for a gunner in the turret, you can battle it out by shooting racquetballs at other tanks. (Separate admission.)

Games of Skill: located throughout the park.

SHOWS

Check with the park for special events.

Stargazer Showplace and Center Stage: a variety of shows and concerts, including the Christian Music Festival, Rock 'n' Roll Reunion, and "The Really Big Show," are held annually in these state-of-the-art theaters. Shown daily is "The Magic in Me to Stay Drug-Free," an astounding magic show based on the illusions of Jeff O'Lear that deals with the subject of substance abuse.

Care Bear Show: animated whimsical show featuring the Care Bears, who also romp through the park.

Middle-Earth Marionettes: a handcrafted marionette and puppet show in which kids participate in the storytelling.

SPECIAL ANNUAL EVENTS

Fireworks: Fourth of July, Memorial Day, Labor Day.

RESTAURANTS

The Coors Jukebox: roast beef sandwiches, sausage sandwiches, burgers, fries, beer, and a '50s-style rock and roll band.

Bain's Deli: two locations feature old family recipes for delicatessen favorites.

Mexican Fiesta: tacos, burritos, fajitas, and nachos, plus pizza, chicken, hot dogs, and fries.

SNACK BARS

Stands located throughout the park serve hot dogs, "TCBY" yogurt, burgers, fries, shrimp-in-a-basket, pizza, ice cream, tacos, steak sandwiches.

Popcorn Wagon

CATERING

Contact Howard Scharf at 1-800-253-8636.

SOUVENIR SHOPS

Dorney Park Exit Gift Shop: T-shirts, mugs, hats, park mementos.

Wildwater Kingdom's New World Novelties: swimwear, T-shirts, park souvenirs.

Gags and Gadgets: magic tricks, joke items, T-shirts, candy.

The Hall of Fame Sport Shop: college and professional sports merchandise and souvenirs.

Country Comforts: country crafts and folk art.

The Rock Shop: rock and roll T-shirts, bumper stickers, and related gifts.

Hat and Shirt Shop: T-shirts, hats.

Coaster Shop: roller coaster T-shirts and souvenirs.

Novelties and Gifts: T-shirts, glassware, porcelain, gift items.

Li'l Folks Fashions: children's clothing and novelties.

Personalities: famous personality clothing, stuffed animals, T-shirts, hats.

It's a Rare Earth: clothing, nature books, tapes of nature sounds and more for the environmentally aware.

DUTCH WONDERLAND

Tucked in the rolling hills of Lancaster County in the heart of Pennsylvania Dutch country, Dutch Wonderland encompasses 44 acres. It has more than 20 rides, including the Giant Slide, Double Splash Flume, Bumper Cars, Ripcord, and boat cruises through the Botanical Gardens. The Great American High-Diving Team performs daily, ending each show with a dive from 95 feet in the air into only 10 feet of water. Bubba Bear and The Badland Band, six furry life-sized animated characters, perform in the amphitheater. A game room equipped with the latest in arcade apparatus tests visitors' skills and reflexes. Other attractions include a reproduction of a real-life circus complete with 5,000 handcrafted miniature characters, and a picnic area inside the park.

ADDRESS AND TELEPHONE

Dutch Wonderland
2249 Route 30
East Lancaster, PA 17602

(717) 291-1888

LOCATION

Dutch Wonderland is located on U.S. Route 30. It is four miles east of Lancaster, approximately 30 miles south of the Pennsylvania Turnpike.

OPERATING SEASONS AND HOURS

Open weekends from Easter to Memorial Day and from Labor Day to October. Hours: Saturday, 10 A.M. to 6 P.M; Sunday, 11 A.M. to 6 P.M. Open daily from Memorial Day to Labor Day. Hours: Monday to Saturday, 10 A.M. to 7 P.M; Sunday, 11 A.M. to 7 P.M.

ADMISSION FEES

Plan A: $10.50—admission, shows, and five rides of your choice.

Plan B: $15.50—admission, shows, and unlimited rides.

TRANSPORTATION AND ACCOMMODATIONS WITHIN THE PARK

None.

GUEST SERVICES

Handicapped-accessible restrooms, telephones, two information booths, lost and found, first aid, public paging system, wheelchair and stroller rentals, free parking.

RIDES

Astro-Liner: feel as if you're in a rocket.

Bumper Cars: drive as recklessly as you like in antique model bumper cars.

Double Splash Flume: take a refreshing dip through channels of water.

Flying Trapeze: enjoy the timeless, weightless feeling of soaring through space as you whirl in the air.

Giant Slide: after climbing 60 steps to reach the top, speed down 165 feet of pure excitement.

Gondola Cruise: on this scenic trip "around the world" see the Eiffel Tower, a Swiss chalet, Big Ben, and the Leaning Tower of Pisa.

Log Boat Cruise: cruise across Castle Lake.

Merry-Go-Round: ride your own prancing horse and listen to a real calliope.

Monorail: enjoy a sky-top view as you circle the park.

Old 99: ride in miniature engines.

Ripcord: this simulated parachute ride takes you up 30 feet, then drops you back down to earth.

River Boat: cruise aboard a miniature old-fashioned paddle wheel boat.

Sky Ride: this ski-lift-style ride offers views of the park.

Space Shuttle: a spaceship that rocks back and forth.

Tug Boat: ride a real tugboat on the Old Mill Stream.

Turnpike: steer and accelerate your own antique auto.

Wonder House: experience a sensation like no other as this house spins around.

Wonderland Special Train Ride: climb aboard for a tour through the park's landscaped grounds.

KIDDIE RIDES

Ball Bath: ball crawl.

Ferris Windmill: miniature Ferris wheel.

Flying Turtle Roller Racers: self-propelled sit skates.

Panda Party: kiddie-go-round.

Silo Slide: not-too-speedy slide for little ones.

ATTRACTIONS AND GAMES

Miniature Circus: watch as more than 5,000 handcrafted characters come to life under the big top in this turn-of-the-century replica depicting circus life.

Wonderland Characters: Cubby the Bear, Hinkle the Chicken, Sparky the Clown, Papa Bear, and Pudgy Penguin frolic through the park all day.

Island of Botanical Gardens: walk over a bridge or ride the gondola to this island where you can see architecture from seven different countries.

Shooting gallery, remote control cars and boats, splash guns, Skee ball, and video games are located throughout the park.

SHOWS

Great American High-Diving Show: world champion divers don colorful costumes and perform rapid-fire acrobatic stunts and hilarious comedy dives. Shown four times daily.

Bubba Bear and the Badland Band: charming animated musical. Shown five times daily.

RESTAURANTS

Park Place Pavilion: roasted chicken, burgers, and more.

Cafeteria Patio: soups, sandwiches, desserts.

SNACK BARS

Stands located throughout the park serve hot dogs, pizza, funnel cakes, popcorn, ice cream cones.

CATERING

Contact Sandy Clark at (717) 291-1888.

SOUVENIR SHOPS

Castle Gift Shop: a 12,000-square-foot house that offers Hummel figurines, glassware, music boxes, jewelry, lamps, artwork, and Amish and Mennonite crafts.

Fudge Kitchen

Bake Shop

HELPFUL TIPS ON MAKING YOUR VISIT MORE ENJOYABLE

To avoid crowds and see all the attractions, it's best to arrive between 11 A.M. and 1 P.M. and plan to spend the entire day.

HERSHEYPARK

Since its inception in 1907, Hersheypark has provided an atmosphere of relaxation and entertainment for the entire family. Located on 87 acres, including the 13-acre wildlife park Zoo-America, the theme park blends tradition with the newest in technology, offering visitors a variety of attractions, from an antique carousel to state-of-the-art thrill rides and entertainment productions. Special attractions include the Museum of American Life, Chocolate World, where visitors can see how chocolate is made, and the Hershey Gardens. Guests can also enjoy the beautiful landscapes, wide assortment of foods, challenging games of skill, and shops that help make Hersheypark one of the most renowned theme parks in North America.

ADDRESS AND TELEPHONE

Hersheypark
100 W. Hersheypark Drive
Hershey, PA 17033

1-800-HERSHEY

LOCATION

To reach Hersheypark, take Interstate 83 north to Route 322 east, then follow the signs to Hershey.

OPERATING SEASONS AND HOURS

Open selected weekends in May, September, and October. Check with the park before arriving.

Open daily from the end of May to Labor Day. Opens at 10 A.M. Closing times vary, so check with the park upon arrival.

ADMISSION FEES

Adults: $20.95. Children ages 3 to 9: $17.95. Children 2 and under: free. Seniors 62 and over: $13.75. Sunset Savings (enter after 5 P.M.): $14.95.

Two-day Ticket (good for two consecutive days): Adults: $31.50. Children ages 3 to 9: $25.50.

TRANSPORTATION AND ACCOMMODATIONS WITHIN THE PARK

Motorized Tram: between the parking lots and Hersheypark entrance.
Hotel Hershey and Hershey Lodge are both full year-round resorts with restaurants, gardens, swimming, golf, and many other facilities as well as activity programs for kids. For information and reservations call 1-800-HERSHEY.

GUEST SERVICES

Restrooms, telephones, adults' and children's stroller rentals, lockers, Guest Relations, information, first aid, lost children's area, lost and found, kennels ($3 per day per pet), sheltered picnic area, audience TV monitors in ride queues and high traffic areas to provide entertainment and information. Visa, MasterCard, American Express, Diners Club, and Discover cards accepted.

RIDES

Canyon River Rapids: fiberglass six-person rubber inner tubes carry you on a white water splash course.
Carousel: features a wheezing Wurlitzer band organ and 66 handcarved horses.
Coal Cracker: fiberglass hydroflume coal-car boat plummets you to a refreshing splashdown.

Comet: flashing light-bedecked wooden coaster on which you brave double drops of 96 feet and 60 feet and reach speeds of 50 miles per hour.

Conestoga: pioneer wagon swings you 79 feet high, then sends you spinning in a dizzying 360-degree rotation.

Cyclops: this centrifugal force spinning wheel sweeps you into the sky.

Dry Gulch Railroad: authentic reproduction of a nineteenth-century steam-powered locomotive takes you on a journey through the Old West.

Fender Bender: ever-popular bumper cars.

Flying Falcon: take a "glide" on the wild side on this new, exhilarating ride that will evoke the smooth serenity of floating 105 feet in the air and the thrill of the twirling, swinging flight of the falcon.

Frontier Chute-Out: giant water ride that sends you sliding, twisting, turning, and tunneling.

Giant Wheel: step into an enclosed gondola for a 130-foot-high view of Hersheypark.

Kissing Tower: a brown and silver cabin with bubbled observation windows that simulates the Hershey Kiss; it lifts you 250 feet for a great park view.

Monorail: elevated trains take you on an audiovisual tour of Hersheypark and Chocolate Town, U.S.A.

Pirate: rock to heights of 66 feet as a swinging pendulum motion carries you to and fro.

Rodeo: swirl in endless circles while drifting up and down.

Rotor: spin at high speed in a room with no corners.

Scrambler: high-speed ride that spins you around in many directions.

Sidewinder: a steel looping roller coaster with six loops in 60 seconds.

Sky Ride: enclosed gondolas resembling coal cars lift you 114 feet into the air and shuttle you from one end of the park to the other.

Skyview: aerial tramway with 20 colorful gondolas.

SooperdooperLooper: soar up, down, and around all 2,614 feet of this 360-degree steel roller coaster.

Starship America: pilot your own space jet in this aerial thrill ride.

Tilt-a-Whirl: lots of tilts and whirls.

Trailblazer: this centrifugal force roller coaster makes a series of tight, curve-splitting turns that tilt you sideways.

Twin Turnpike Ride: drive your own antique car on a two-lane turnpike.

Wave Swinger: whirls you through the air around a central hand-painted tower.

KIDDIE RIDES

Antique Livery Stables: ponies to delight the little ones.

Auto Scooters: self-drive minivehicles.

Balloon Flite: tykes are airborne.

Convoy: a truck journey.

Dinosaur-Go-Round: a prehistoric version of the merry-go-round.

Granny Bugs: colorful bugs in a circular ride.

Helicopters: tiny copters.

Ladybug: another "bug" ride.

Mini Himalaya: soaring on a make-believe breeze.

Red Baron: flying thrills.

Swing Thing: miniswings.

Tiny Timbers: kiddie log flume water ride with a seven-foot splashing slide.

Traffic Jam: another driving adventure.

ATTRACTIONS AND GAMES

Tudor Square: English Tudor town with cobblestones, leaded glass windows, and wooden beams.

Rhineland: graceful archways and lovely courtyards replicate an eighteenth-century village, complete with shops.

Der Deutschplatz: walk among leather tanners, woodcutters, stained glass makers, and candle makers in a Craftbarn reminiscent of the nineteenth-century Pennsylvania Dutch country.

Pioneer Frontier: re-creation of a Western town, complete with general store and blacksmith.

ZooAmerica: more than 200 animals of 75 species in the North American Wildlife Park. Five areas represent the themes of major regions of America.

Chocolate-Product Characters: Costumed Mr. Hershey Bar, Mr. Golden Almond

Bar, Miss Kiss, and Miss Reese's Peanut Butter Cup stroll the park.

Hershey Museum: learn about Hershey—the man, the community, and the industry—and see exhibits in the American Indian and Pennsylvania Dutch galleries.

Hershey Gardens: six gardens with different themes spread over 23 acres. Highlights are the rose garden and the Japanese garden.

Games: challenges from pinball to ring toss are located around the park.

SHOWS

Dolphin and Sea Lion Show: comical cast of dolphins and sea lions demonstrate their talents.

Chocolate World: tour of a simulated chocolate-making plant.

Dance, Dance, Dance: see a variety of dance performances including a salute to the Olympics with the sounds of Tina Turner and Whitney Houston, a nostalgic trip South of the Border, a showstopping "Birth of the Blues" number, and a tap-dancing finale featuring the music of Irving Berlin.

Hersheypark Jukebox: from '40s nostalgia to the present. A spectacular light show and Day-Glo costumes bring each decade to life. Features the music of legends such as the Supremes, Beach Boys, Aretha Franklin, and Rolling Stones.

The Sarsaparilla Revue: a fun-loving Gay '90s revue with high-kicking chorus girls, a blues singer, and a barbershop quartet. Features the songs of Stephen Foster, the ragtime music of Scott Joplin, and the riverboat tunes of "Showboat."

Hello, America: a songfest and sing-along with songs representing the music of the Great Immigration, from the 1880s through the 1920s. Evokes the melting pot sounds of America.

Frank DiNunzio's Riverside Rascals: an authentic Dixieland band.

Top Name Entertainers: Hersheypark welcomes a range of special performers each season. Check the park for its performance schedule.

SPECIAL ANNUAL EVENT

Fourth of July: fireworks display.

RESTAURANTS

Tudor Rose Tavern: sandwich board, dinner entrees, chicken, meats, soup and salad bar, desserts, lighter menu choices for dieters, cocktails, beer, wine, hot and cold drinks.

Rhineland Restaurant: pizza, steak sandwiches, burgers, chicken strips, fries, drinks.

Craftbarn Kitchen: burgers, fries, chicken strips, funnel cakes, ice cream cones, sundaes, drinks.

Country-Style Cafe: fried chicken, barbecued roast beef, baked stuffed potatoes, corn on the cob, drinks.

Trailblazer Saloon: steak sandwiches, popcorn, nachos, whole dill pickles, drinks.

Links 'n' Drinks: sausages, hot dogs, snacks, cold drinks.

Dawgs Ahoy: hot dogs, dill pickles, fries, drinks.

The Oasis: hot dogs, hand-dipped ice cream, soft pretzels, drinks.

Paddleboat Cafe: chicken strips, burgers, hot ham and cheese sandwiches, fries, soft-serve ice cream, cones, sundaes, floats, drinks.

San Giorgio Pasta House: hot and cold pasta and sauces.

Minetown Vittles: pizza, chicken strips, burgers, fries, drinks.

Ben & Jerry's Ice Cream

SNACK BARS

Stands located throughout the park serve ice cream, hot dogs, soft pretzels, tacos, funnel cakes, fries, cotton candy, popcorn, drinks.

CATERING

Contact Susan Kunisky at (717) 534-3355.

SOUVENIR SHOPS

Chocolate House
Hat Shop: hats, sunglasses, tote bags.
Right Stuff: shirts, posters, sunglasses, jewelry.
Hershey Gifts & Souvenirs: carousel horses, jewelry, film, Hershey chocolate products.
Aunt Sally's Sundries: hats, T-shirts, souvenirs.
Canyon River Rapids: shirts, towels, raingear, footwear.
Dutch Souvenirs: film, T-shirts, glassware, Hershey chocolate.
The Parasol Place: personalized parasols.
Comet Cover-Up: hats, shirts.
Looper Souvenirs: ride-related mementos, T-shirts.
Aquatheatre Souvenirs: mementos of dolphin show, shirts, novelty items.
Tower Souvenirs: T-shirts, toys, glassware.
Craftbarn Shops: items of wood, crockery, candles, leather goods, stained glass.
ZooAmerica Gift Shop: zoo-related mementos, plush items, T-shirts.

HINTS FOR TRAVELING WITH CHILDREN, ELDERLY, HANDICAPPED

Most Hersheypark rides can be enjoyed by guests with disabilities, provided they meet the various restrictions posted at each ride. For a list of restrictions stop at Guest Relations or Rides Office inside the park. If a ride entrance is unsuitable to a guest with a wheelchair, operators will direct entrance via special routes where available; do not hesitate to ask the ride operator for Easy Access Admittance. Hosts and hostesses will provide assistance and direction to disabled guests at all shows.

IDLEWILD PARK

Idlewild Park is a 410-acre family amusement center noted for its natural setting. The center consists of five areas, each with a different theme: Storybook Forest, a storybook fantasy land for children; Jumpin' Jungle, a "woodsy" parent-child participation play area; Hootin' Holler, a Western town featuring live entertainment; Ole Idlewild, an amusement area filled with classic and thrill rides; and H$_2$OHHH Zone, one of western Pennsylvania's largest water parks, now with an all new area for kids. The park also offers a new attraction, Mister Rogers' Neighborhood of Make-Believe, featuring a ride on the Neighborhood Trolley. There is also Raccoon Lagoon, a kiddie play area.

ADDRESS AND TELEPHONE

Idlewild Park
Route 30 East
Ligonier, PA 15658

(412) 238-3666

LOCATION

Idlewild is located on the Lincoln Highway (U.S. 30), three miles west of Ligonier, Pennsylvania.

OPERATING SEASONS AND HOURS

Open Tuesday to Sunday from the end of May to Labor Day. Opens at 10 A.M. Closing times are announced daily. They vary between 7 P.M. and 10 P.M., so check with the park upon arrival.

ADMISSION FEES

General: $12. Children 2 and under: free. Seniors 55 and over: $6.

TRANSPORTATION AND ACCOMMODATIONS WITHIN THE PARK

None.

GUEST SERVICES

Restrooms, telephones, guest services booth, stroller rental, first aid, locker rental, lost and found. Visa and MasterCard accepted.

RIDES

Antique Cars: drive your own car on a track.
Black Widow: spin about at the end of the spider's legs.
Carousel: choose your galloping mount.
Ferris Wheel: a park favorite.
Loyalhanna Limited: take a trip through the forest and around the park in this beautiful steam train.
The Miniature Train: ride around the lake, Rafter's Run, and the H$_2$OHHH Zone.
Paddle Boats: paddle around in the H$_2$OHHH Zone.
Paratrooper: spin around in this popular umbrella ride.
Rafter's Run: raft down a twisting tube into water in the H$_2$OHHH Zone.
Rollo Coaster: a wooden coaster.
Satellite: stand up and spin; centrifugal force won't let you fall.
Scooter Cars: classic bumper cars.
Steam Trains: two trains tour the park.
Water Slides: swoop down six water slides in the H$_2$OHHH Zone.

KIDDIE RIDES

At Raccoon Lagoon:
Flivvers: little boats.
Go Carts: they go on a track.
Little Cars: cars run on a minitrack.
Little Planes: ride around.
Little Whip: mini crack-the-whip ride.
Mini Ferris Wheel: a classic.

ATTRACTIONS AND GAMES

Storybook Forest: 12 wooded acres with a walk-through attraction featuring live costumed performances depicting such storybook classics as Snow White, Little Red Riding Hood, Bambi, Three Little Pigs, and Little Boy Blue.
Confusion Hill: a walk-through house in an old gold-mining town where everything's out of kilter, including the water that runs uphill.
Mister Rogers' Neighborhood of Make-Believe: a 12-minute trolley tour to visit many of the friends who live in Mister Rogers' Neighborhood, including Daniel the Tiger and Prince Tuesday.
Hootin' Holler: a Wild West town with shops, eateries, and live entertainment.
Swimming Pool: large swimming pool with a children's activity area in H$_2$OHHH Zone.
Jumpin' Jungle: children's play area featuring a rope ladder to a tree house, ball crawl, miniboats, swinging bridge, swings, and slides.
Miniature Golf
Video Arcade
Games of Skill: located throughout the park, including Skee ball, dart and ring game.

SHOWS

Shows are performed hourly in the afternoon.

At Hootin' Holler.
Shoot-'em-Up: a live shoot-out with the Wild Bunch.
Country Music: the Wild Bunch performs.

On the Main Stage:
Express: a musical performance.
Rock 'n' Roll Is Here to Stay: a rock 'n' roll band.

Evening shows:
Swing That Music
Hot Stuff

SPECIAL ANNUAL EVENTS

Fourth of July: fireworks.
Old-Fashioned Day: antique-car parade through the park on a Wednesday in mid-July.

RESTAURANT

Pasta Warehouse: spaghetti, subs, pizza, salads.

SNACK BARS

Big Zack: sandwiches, salads.
Potato Patch: fries, drinks.
Ice Cream Parlor
Fudgerie
   Other stands located throughout the park serve cotton candy, burgers, hot dogs, pretzels, barbecued chicken, corn on the cob.

CATERING

Contact Dan Siler at (412) 238-3666.

SOUVENIR SHOPS

Three gift/souvenir shops sell hats, T-shirts, sweatshirts, sunglasses, novelties, and Idlewild mementos.

KENNYWOOD PARK

Kennywood Park bills itself as the roller coaster capital of the world. The park features a variety of thrill rides, including the new Steel Phantom, the fastest roller coaster with the longest drop in the world; three wooden coasters; and a water coaster. There are also games, arcades, boating on the lagoon, and a fully landscaped miniature golf course. In addition, visitors can walk through an area of lush gardens, fountains, and shade trees. A 26-foot floral clock and a floral calendar are two of the park's special displays. Entertainment includes circus acts, a circus sideshow, and musical revues.

ADDRESS AND TELEPHONE

Kennywood Park
4800 Kennywood Boulevard
West Mifflin, PA 15122

(412) 461-0500

LOCATION

To get to Kennywood, which is east of Pittsburgh, take Interstate 376 (Pennsylvania-Lincoln Parkway) to Swissvale, exit 9, and follow signs to the park.

OPERATING SEASONS AND HOURS

Open weekends from mid-April to mid-May. Open daily from mid-May to Labor Day. Hours: noon to 10 P.M.

ADMISSION FEES

Unlimited rides: Weekends, $16. Weekdays, $13. Children 3 and under, free. General admission (rides not included): $3.50. Ride tickets booklet (includes 25 tickets; rides are 1 to 7 tickets each): $5.

TRANSPORTATION AND ACCOMMODATIONS WITHIN THE PARK

None.

GUEST SERVICES

Restrooms, telephones, information booth, first aid, lockers, strollers, wheelchairs, lost and found, lost parents area, diaper-changing and nursing facilities, automated teller machine. Visa and MasterCard accepted.

RIDES

Auto Race: ride your own antique auto.

Balloon Race: float in a hot air balloon on this relaxing family ride.

Choo-Choo: a train with a hillbilly theme.

Enterprise: flip upside down on this thriller.

Flying Carpet: spin 360 degrees on a magic carpet.

Gold Rusher: speed through this dark mine.

Grand Prix: crash and boom in bumper cars.

Haunted Hideaway: a dark water ride with a Western theme.

Jack Rabbit: a nationally rated wooden coaster.

Kangaroo: enjoy this flying coaster ride.

Le Cachot: spooky dark ride with a dungeon theme.

Log Jammer: splash down an arrow log flume.

Merry-Go-Round: a Kennywood trademark.

Musik Express: a thrilling Himalayan-style ride.

Noah's Ark: walk through this dark ride with a Noah's Ark theme.

Pirate: board a ship that swings 180 degrees.

Racer: zoom along this twin racing coaster with reverse curve; start on the right track and finish on the left.

Raging Rapids: experience the thrill of white water rafting.

Rotor: a centrifugal force ride that lets you circle at top speeds.

Sky Diver: ride to the sky in this paratrooper ride.

Steel Phantom: the fastest roller coaster with the longest drop in the world.

Swing Around: this ride's arms swing from vertical to horizontal in a 360-degree turn.

Thunderbolt: rated among the world's best coasters, it features a final 90-foot drop.

Tri-Star: a whirling dervish.

Turnpike: drive your own antique car.

Turtle: an old-fashioned tumblebug ride.

Wave Swinger: ride the Bavarian swings.

Whip: crack the whip on this all-time favorite.

Wonder Wheel: a 90-foot gondola Ferris wheel.

KIDDIE RIDES

Cadillacs: pint-sized cars.

Ferris Wheel: a miniversion for tykes.

Flying Saucers: small spaceships.

Herschell Boats: fun for cruising.

Hondas: motorcycle rides.

Kiddie Swings: a small Bavarian swing ride.

Kiddie Whip: a small, oval crack-the-whip.

Merry-Go-Round: downsized version for little ones.

Parachute Drop: adults can accompany kids in this simulated parachute as it slowly rises 15 feet and then drifts down to earth.

Red Baron: a self-piloting minibiplane.

Safety City: a 4 × 4 ride with a Pittsburgh Downtown Golden Triangle theme.

Turtle: a little tumblebug ride.

ATTRACTIONS AND GAMES

Paddleboats: rent your own and paddle around the lagoon in the park's center.

Miniature Golf Course: play a beautifully landscaped, obstacled course.

Arcades: more than 30 games of skill.

SHOWS

Musical Revues: Raz'mataz and Flash perform musical revues featuring the following performances: The Beat Goes On (music of the decade), Country U.S.A., Heart of Rock 'n' Roll, Dixieland Jazz, You're in the Army Now (military tunes), and School Days (nostalgia). Shows are performed eight times a day.

Old-Fashioned Calliope Concert: Riverboat music performed by "Beethoven." Shows are given at Little Gazebo four times a day.

Circus Acts: the finest in thrills, chills, and spills. Two different circus acts are performed twice a day.

SPECIAL ANNUAL EVENT

Fourth of July: fireworks

RESTAURANT

Patio Cafe: chicken, burgers, salads, spaghetti, desserts, drinks.

SNACK BARS

Submarines: Italian, turkey, ham, and cheese hoagies.
Star: funnel cakes, cookies, ice cream.
Lemon Squeeze: pretzels, lemonade.
Taco: tacos, nachos.
Midway: Philly beef and cheese, hot dogs, pretzels, chicken corn dogs, cotton candy.
Sweet Treat: ice cream, waffles, doughnuts, brownies, popcorn, candy apples.
Burger Side: burgers, fries, hot dogs.
Kandy Kaleidoscope: chocolates, cookies, fudge, brownies.
Big Dipper: ice cream, cookies.
Fruit Gazebo: fruits, sorbets, juices, yogurts, slush.
Lucky: corn dogs, cheese on a stick, funnel cakes.
Potato Patch: fries, drinks.
Pagoda Hot: hot dogs, chicken, sausage, fries, meatball sandwiches, cookies, onion rings.
Pagoda Cold: ice cream, popcorn, slush.
Golden Nugget: dip cones, Sno cones, licorice whips, cotton candy.
Pizza

CATERING

Contact the Refreshment Department at (412) 461-0500.

SOUVENIR SHOPS

Gift Shop: hats, T-shirts, film, souvenirs, glassware, sundries.
Midway Portable Stand: glow lights, rose lights, and other novelties.

SESAME PLACE

Sesame Place is a unique play park for families with children ages 3 to 13. The seven-acre park, complete with the characters and ambiance of television's "Sesame Street," blends wholesome physical play, water activities, and rides with stimulating science exhibits, challenging computer games, and live entertainment, featuring the "Big Bird & Company" musical revue. Other kid-appealing attractions are Sesame Neighborhood, a replica of the "Sesame Street" TV set, and regular appearances by some of Jim Henson's "Sesame Street" Muppet characters, including Bert, Ernie, Grover, Prairie Dawn, Cookie Monster, and the Honkers. The all new Sesame Island is a colorful, Caribbean-themed entertainment and play area with rides, restaurants, entertainment, and a gift shop.

ADDRESS AND TELEPHONE

Sesame Place
P. O. Box 579
Langhorne, PA 19047-0579

(215) 757-1100

LOCATION

Sesame Place is located on New Oxford Valley Road off U.S. Route 1, near Oxford Valley Mall in Langhorne, Pennsylvania, seven miles southwest of Trenton, New Jersey.

OPERATING SEASONS AND HOURS

Open weekends in September and early October. Open daily from May to early September. Opens at 10 A.M. (9 A.M. in July and August). Closing times vary, so check with the park upon arrival.

ADMISSION FEES

Adults: $15.95. Children: $17.95. Children 2 and under: free. Seniors: $10.95.

TRANSPORTATION AND ACCOMMODATIONS WITHIN THE PARK

None.

GUEST SERVICES

Restrooms, telephones, information booth, wheelchairs, locker rental, lost and found, first aid. Visa, MasterCard, and American Express cards accepted.

RIDES

Amazing Mumford's Water Maze: crawl through a series of colorful tubes while experiencing a gentle water spray.

Big Bird's Rambling River: relaxing single or double inner tube ride down a 1,000-foot swirling river with bubbling geysers along the way.

Big Slipper: zoom through two intertwining body flumes to a splash pool finale.

Cookie Mountain: scale down a tall vinyl cone.

Count's Ballroom: "swim" through a sea of 80,000 colorful plastic balls on a trampoline surface.

Ernie's Bed Bounce: bounce on a large, springy air mattress.

Ernie's Waterworks: a fun-filled maze of colorful pipes, leaping jets, globes of water and participatory fountains.

Nets & Climbs: climb on hundreds of yards of cargo netting connected by 200 feet of suspended net tunnels.

Runaway Rapids: soar along a 350-foot churning, turning course that simulates a white water tubing experience.

Sesame Slab Slides: shoot down slides of different grades.

Sesame Streak: slide down two twisting, turning chutes in one- or two-person tubes, then splash down into a pool.

Slippery Slopes: a slick 15-foot drop into a splash pool.

KIDDIE RIDES

Count's Fount: wading pools with nets, slides, a Muppet fountain, and a mini lazy river.

Rubber Duckie Rapids: a tamer version of the white water tube ride.

Rubber Duckie Pond: an activity slide in a shallow pool for children under 5.

ATTRACTIONS AND GAMES

Sesame Neighborhood: an outdoor, full-sized replica of the storefronts and building facades found on TV's "Sesame Street."

Sesame Island: an all new, colorful, Caribbean-themed entertainment and play area featuring rides, restaurants, entertainment, and a gift shop.

Sesame Seaport: waterfront wharf area.

Sesame Studio and Science Exhibits: educational exhibits that introduce children to concepts about light, sound, and motion.

Shadow Room: pose against a liquid crystal wall surface; as you step away, your shadow remains.

Pedal Power: light up a neon board by pedaling a bike.

Zoetrope: this device turns children's hand-drawn images on narrow strips of paper into a moving picture.

Foot Notes: step on a colored light projected onto the floor and create a musical tone.

Rainbow Room: play and perform before a screen that captures your movements, displaying a rainbow of color.

The Computer Gallery: more than 50 challenging computer games housed in a two-level gallery.

Create a Puppet Show: youngsters can use their imagination to produce their own puppet show.

Good Ship Sesame: a 60-foot whimsical replica of a cruise ship where the In-Tunas, a four-part harmony troupe of singers, perform.

Oscar's Trash Can Bandstand: children can play authentic steel drums.

Sand Castle Beach

Little Bird's Birdbath: a pond with cascading water umbrellas and an area where parents can lounge while watching the kids.

Little Bird's Court and Big Bird's Court: play activity area for preschoolers including a crawl-through maze, modular climb-through fort, mini ball crawl, and activity tables.

SHOWS

Big Bird & Company: a lively musical revue featuring Big Bird and his Sesame Street friends.

Sesame Place Animal Actors: talented macaws and cockatoos sing, talk, impersonate other animals, and demonstrate their skills.

Sesame Players: a creative presentation of interactive stories designed for kids.

Sesame Brass Band: hear performances throughout the summer.

Paradise Playhouse: an exotic tropical bird revue.

Sesame Production Company: a special effects video adventure in which kids can see themselves on TV as their image is mixed with a prerecorded videotape.

RESTAURANTS

Sesame Food Factory: whole wheat pizza, croissant sandwiches, carob chip cookies, muffins.

Captain Ernie's Cafe: burgers, sandwiches, baked "fries."

Sesame Sandwich Shop: baked "fries," chicken salad pita pockets.

SNACK BARS

Snuffy's Sandbar: fruit drinks.

Food carts located throughout the park sell popcorn, pretzels, ice cream, lemonade, soft drinks.

CATERING

Not available.

SOUVENIR SHOPS

Mr. Hooper's Emporium: Sesame Street products and Sesame Place souvenirs.

Sesame Swim Shop: water-related merchandise.

Trader Bert's Treasures: swim essentials and souvenirs.

HELPFUL TIPS ON MAKING YOUR VISIT MORE ENJOYABLE

To beat the crowds, arrive early or in the late afternoon in July and August. Bring a picnic if you like.

SHAWNEE PLACE PLAY & WATER PARK

Shawnee Place Play & Water Park is a theme park where children can explore and have fun through creative and wholesome play. The park offers more than 15 unique, hands-on play elements especially suited to children ages 3 to 13. Attractions include two exciting water slides with refreshing splashdown pools and a scenic chairlift ride. Visitors can watch shows performed daily in the magic theater and picnic in specially designated areas complete with horseshoe pits and whiffleball field.

ADDRESS AND TELEPHONE

Shawnee Place Play & Water Park
P. O. Box 93
Shawnee on Delaware, PA 18356

(717) 421-7231

LOCATION

Shawnee Place is three miles east of Stroudsburg, Pennsylvania. To get there, take Interstate 80 to exit 52, Route 209 north. Follow signs to Shawnee Place and Shawnee Mountain.

OPERATING SEASONS AND HOURS

Open weekends in September and October. Open daily from Memorial Day to Labor Day. Hours: 10 A.M. to 5 P.M.

ADMISSION FEES

General: $9.50. Spectator: $3.50.

TRANSPORTATION AND ACCOMMODATIONS WITHIN THE PARK

A shuttle bus is available to and from Shawnee Inn and Shawnee Village, located three miles from the park. Call (717) 421-1500 for motel reservations and information.

GUEST SERVICES

Restrooms, telephones, information desk, first aid, lockers, lost and found, security, baby strollers, changing facilities, wheelchair access. Visa, MasterCard, and American Express cards accepted.

RIDES

Ball Crawl: large- and small-sized.
Beverly Bounce: enjoy the balloon bounce.
Cable Glide: hang and glide from cables.
Chairlift: enjoy the view while riding to the summit of Shawnee Mountain.
Cloud Bounce: soar and bounce.
Curly Water Slide: travel through twists and turns on this water slide.
Punch Bag Forest: safe punching fun.
Slab Slide: zip down this refreshing ride.
Straight Water Slide: no curls here, just straight speedy sliding.
Tube Slide: whoosh through a tube into a splashdown pool.
Venture Canoe Ride: a mini canoe cruise in a slow-moving water flume.

GAMES

Video Game Room

SHOWS

Magic Shows: magic tricks performed four times daily in Magic Theatre.
Meet clowns and costumed characters as you stroll around the park.

SPECIAL ANNUAL EVENTS

Fourth of July: fireworks.
Shawnee Craft Fair: in September.

RESTAURANTS

Hickory Licks: steaks, ribs, chicken.
Hope Lodge Cafeteria: burgers, hot dogs, pizza, chicken nuggets, pretzels, nachos, sandwiches, salads, ice cream, fruit, chips, soft drinks.

SNACK BARS

Greenhouse Pizza Bar: pizza, popcorn.

CATERING

Contact Group Sales at (717) 421-7231, ext. 23.

SOUVENIR SHOPS

Shawnee Gift Shop

TIP ON TRAVELING WITH CHILDREN, ELDERLY, HANDICAPPED

The park offers wheelchair accessibility.

VIRGINIA

BUSCH GARDENS, THE OLD COUNTRY

Busch Garderns, The Old Country is a 360-acre family theme park that brings old-world Europe to life in quaint villages to nearly 2 million guests each year. Strolling costumed characters, authentic foods, musical entertainment, and shops featuring imported gifts and souvenirs re-create the festive atmosphere of the Old Country. The park, located in historic Williamsburg, Virginia, also features a wide selection of rides, including the Roman Rapids white water rafting adventure in the Festa Italia section, the Loch Ness monster double-looping steel roller coaster in the Heatherdowns (Scotland) area, and Questor, the first fantasy ride of its kind in the mid-Atlantic region and the largest in the world. The newest ride is the Drachen Fire, a steel roller coaster that turns riders upside down six times.

ADDRESS AND TELEPHONE

Busch Gardens, The Old Country
One Busch Gardens Boulevard
Williamsburg, VA 23187-8785

(804) 253-3350

LOCATION

Take I-64 to Williamsburg; Busch Gardens is located three miles east of Williamsburg.

OPERATING SEASONS AND HOURS

Open weekends from mid-March to mid-May. Open daily from mid-May to Labor Day. Open Friday to Tuesday in September and October. Hours: main entrance opens 9:30 A.M. Villages open 10 A.M. Closing times vary, so check with the park upon arrival.

ADMISSION FEES

One-day ticket: $22.95. Two-day ticket: $28.95. Season pass: $64.95. Children 2 and under: free. Arrive after 5 P.M.: $18.95.

TRANSPORTATION AND ACCOMMODATIONS WITHIN THE PARK

Eagle One computer-operated sky bus (monorail).

GUEST SERVICES

Restrooms, telephones, information booths, check cashing, first aid, kennels, locker rental, lost and found, message centers, stroller and wheelchair rental. Visa, MasterCard, and Discover cards accepted.

RIDES

Aeronaut Skyride: climb high for an overview of the entire park.

Balmoral Castle and Die Hochbiengen: board these replicas of European locomotives.

The Battering Ram: board a boat that swings higher and higher.

Big Bad Wolf: suspended roller coaster hits speeds up to 48 miles per hour and barely misses rooftops of a Bavarian village.

Blimp Debarcadere Skyride: takes you to the treetops.

Catapult: get all scrambled up.

Da Vinci's Cradle: rocks you from side to side, then careens over a 360-degree circuit.

Die Autobahn: try these stylish bumper cars.

Der Wirbelwind: thrill to this exciting wave swinger.

Die Schwartze Spinne: spine-tingling spider ride.

Drachen Fire: all new steel roller coaster that turns riders upside down six times.

Eagle One: monorail offers views and easy transportation.

The Flying Machine: try to catch your breath on this circular thriller.

Gladiator's Gauntlet: move in a taffy-pull motion on this 46-foot-high attraction.

Kinder Karrussell: antique merry-go-round.

Le Mans Raceway: drive replica race cars through hairpin turns and tunnels.

Le Scoot: heart-pounding log flume.

Loch Ness Monster: ride this serpentine steel coaster over a 114-foot drop, through a dark tunnel, and around two loops.

Questor: a fantasy adventure ride with Alwynan, the 800-year-old gnome who will guide you in a search for the elusive crystal of Zed. Bore deep into the earth and travel under water and through the sky. This is the largest flight simulator in the world.

Rhine River Cruise: scenic boat ride.

Roman Rapids: swirl through ancient ruins complete with misty fog, geyser, and spouting aqueduct.

Sea Dragons: experience the thrill of this swirling ride.

Tradewind: reach high speeds in this circular ride.

Turkish Delight: spin in whirling teacups.

KIDDIE RIDES

Das Wirbelwindchen: kiddie swings.

Die Autobahn Jr.: pint-sized bumper cars.

Der Roto Baron: airplanes lift kids into the air.

Elephant Run: a fun-filled favorite.

Grimm's Hollow: play area and rides designed for the park's youngest visitors.

Li'l Clydes: for smaller equestrians.

The Little Balloons: balloon ride for tykes.

The Little Gliders: a scaled-down hang glider ride.

ATTRACTIONS AND GAMES

Eagle's Nest: play area for the youngest guests with Punching Bag Forest, Cloud Bounce, and Bawl Crawl.

Highland Stables: home of the world-famous Clydesdale horses.

The Royal Preserve: petting zoo and menagerie.

Remote-o-Boat: remote control boats.

Turvey Manor: coin-operated arcade.

The Battlements: electronic shooting gallery.

High Striker Game: test your strength.

Der Budenstrasse: skill games.

Skeeball to Basketball: games for all ages.

SHOWS

Stage Struck: lavish musical revue.

The Enchanted Laboratory of Nostramos the Magnificent: watch the wizardry of the Middle Ages.

Carvalho's Bird Revue: exotic bird show.

Tailors of Threadneedle: audience members star in this rousing Renaissance show.

Feats Too Big: a spectacular variety show.

Keepin' with Kountry: a dynamic show combining old and new country music favorites.

King Arthur's Chamber: storyteller weaves tales of King Arthur and his knights.

Le Palais Royal Concerts: big name concert· talent.

High Steppin' Country: traditional country music.

Festhaus Musicians and Performers: lively Schuhplatter dancers and oompah band.

Bel Canto Italiano: tribute to the folk songs of Italy and Italian opera.

SPECIAL ANNUAL EVENT

Busch Gardens Physics Fair: in May visitors experience the thrill of science while using roller coasters and other examples to learn about physics.

RESTAURANTS

Three River Smokehouse: hickory-smoked barbecued beef, spare ribs, chicken.

Das Festhaus: Black Forest cake, knockwurst.

Restaurante Della Piazza: pasta, veal parmigiana, other Italian specialties.

Le Coq d'Or: French-fried chicken.

The Squire's Galley: English breakfast, burgers, fries.

Mackinak Cafe: burgers, fries.

SNACK BARS

The Muffin Man: muffins, pastries, espresso, cappuccino.

London Dairy: ice cream.

M. Sweets & Son: fudge.

Pigs-in-a-Kilt: corn dogs, fries.

Loch Ness Drinks: popcorn, soft drinks.

La Grande Glace: ice cream.

The Tournament Table: 25 unique European favorites.

The Wilkommenhaus: ice cream, frozen yogurt.

Das Gingerbread Haus: candy.

Das Edelweiss: Old Country cakes and desserts.

Vino e Caffe: European wines, espresso, cappuccino.

La Cucina: pizza, beef sandwiches, sausage, salads, desserts.

Le Grand Gourmet: international desserts, espresso, cappuccino.

CATERING

Contact Group Sales at (804) 253-3350.

SOUVENIR SHOPS

White Swan Cottage: David Winter collectibles.

The Emporium: Busch Gardens mementos.

Coat of Arms: Anheuser-Busch beer brand gifts.

Tweedside Gifts: imported Scottish gifts and mementos.

Loch Ness Ltd.: Loch Ness memorabilia.

McTavish Gifts: Clydesdale mementos.

Oktoberfest Gifts: Oktoberfest mementos, glassware, personalized embroidery.

Big Bad Wolf Gifts: Big Bad Wolf memorabilia.

Roman Rapids Gifts: ride mementos.

Other shops located throughout the park sell a variety of merchandise including hats, T-shirts, beer steins, glassware, soaps, scents, toys, stuffed animals, jewelry, music boxes, and crafts.

KINGS DOMINION

Kings Dominion is a 320-acre theme park with six themed areas, each featuring a variety of rides, live shows, shops, games, and eateries. Themes include International Street, featuring rides, shops, and restaurants of various countries; Old Virginia, where you step back into the antebellum era; Candy Apple Grove, offering turn-of-the-century games, arcades, and thrill rides; Hanna-Barbera Land, a special child-oriented section hosted by Yogi Bear and his buddies; Safari Land, reminiscent of the Serengeti and the African veldt, featuring more than 300 exotic birds and animals plus many action rides; and the all new water park featuring water slides, a lazy river, and other "bathing suit required" experiences.

ADDRESS AND TELEPHONE

Kings Dominion
Doswell, VA 23047

(804) 876-5000

LOCATION

Kings Dominion is located 20 miles north of Richmond, Virginia, and 75 miles south of Washington, D.C., on Interstate 95.

OPERATING SEASONS AND HOURS

Open weekends from the end of March to May and September and October. Open daily from June to Labor Day. Opens at 9:30 A.M. Closing times vary, so check with the park upon arrival.

ADMISSION FEES

Adults: $21.95. Children ages 3 to 6: $13.95. Children 2 and under: free. Seniors 55 and over: $16.95.

TRANSPORTATION AND ACCOMMODATIONS WITHIN THE PARK

Kings Dominion Campground: 225-site, on-premises, full-service campground. For reservations call (804) 875-5355.
King's Quarters: located adjacent to park, this hotel offers 248 family-sized guest rooms. Call (804) 376-3321 for reservations.
Free shuttle service to Kings Dominion from lodgings.

GUEST SERVICES

Restrooms, telephones, locker rental, stroller and wheelchair rental, lost and found, lost parents center, kennels. Visa, MasterCard, American Express, and Discover cards accepted.

RIDES

Anaconda: six loops and an underwater tunnel highlight this twisting, turning roller coaster.
Avalanche Bobsled: ride your own bobsled; no two trips are the same.
Boulder Bumper Cars: collide carefree.
Carousel: antique wooden carousel.
Diamond Falls: spill over waterfalls.
Grizzly: thrill-packed bear of a coaster.
Monorail: in Safari Village you trek through 120 acres of animal preserve.
Rebel Yell: screams guaranteed on twin racing roller coasters.
Riptide: drop three stories in three seconds, then shoot the chutes.
Shenandoah Log Flume: wet and wild flume ride.
Shockwave: stand up and turn upside down on this breathtaking coaster.
Sky Pilot: strap yourself into the cockpit, close the hatch, soar 60 feet into the air, then revolve around a tower at 10 revolutions per minute. You control dips and whirls.
Splashdown: splash down on this water action ride.
White Water Canyon: prepare to get soaked on this wet, wild, white water rafting experience.
   Other rides include the Eiffel Tower, Blue Ridge Tollway, Apple Turnover, Berserker, Old Dominion Train Ride, Time Shaft, Haunted River, Scrambler, Wave Swinger.

KIDDIE RIDES

Boulder Bumpers: little bumper cars.
Captain Cave Man's Clipper: miniature swinging ship ride.
Captain Skyhook: parachute ride for little ones.

Fred's 4 × 4's: kids ride around in a 4 × 4 on this auto course.

Huck's Hot Rods: a Grand Prix drive course.

Parrot Troopers: swing into the sky in your own parrot.

Scooby Doo Coaster: kid-sized coaster.

Smurf Mountain: dark train ride features the Smurfs.

Snagglepuss' Sea Planes: go up in an airplane, land in water, ride round and round.

Yogi's Cave: not too scary dark walk-through.

Yogi's Yacht Club: a boat ride for kids.

ATTRACTIONS AND GAMES

Scooby's Play Park: participatory play area.

Serengeti Plains: 120 acres of a natural habitat animal preserve, with more than 300 exotic birds and beasts.

Games of Skill: located throughout the park, including basketball, coin pitch, and arcade games.

SHOWS

Kings Dominion features more than a dozen live shows, each performed throughout the day, including a Broadway-style revue, country and popular music shows, and several children's shows. There is also an 8,000-seat outdoor amphitheater called The Show Place where approximately 15 major concerts are held each season.

SPECIAL ANNUAL EVENT

Spring Cheerleading Championships: in April.

Check with the park for other seasonal events.

RESTAURANTS

Restaurante Mexicana: Mexican foods, tacos, burritos, beer, wine, drinks.

Country Kitchen: fried chicken, shrimp, barbecued chicken, ribs, corn, coleslaw, desserts, beer, drinks.

Victoria Gardens: pizza, lasagna, subs, salads, desserts, beer, soft drinks.

Hungry Hippo: hot dogs, burgers, fries, desserts, beer, drinks.

Livingston's: chicken, baked ziti, lasagna, salads, beer, soft drinks.

SNACK BARS

Alpine Cafe: eggs, sausage, biscuits, deli sandwiches, potato salad, strudel, beer, soft drinks.

Ice Cream Cones

Yogurt: frozen yogurt, funnel cakes, soft drinks.

Tower of Pizza: pizza, salad, pretzels, beer, soft drinks.

Waffle Works: homemade cones with ice cream and toppings, Belgian waffles.

Lunch Basket: hot dogs, corn dogs, burgers, fries, onion rings, pies, beer, drinks.

Smurf Goodies: hot dogs, candy apples, ices, soft drinks.

BBQ Gazebo: barbecue, tacos, nachos, soft drinks.

Mason-Dixon Kitchen: burgers, chicken.

Old Virginia Corn Dog Stand: corn dogs, pretzels, soft drinks.

Pop & Pups: corn dogs, hot dogs, fries, soft drinks.

Sweet Tooth: cotton candy, candy apples, ice cream, soft drinks.

Apple Ida's: shrimp, corn dogs, chicken nuggets, onion rings, fries, soft drinks.

Uncle Ray's: lemonade.

Dinner Bell: burgers, fries, pies, soft drinks.

Jungle Jim's: fries, shrimp, beer, soft drinks.

Avalanche Soft Serve: ice cream.

Stanley's Pizza: pizza, salad, beer, soft drinks.

CATERING

Contact Food Service at (804) 876-5000.

SOUVENIR SHOPS

Anaconda Safari Supply: T-shirts, headwear, roller coaster souvenirs.

Main Gate Souvenirs: park memorabilia.

Sports Store: sportswear and gifts featuring National Football League, National Basketball Association, baseball, hockey, and college teams.

The Hanna-Barbera Collection: activewear, gifts, and toys.

Surf Gear: thousands of shirts, shorts.

Hanna-Barbera Toy Shop: toys, souvenirs, apparel, and headwear.

Old Virginia Trading Post: American Indian and Western-style gifts and sunglasses.

Canyon Supplies: park mementos and sportswear featuring the park's White Water Canyon ride.

Shockwave Gear: souvenirs celebrating the stand-up coaster.

Elephant's Trunk: giftware, jewelry, hats, beachwear.

Avalanche Outfitters: shirts and souvenirs with the Avalanche Bobsled ride theme.

HELPFUL TIPS ON MAKING YOUR VISIT MORE ENJOYABLE

Plan to arrive early and spend the entire day. Pick up a Shopping and Dining Guide/Map at the parking gate. Dress with wet water rides in mind (swimsuits aren't necessary). If you come on a weekend, Sunday is not as busy as Saturday. Picnics are not allowed inside the park, but there is limited picnic space just outside the front gate.

OCEAN BREEZE FUN PARK

Eighty-seven-acre Ocean Breeze Fun Park offers a combination of themes: Wild Water Rapids, a large water park with a variety of slides and a half-acre wave pool; Motorworld, a motor park with go-carts, ¾-scale Grand Prix car rides, and junior amusement rides; Shipwreck Golf, a 36-hole miniature golf course; and Strike Zone, a nine-cage batting facility. Approximately half a million guests visit Ocean Breeze each year to enjoy the range of activities and attractions.

ADDRESS AND TELEPHONE

Ocean Breeze Fun Park
849 General Booth Blvd.
Virginia Beach, VA 23451

(804) 425-1241 or 1-800-678-WILD

LOCATION

The park is located 1½ miles south of the oceanfront on Pacific Avenue past the Rudee Inlet Bridge. Take exit 8 off the Virginia Beach Expressway (I-44) to 700 S. Birdneck Road. TRT trolley service is available directly from the oceanfront to the park.

OPERATING SEASONS AND HOURS

Open weekends from Easter to Memorial Day and from Labor Day to Halloween. Open daily from Memorial Day to Labor Day. Hours: 10 A.M. to 10 P.M. on Friday and Saturday; 10 A.M. to 8 P.M. the rest of the week.

ADMISSION FEES

Gold Pass (good for all attractions except Grand Prix): $30. Children 3 and under: free. Seniors 55 and up: $8.95.

Tickets for Grand Prix ride can be purchased before each turn around the track.

TRANSPORTATION AND ACCOMMODATIONS WITHIN THE PARK

Tram service continually transports guests from park to park.

GUEST SERVICES

Restrooms, telephones, information booth, first aid, lockers, lost and found. Visa and MasterCard accepted.

RIDES

At Wild Water Rapids:

Activity Pool: try the logroll, four short slides, small twister flume, and obstacle course.

Lightning Bolts: zoom down these twin slides at speeds up to 40 miles per hour.

Rock River Rapids: experience a river rapids ride.

Twisters: slip down each of six slick, twisting water flumes on your mat or inner tube.

At Motorworld:

Family Track: the whole family can ride in go-carts.

Grand Prix Track: drive your own ¾-scale Formula One car. (Must have valid driver's license.)

Rookie Racers: fun go-carts for beginners.

Slick Track: spin out in real go-carts.

Speed Racers: race in extra-fast go-carts.

KIDDIE RIDES

At Wild Water Rapids:

Lazy River: cruise gently in a miniriver.

At Motorworld:

Airplane: miniplanes zoom around.

Convoy Truck: kids ride in little trucks.

Dino the Dinosaur: up, down, and around.

Flying Elephants: up and down and circle around.

Go Carts: little carts for children ages 3 to 6.

Himalaya: a ride up little hills and down valleys.

Parachute: kiddies can rise up two stories and then float down to earth.

Train Ride: a gentle train ride on a small track.

ATTRACTIONS AND GAMES

Runaway Bay Wave Pool: splash and dip in a ½-acre wave pool, in Wild Water Rapids.

Activity Area: tyke-sized body slides, chutes, tire swings, tunnels, and forts just for the younger set, in Wild Water Rapids.

Video Arcade

Midway: games of skill, including Skee ball and hoop shoot.

Shipwreck Golf: test your golfing skills at this 36-hole championship miniature golf course.

Strike Zone: step into batting cages and test your skill, from major league to tricky softball pitching to the minor leagues. Little League pitching for kids.

SHOWS

Daily shows and weekend events. Check with the park for its performance schedule and show times.

SPECIAL ANNUAL EVENT

Motorworld Grand Prix Races: on Memorial Day.

RESTAURANTS

Ocean Breeze Main Restaurant: hot dogs, pizza, burgers, fries, barbecue.

Runaway Bay Cafe: steaks, tuna subs, brisket, burgers, beer, spirits.

SNACK BARS

Drive In: sandwiches, beer.

Ted's Filling Station: ice cream, pretzels, drinks.

Ice Cream & Yogurt Stand
Roaming carts throughout the park serve ice cream, popcorn, drinks.

CATERING

Call (804) 425-1241.

SOUVENIR SHOPS

Wet Willie's: beachwear, seashells, T-shirts.

Speedy Zambini's: mementos for car buffs, T-shirts, jackets, caps.

HINTS FOR TRAVELING WITH CHILDREN, ELDERLY, HANDICAPPED

The park has facilities to refrigerate medications. No personal flotation devices are allowed in the park; the park supplies life vests.

HELPFUL TIPS ON MAKING YOUR VISIT MORE ENJOYABLE

Enjoy the water park in the hot daytime and go to Motorworld in the cooler evenings. Shipwreck Golf and Strike Zone are enjoyable anytime.

WATER COUNTRY USA

Water Country USA is a 40-acre family theme park with a variety of temperature-controlled water rides, pools, and attractions, including the double-tube Amazon, the giant Surfer's Bay wave pool, and two live shows featuring the U. S. High-Diving Team. The park also features Polliwog Pond, a specially designed area for small children and home of Lillypad Landing, a stage hosting children's entertainment. Water Country USA also provides an acre of sun decks, lounge chairs, arcades, and eateries.

ADDRESS AND TELEPHONE

Water Country USA
P. O. Box 3088
Williamsburg, VA 23187

1-800-343-SWIM

LOCATION

Water Country is located three miles east of Williamsburg. From Route 60 or Highway 143, take Route 199 east, cross over I-64, and go ¼ mile to the park.

OPERATING SEASONS AND HOURS

Open weekends in May through Memorial Day and from Labor Day through mid-September. Open daily from Memorial Day to Labor Day. Opens at 10 A.M. Closing times vary, so check with the park upon arrival.

ADMISSION FEES

Adults: $16.95. Children ages 4 to 12: $14.95. Children under 4: free. After 3 P.M.: $8.95.

TRANSPORTATION AND ACCOMMODATIONS WITHIN THE PARK

None.

GUEST SERVICES

Restrooms, telephones, bathhouse, first aid, lockers, free life vests, free tubes where required. Visa and MasterCard accepted.

RIDES

Adventure Isle: this obstacle course keeps you moving with agility ladders, inner tube walks, and fast and furious hydrochutes.

Amazon: you and a friend fly down the figure-eight slide on a double inner tube and are propelled 500 feet through tunnels, waterfalls, and a 360-degree loop at speeds of 20 to 25 miles per hour.

Double Rampage: climb aboard a water sled, then hold tight as you shoot down 75 feet and skim at lightning speed across 120 feet of water.

The Jet Stream: spin and slide 25 miles per hour down four winding flumes into a splash pool.

Rambling River: drift through shady, scenic woodlands while soaking up the sun and enjoying the view.

Runaway Rapids: enjoy the thrill of churning, frothy torrents that sweep and swirl you from pool to pool.

Sonic Whip: shoots riders down and around a 180-degree curved tube into a splash pool.

KIDDIE RIDES

Playport: a bouncy obstacle course complete with Boppin' Boppity Bags, Bubble Mountain, Cargo Climb, and Ballbath.

Polliwog Pond: a colorful water fantasy land filled with red mushroom fountains, yellow rain tunnels, and bright inner tubes.

ATTRACTIONS AND GAMES

Surfers Bay: enjoy the largest wave pool in Virginia, with four-foot waves.

Sun Deck: offers 1,000 lounge chairs for relaxing under the sun.

Gator Games: favorite video games.

Guppy Games: arcade in children's area featuring video and pinball games for small children.

SHOWS

U. S. High-Dive Team: world-class high divers perform feats of daring and skill.

Lillypad Landing: shaded theater featuring varying live entertainment geared to young children.

The park also has another live show that varies each year.

RESTAURANTS

Sun Deck Cafe: breakfast, lunch, and dinner including danish, burgers, hot dogs, nachos, fries, salads, drinks.

Pizza Port: pizza, onion rings, curly fries, drinks.

Down the Hatch: sausage sandwiches, subs, burgers, hot dogs, fries, drinks.

Lite House: frozen yogurt, hand-dipped ice cream.

Seabreeze: soft-serve ice cream.

SNACK BARS

Snack stands located throughout the park serve ice cream, popcorn, soft drinks.

CATERING

Contact the Marketing Department at (800) 343-SWIM.

SOUVENIR SHOPS

W. D. Duds: clothing, swimsuits, sunglasses, towels, T-shirts, suntan products.

Fun Bums: souvenirs, children's novelty toys, collectibles, candy.

HINT FOR TRAVELING WITH CHILDREN, ELDERLY, HANDICAPPED

The park is wheelchair accessible, although some attractions are not appropriate for the handicapped.

SOUTHEAST

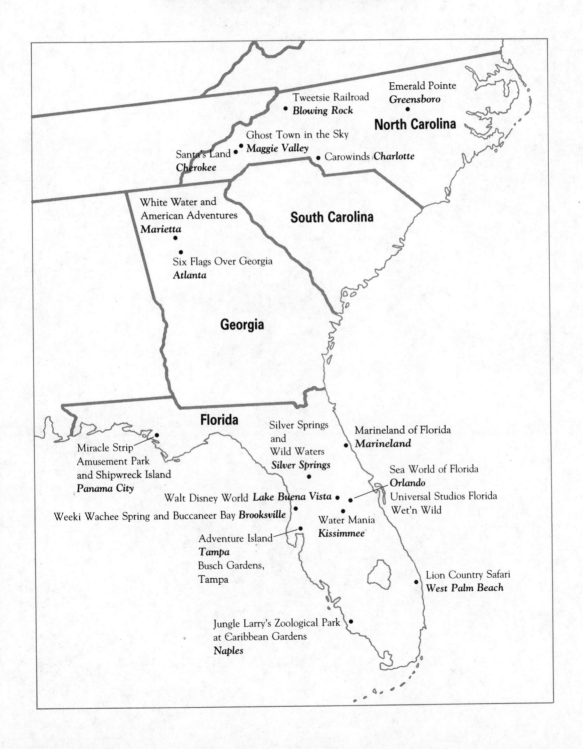

Tweetsie Railroad
• *Blowing Rock*

Emerald Pointe
Greensboro
•

North Carolina

Ghost Town in the Sky
Santa's Land • • *Maggie Valley*
Cherokee

• Carowinds *Charlotte*

White Water and
American Adventures
Marietta
•

South Carolina

•
Six Flags Over Georgia
Atlanta

Georgia

Florida

Silver Springs
and
Wild Waters
Silver Springs

Marineland of Florida
• *Marineland*

Miracle Strip
Amusement Park
and Shipwreck Island
Panama City

Sea World of Florida
Orlando
Universal Studios Florida
Wet'n Wild

Walt Disney World *Lake Buena Vista* •

Weeki Wachee Spring and Buccaneer Bay *Brooksville*

Water Mania
Kissimmee

Adventure Island
Tampa
Busch Gardens,
Tampa

Lion Country Safari
• *West Palm Beach*

Jungle Larry's Zoological Park
at Caribbean Gardens
Naples

FLORIDA

ADVENTURE ISLAND

Adventure Island is a 19-acre outdoor water theme park located ¼ mile northeast of Busch Gardens, Tampa. The park features giant speed slides, body flumes, inner tube slides, a wave pool, diving platforms, and water games set amid tropical lagoons and white sand beaches. Other attractions include a games arcade, picnic and sunbathing area, and outdoor cafe.

ADDRESS AND TELEPHONE

Adventure Island
P. O. Box 9158
Tampa, FL 33674

(813) 987-5600

LOCATION

Adventure Island is 4 miles north of Tampa. Exit from I-275 at Fowler Avenue and travel east to park. Exit from I-75 at Fowler Avenue and travel west to park.

OPERATING SEASONS AND HOURS

Open daily from mid-March to mid-September. Open weekends from mid-September to October. Hours: 10 A.M. to 5 P.M. Check the park for extended hours in June, July, and August.

ADMISSION FEES

Adults: $15.95. Children ages 3 to 9: $13.95. Children 2 and under: free. After 3 P.M.: $9.95.

TRANSPORTATION AND ACCOMMODATIONS WITHIN THE PARK

None.

GUEST SERVICES

Restrooms, telephones, locker rental, picnic area.

RIDES

Aqua Tube Slide: ride this all new giant spiraling slide through harrowing hairpin turns and twists into a splash pool.

Barratuba: twist and turn in an inner tube down a 450-foot slick-surfaced water course.

Calypso Coaster: spiraling water slide emptying into the "Rambling Bayou" river float.

Caribbean Corkscrew: twist and shout down an exciting criss-cross course on this new adventure of a double tube water slide that takes riders on a slippery journey which starts from a height of 38 feet and ends with a splash.

Everglides: ride this 72-foot double slide on water sleds that hydroplane up to 100 feet over a splash pool.

Gulf Scream: hurl down a 210-foot fiberglass slide into a bracing splash pool.

Rambling Bayou: float down a rambling river in a giant-sized inner tube around bends, under bridges, and through a man-made rain forest.

Runaway Rapids: ride this 34-foot-high mountainous structure featuring five separate curving, twisting water flumes.

Tampa Typhoon: experience the sensation of a sheer drop from a seven-story tower in this free-fall body slide.

Water Moccasin: splash your way down a triple-tube slide that cascades through a spiral before splashdown into a pool.

KIDDIE RIDES

Fountain of Youth: this newly expanded area can now be enjoyed by adults as well. Kids can splash in a giant fountain and enjoy pint-sized slides, pools, water cannons, and swings.

ATTRACTIONS AND GAMES

The Endless Surf: try body-or rubber-raft-surfing in this 1,700-square-foot wave pool.

Paradise Lagoon: a 9,000-square-foot swimming pool fed by cascading waterfalls and offering diving platforms, cable drop, cannonball slide, and translucent tube slides.

Games Arcade: games of skill and video challenges.

RESTAURANT

Surfside Cafe: sandwiches, pizza, desserts, soft drinks.

SNACK BAR

Gulf Scream Cafe: sandwiches, pizza, desserts, soft drinks.

CATERING

Contact Group Sales at (813) 987-5000.

SOUVENIR SHOP

Island Trader: sportswear, beachwear, water-related items, and Adventure Island memorabilia.

HELPFUL TIP ON MAKING YOUR VISIT MORE ENJOYABLE

Arrive early to select the best picnic spot, then rent a locker for wallets and other valuables.

BUSCH GARDENS, TAMPA

A 300-acre family entertainment center and theme park, Busch Gardens, Tampa features thrill rides, live entertainment, animal shows, exhibits, shops, restaurants, and games. All the attractions are located within seven distinct theme areas that capture the charm and spirit of turn-of-the-century Africa, including the Serengeti Plain, Nairobi, the Congo, and Timbuktu. The park also ranks among the top zoos in America, exhibiting more than 3,700 animals.

ADDRESS AND TELEPHONE

Busch Gardens, Tampa
P. O. Box 9158
Tampa, FL 33624

(813) 987-5082

LOCATION

Busch Gardens can be reached from Orlando by taking I-4 west to I-75 north. Take I-75 to Fowler Avenue, exit 54, and follow signs to Busch Gardens. From I-275 in Tampa take exit 33, Busch Boulevard. The park is located at 40th Street.

Many motor coach sightseeing companies feature the park as a regular destination. For information call Busch Gardens at (813) 987-5000 or inquire at your hotel.

OPERATING SEASONS AND HOURS

Open daily year-round. Hours: 9:30 A.M. to 6 P.M. Hours during the summer and on selected holidays: 9 A.M. to 9 P.M. Closing times may vary, so check with the park upon arrival.

ADMISSION FEES

Adults: $26.95. Children ages 3 to 9: $22.95. Children 2 and under: free.

TRANSPORTATION AND ACCOMMODATIONS WITHIN THE PARK

An electric monorail transports visitors across the Serengeti Plain.

GUEST SERVICES

Restrooms, telephones, information booth, first aid, kennels, lost and found, locker rental, message center, stroller and wheelchair rental, electric vehicle rental. Visa, MasterCard, and Discover cards accepted.

RIDES

Congo River Rapids: a feisty white water raft ride.
Monstrous Mamba: African-style thrill ride.
Phoenix: climb aboard for a classic boat swing ride.
Python: scream away in a 1,200-foot roller coaster with a 360-degree double spiral.
Questor: take a journey to the earth's core in a ride that combines flight simulator technology, a fast-paced adventure film, audio animation, and special effects.
Sandstorm: feel as if you're in an African storm.
Scorpion: experience this 360-degree loop roller coaster.
Skyride: get a treetop view of the park.
Stanley Falls Log Flume: a wet and wild water ride.
Swinging Vines: swing and swoop through a tangle of a ride.
Tanganyika Tidal Wave: ride the waves in a water adventure.
Trans-Veldt Railroad: journey on an authentic steam train.
Ubanga-Banga: African-style bumper cars.

KIDDIE RIDES

Bawl Crawl: an endless pool of balls.
Bush Flyers: kids can fly their own airplanes.
Carousel Caravan: there are 58 Arabian horses, eight camels, and two benches on this lovely carousel.
Cloud Bounce: air bounce.
Desert Runners: minirunners on a track give kids jumping experience on a two-minute motorcycle ride.
Dune Buggy: cars travel through a miniature "Dwarf Village."
Kiddie Canoe: kids ride in a big canoe.
Little Rammer: a pair of boatlike vessels swing from the apex like pendulums.
Pygmy Bats: mini hang gliders that follow a circular course.
Pygmy Goats: a spinning "teapot" ride.
Pygmy Vines: a pint-sized version of Swinging Vines.

ATTRACTIONS

Gorilla Habitat: families of chimpanzees and gorillas live in this all new, lush, expansive rain forest that simulates their natural African habitat.

Serengeti Plain: 500 head of African big game roam freely across the veldtlike plain. See camels, elephants, zebras, giraffes, chimpanzees, and more.

Nairobi Field Station Animal Nursery: observe experts caring for newborn animals.

SHOWS

Big Band Sounds and Dance: tap your toes and dance in your seat to the big band sound of Busch Gardens' own orchestra while dancers do routines from the '40s.

Around the World on Ice: elaborately staged ice show takes audiences on a six-country tour.

Sounds of the '60s: a musical revue.

Dolphins of the Deep: bottlenose dolphins Bud and Mickey join forces with Sniffles the Sea Lion to showcase their tricks.

World of Birds: watch trained exotic macaws and cockatoos perform.

International Show: dancing and singing from several countries.

Stanleyville Variety Show: lively entertainment by jugglers, acrobats, ice dancers, dance troupes, and performing animals.

Snake Charmer: Charmer and her slithering companion captivate guests in the Sultan's Tent.

The Mystic Sheiks of Morocco: musical entertainment from an eight-piece, all-brass marching band.

Congo Comedy Corps: the audience joins in the fun led by a troupe of comical characters in the Stanleyville Theater.

RESTAURANTS

Crown Colony House: a full-service restaurant with chicken, seafood dishes, and more.

Hospitality House: sandwiches, pizza.

Zagora Cafe: sandwiches, burgers, fries, desserts.

Smokehouse Bar-B-Que: chicken, ribs, beef.

Das Festhaus: German cuisine, pastries, pizza.

SNACK BARS

Ice Cream Parlor

Boujad Bakery: pastries, cappuccino.

Zambezi Cafe: burgers, fries, desserts.

Bazaar Cafe: roast beef sandwiches, fries, drinks.

Vi Vi Storehouse: fried chicken, sandwiches, fries, desserts, soft drinks.

Oasis Juice Bar

Python Ice Cream

Bird Gardens Bakery: pastries, drinks.

Kenya Canteen: ice cream, cotton candy, nachos, drinks.

CATERING

Contact Donna Walters, Special Events Office, at (813) 988-5171.

SOUVENIR SHOPS

Moroccan Emporium: Busch Gardens memorabilia and gifts.

Label Stable: Anheuser-Busch novelties plus Clydesdale collectibles.

Continental Curios: handcrafted African gifts of brass, leather, wood, and clothing.

Crown Colony Gift Shop: apparel, old-world decorative gifts.

Bavarian Colony Shop: Hummel figurines, crystal, and other gifts.

Monorail Gift Shop: gifts, Clydesdale collectibles, apparel.

West African Trading Company Ltd.: gifts and apparel from 24 countries.

Crafts Bazaar: handcrafted jewelry, wood, gifts.

Stanleyville Bazaar: souvenirs and gifts.

Bird Gardens Gift Shop: Busch Gardens mementos.

Gulf Wind Trader: beachwear and nautical gifts.

HELPFUL TIP ON MAKING YOUR VISIT MORE ENJOYABLE

Arrive early to beat the crowds and plan to spend seven to eight hours touring the park.

JUNGLE LARRY'S ZOOLOGICAL PARK AT CARIBBEAN GARDENS

Jungle Larry's is a 52-acre zoological and botanical garden theme park with an annual attendance of 100,000 to 250,000. Founded originally as botanical gardens in 1919, it was taken over and expanded by the Jungle Larry family in 1969. Today the park features rare endangered animal species, special breeding programs, tram rides, animal performances, lectures, a bird circus, animal feeding, an animal training center, a petting farm, picnic area, and gift shop.

ADDRESS AND TELEPHONE

Jungle Larry's
1590 Goodlette Road
Naples, FL 33940

(813) 262-5409

LOCATION

To get to Jungle Larry's, take Route 41 to Naples, turn east at Fleischman Boulevard, and proceed one block to the park. Or take I-75 to exit 16. Proceed west on Pine Ridge Road to Goodlette Road, turn south, and drive three miles to the park.

OPERATING SEASONS AND HOURS

Open daily all year except Thanksgiving Day and Christmas Day. Hours: 9:30 A.M. to 5:30 P.M.

ADMISSION FEES

Adults: $9.95. Children ages 3 to 15: $5.95.

TRANSPORTATION AND ACCOMMODATIONS WITHIN THE PARK

None.

GUEST SERVICES

Restrooms, wheelchairs, picnic area. Visa, MasterCard, and American Express cards accepted.

RIDES

Tram Tour: take a guided tour with inside information on the animals.

KIDDIE RIDES

None.

ATTRACTIONS AND GAMES

Petting Zoo: get up close and feed the deer, llamas, and miniature donkeys.
Tropical Gardens: 52 acres of winding gardens, shady banyan trees, palms, bamboos, and more. At every turn encounter animals such as lions, leopards, anteaters, alligators, cougars, monkeys, plus macaws and cockatoos.
Kiddie Playground

SHOWS

Wild Animal Show: internationally acclaimed trainers put the big cats through their paces.
Elephant Show: see elephants perform.
Alligator Lecture: see the crocodilians feed; touch a live baby gator.

Tropical Bird Circus: see beautiful exotic birds.

Wildlife Encounter: educational lecture with baby animals.

RESTAURANTS

None.

SNACK BARS

Stands located throughout the park sell ice cream, snacks, juices, drinks.

CATERING

Contact (813) 265-5409.

SOUVENIR SHOP

Zoological gifts, plush animals, and park memorabilia.

LION COUNTRY SAFARI

Lion Country Safari is a 500-acre wildlife preserve and entertainment park. Visitors drive through the preserve to view the more than 1,000 free-roaming animals from all over the world. Guests can repeat their preserve trips as often as they like throughout the day. The park also features boat rides, miniature golf, a carousel, petting zoo, baby animal nursery, exotic bird aviary, and gift shops.

ADDRESS AND TELEPHONE

Lion Country Safari
P. O. Box 16066
West Palm Beach, FL 33416-6066

(407) 793-1084

LOCATION

Take I-95 to exit 50, U.S. 98/441, then go west 18 miles. The park will be on your right.

OPERATING SEASONS AND HOURS

Open daily year-round. Hours: 9:30 A.M. to 5:30 P.M. (The last vehicle is admitted at 4:30 P.M.)

ADMISSION FEES

Adults: $11.95. Children ages 3 to 15: $9.95. Children under 3: free. Seniors over 65 and members of the American Association of Retired Persons (AARP): $8.55.

TRANSPORTATION AND ACCOMMODATIONS WITHIN THE PARK

Rental cars are available for guests with convertibles.

GUEST SERVICES

Restrooms, telephones, information booth, lost and found, kennels, wheelchairs, stroller rental. Visa, MasterCard, and American Express cards accepted.

RIDES

African Safari Queen: take a narrated boat cruise around the island and see flamingos, monkeys, apes, and other animals.

Carousel: an old-fashioned park favorite.

Paddleboat Ride: cruise along in a paddleboat.

KIDDIE RIDES

Merry-Go-Round: coin-operated and mini-sized.

Rocking Horse: coin-operated single horse.

ATTRACTIONS AND GAMES

Remote Control Boats: be the captain of a miniature boat.
Petting Zoo: pet and feed baby animals.
Monkey Feeding: feed monkeys by swinging buckets of feed they can catch.
Dinosaur Park: see life-sized replicas of prehistoric creatures.
Safari Miniature Golf
Games: video challenges and Skee ball.

SHOWS

Alligator Feeding: 1 P.M. and 3 P.M.
Vulture Feeding: 4 P.M.
Pelican Feeding: 3:30 P.M.
Tortoise Wash: see tortoises get a shower, at 2 P.M.
Siamang Feeding: 3 P.M.

RESTAURANT

Cafeteria: burgers, hot dogs, salads, fried chicken, pizza.

SNACK BARS

Hippo Hut: pizza, hot dogs, ice cream, drinks.
Camera Shop & Outpost: popcorn, drinks.
Ice Cream Shop

CATERING

Not available.

SOUVENIR SHOPS

Old & New Curios Shop: African curios, T-shirts, park souvenirs.
Camera Shop: film, cameras, park souvenirs.
Outpost: camera rentals, film, park mementos.

HELPFUL TIPS ON MAKING YOUR VISIT MORE ENJOYABLE

Come in the morning when the animals are most active. Remember, you can drive through the preserve as many times as you want. Allow at least three hours for your stay. And bring your camera; the preserve has excellent photo opportunities.

MARINELAND OF FLORIDA

Marineland of Florida, listed in the National Register of Historic Places, is America's original marine life attraction. Founded in 1938, the park has been giving visitors an opportunity to take a close-up look at many varieties of sea life in their natural habitat for over 50 years. For instance, guests watch dolphins leap through the air, peruse the playful penguins, and watch otters, sea lions, and electric eels as they dart and dive about. For a change of pace, guests can stroll on the boardwalk for a relaxing view of the Atlantic Ocean.

ADDRESS AND TELEPHONE

Marineland of Florida
9507 Ocean Shore Boulevard
Marineland, FL 32086-9602

(904) 471-1111

LOCATION

Marineland of Florida is located on Highway A1A between St. Augustine and Daytona Beach.

OPERATING SEASONS AND HOURS

Open daily year-round. Hours: 9 A.M. to 6 P.M.

ADMISSION FEES

Adults: $12. Children ages 3 to 11: $7.

TRANSPORTATION AND ACCOMMODATIONS WITHIN THE PARK

Marineland's Quality Inn Motel: oceanfront rooms, beachside pools, secluded beach, and lighted tennis courts.
Yogi Bear Camp Resort: pool, full hookups, miniature golf, groceries, playground, fuel.
Marineland Marina: complete docking facilities, located adjacent to the park on the Intracoastal Waterway.

GUEST SERVICES

Restrooms, telephones, kennels, baby stroller rental, wheelchairs. Visa, MasterCard, American Express, Discover, and Diners Club cards accepted.

RIDES

None.

ATTRACTIONS AND GAMES

Wonders of the Sea and Secrets of the Reef: exhibits featuring beautiful and unusual marine specimens.
Wonders of the Spring: 35,000-gallon re-creation of a Florida freshwater spring.
Whitney Park: home of Marineland's sea lions and penguins.
Herrick Sea Shell Museum: view colorful and intricate shells gathered from all over the world.
Playport: children's activity area with ball crawl and air bounce.

SHOWS

Aquarius Theatre: "Sea Dream," a 3-D film about the undersea world.

Jumping Dolphins Show: trained dolphins perform on the top deck of Circular Aquarium.
Educated Dolphin Show: see just how smart real dolphins can be.
Underwater Feeding: view divers through 200 portholes as they feed sharks, rays, and other marine life.
Sea Lion Training: a 10-minute sea lion show at Whitney Park.
Penguin Feeding: watch penguins gulp down fish at Whitney Park.

RESTAURANTS

Dolphin Restaurant and Moby Dick Lounge: breakfast, lunch, and dinner menus, including prime ribs, seafood, lobster, steak, chicken, burgers, fries, salads, alcoholic beverages, soft drinks.
Sandpiper: sandwiches, fries, shrimp, clams, chicken fingers, barbecued pork, burgers, beer.

SNACK BARS

Periwinkle: nachos, hot dogs, ice cream, candy, beer.
Sea Breeze: nachos, hot dogs, ice cream, chocolate bars, beer.
Aquarius: nachos, hot dogs, ice cream, candy, beer.

CATERING

Contact Group Sales at (904) 471-1111.

SOUVENIR SHOPS

Ocean Shore Gift Shop: marine gifts, Marineland mementos.
Beachcomber Gift Shop: marine gifts, Marineland mementos.
Shell Shop: ocean shells.

HINT FOR TRAVELING WITH CHILDREN, ELDERLY, HANDICAPPED

Marineland is wheelchair accessible for everything except top-deck shows.

HELPFUL TIP TO MAKE YOUR VISIT MORE ENJOYABLE

Be sure to arrive before 3 P.M. to see all shows and exhibits.

MIRACLE STRIP AMUSEMENT PARK AND SHIPWRECK ISLAND

Miracle Strip Amusement Park has been providing evening and weekend entertainment to families since 1963. The park offers many rides, games, snack bars, and attractions, including a 2,000-foot-long wooden roller coaster that features a 65-foot incline and a dark tunnel, and a walk-through haunted house. The park covers 15 acres in Panama City. Shipwreck Island is a six-acre water theme park including a wave pool and Shipwreck, a wrecked ship ride that swings you off a cable and into eight feet of water. Go to Shipwreck Island for the day and Miracle Strip for the evening.

ADDRESS AND TELEPHONE

Miracle Strip and Shipwreck Island
P. O. Box 2000
Panama City, FL 32402

(904) 234-5810 or (904) 234-0368

LOCATION

Miracle Strip and Shipwreck Island are located at 12000 West Highway 98 in Panama City. From Pensacola, take Highway 98 east to Panama City and follow signs to the park.

OPERATING SEASONS AND HOURS

Open daily from June to Labor Day.
   Miracle Strip Hours: Monday to Friday from 6 P.M. to 11:30 P.M.; Saturday from 1 P.M. to 11:30 P.M.; Sunday from 3 P.M. to 11:30 P.M.
   Shipwreck Island Hours: 10:30 A.M. to 6 P.M.
   Open selected weekends in April and May, but hours vary, so check with the park before arriving.

ADMISSION FEES

For Miracle Strip: Adults: $12. Children 10 and under: $10. Nonriders 5 and over: 75%. Nonriders 4 and under: free.
   For Shipwreck Island: Adults: $13. Children ages 5 to 10: $11. Children 4 and under and seniors 60 and over: free.

TRANSPORTATION AND ACCOMMODATIONS WITHIN THE PARK

None.

GUEST SERVICES

Restrooms, telephones, information and guest relations booth, lost and found, first aid, strollers, lockers and life vest rental at Shipwreck Island. Visa and MasterCard accepted.

RIDES

At Miracle Strip:
Abominable Snowman: ride a scrambler that features rock and roll music and a light show.
Bumper Cars: a park classic.
Dante's Inferno: ride in a circle to rock and roll music.
Dungeon: an enclosed tilt-a-whirl with rock and roll music and a light show.
Ferris Wheel: see the park from treetop level.
Haunted Castle: dare to brave this haunted dark ride.

Log Flume: soar down this 1,200-foot-long flume.

Paratrooper: a park favorite.

Roller Coaster: this 2,000-foot wooden coaster features a 65-foot hill and a dark tunnel.

Sea Dragon: swing 80 feet in the air.

Spider: spin at the end of a spider's leg.

Wave Swinger: swing around in the air.

At Shipwreck Island:

Lazy River: lie on a tube and float down a 160-foot lazy river that runs through Shipwreck Island.

Rapid River Run: tube down the rapids.

Shipwreck: a wrecked ship swings you off a cable into eight feet of water.

Speed Slide: race down two 65-foot-high slides.

Zoom Flume Water Slide: slide down three water flumes on a mat.

KIDDIE RIDES

At Miracle Strip:

Bi-Planes: kids can pilot a miniplane.

Junior Bumper Cars: pint-sized bumper cars.

Junior Hot Rods: little hot rods.

Little Swings: a swing ride for tiny tykes.

Merry-Go-Round: colorful horses in a circle.

Ruggy Buggies: fun on a buggy.

At Shipwreck Island:

Tadpole Hole: designed for kids 10 and under; features an elephant slide, fort, water cannons, tunnels, and rope bridge.

ATTRACTIONS AND GAMES

Old House: walk-through haunted house.

Wave Pool: enjoy 12 minutes of waves, then 12 minutes of calm swimming. At Shipwreck Island.

Skull Island: activity pool for all ages. At Shipwreck Island.

Midway Games: 10 games of skill.

Arcades: everyone's favorite arcade games. At Miracle Strip and at Shipwreck Island.

SHOWS

Youth Choirs: visiting church youth choirs perform in the Miracle Strip park at 8 P.M. on selected nights.

RESTAURANTS

At Shipwreck Island:

Pizza Shack: pizza, corn dogs, fries, beer, drinks.

The Ship's Grill: steak sandwiches, shish kebab, shrimp kebab, grouper sandwiches, burgers, fries, onion rings, coleslaw.

The Dawg House: hot dogs, onion rings, beer, soft drinks.

Spring House: nachos, drinks.

SNACK BARS

Stands located throughout Miracle Strip serve tacos, nachos, hot dogs, pizza, chicken fingers, burgers, corn dogs, ice cream, cotton candy, popcorn, soft drinks.

At Shipwreck Island:

The Galley: smoked ribs, chicken, chicken fingers, fries, onion rings, nachos, barbecue sandwiches, beer, soft drinks.

Ice Cream Hut: waffle cones, sundaes.

CATERING

Contact Ken Rudzki at (904) 234-3333.

SOUVENIR SHOPS

At Miracle Strip:

Gift Shop: sun fashions, park mementos, T-shirts.

At Shipwreck Island:

The Ship's Store: suncare products, T-shirts, souvenirs.

Beach Shack: suncare products, T-shirts, park mementos.

HELPFUL TIP ON MAKING YOUR VISIT MORE ENJOYABLE

To avoid the heaviest crowds, it's best to visit on Sunday and Friday; the busiest days are Tuesday and Saturday.

SEA WORLD OF FLORIDA

Sea World of Florida is a 135-acre marine life park and family entertainment center. The park presents seven shows and more than 20 exhibits all year long, including "Shamu: New Visions," a new killer whale show starring Baby Namu, a young killer whale born July 11, 1989. Among the park's most popular attractions are the new Terrors of the Deep, featuring the world's largest collection of dangerous undersea creatures, the Penguin Encounter, and dolphin and seal community pools. Other Sea World favorites are the Whale and Dolphin show, comedic Sea Lion and Otter show, and performances by champion water skiers.

ADDRESS AND TELEPHONE

Sea World of Florida
7007 Sea World Drive
Orlando, FL 32821

(407) 351-3600

LOCATION

Sea World of Florida is located 10 minutes south of downtown Orlando at the intersection of I-4 and the Bee Line Expressway. Many nearby hotels provide shuttle transportation to and from Sea World; check at the concierge desk in your hotel.

OPERATING SEASONS AND HOURS

Open daily year-round. Hours: 9 A.M. to 8 P.M. Closing times vary during peak seasons and holidays, so check with the park upon arrival.

ADMISSION FEES

Adults: $28.55. Children ages 3 to 9: $24.30. Children under 3: free.

TRANSPORTATION AND ACCOMMODATIONS WITHIN THE PARK

Free tram service from the parking lots to the front entrance.

GUEST SERVICES

Restrooms, telephones, first aid, lost and found, free kennels, parking, locker rental, strollers, wheelchairs, diaper-changing areas, foreign currency exchange, automated teller machine. Visa and MasterCard accepted.

RIDE

Sky Tower: ride to the top of the park for a panoramic view.

ATTRACTIONS

Cap'n Kids World: this unique play area with a nautical theme features a 55-foot pirate's galleon with water cannons, rigging nets for climbing, water traverse, and ball crawl.
Penguin Encounter: observe penguins in their own five-acre site.
Terrors of the Deep: nearly a thousand moray eels, three dozen sharks, and other dangerous undersea creatures surround you at this all new attraction.
Dolphin Community Pool: interact with Atlantic bottlenose dolphins.
Seal and Stingray Community Pools: feed and pet these special marine creatures.
Tropical Reef and Caribbean Tide Pool: more than 5,000 tropical fish create aquatic rainbows in the 160,000-gallon Tropical Reef.
Clydesdale Hospitality Hamlet: the world-famous Clydesdale horses will thunder their way into your heart.

SHOWS

Shamu: New Visions: a living documentary about killer whales.

Whale and Dolphin Discovery: whales and dolphins perform together.

Clyde and Seamore 10,000 B.C.: sea lions star with otters and a walrus in this "pre-hysterical" show.

Gold Rush Ski Show: thrilling performances by top-flight water skiers.

Night Magic: after the sun goes down, watch an entertainment lineup that includes a Polynesian Luau dinner show, a sea lion and otter show, "Shamu's Night Magic" show, and a fireworks and laser show.

SPECIAL ANNUAL EVENT

Night Before Citrus: New Year's Eve celebration with music, shows, fireworks, party favors, and champagne toasts.

RESTAURANTS

Bimini Bay Cafe: American and Caribbean cuisine, steaks, cocktails.

Luau Terrace: Polynesian luau. For reservations call (407) 351-3600, ext. 195, or 1-800-227-8048.

Spinnaker Cafe: burgers, fish, chicken sandwiches, soft drinks.

Chicken 'n' Biscuit: fried and barbecued chicken and trimmings, beer.

Pizza 'n' Pasta: pizza, spaghetti, Italian sausage sandwiches, salads, beer, soft drinks.

Waterfront Sandwich Grill: hot dogs, burgers.

SNACK BARS

Snack kiosks located throughout the park sell ice cream, tacos, sandwiches, popcorn, hot dogs, candy, frosted lemonade, soft drinks.

CATERING

Contact Group Sales at (407) 363-2200.

SOUVENIR SHOPS

Shamu Emporium: Shamu souvenirs, including T-shirts, mugs, plush toys, key chains.

Fascinations: men's, women's, and children's clothing.

Penguin Gift Shop: Penguin memorabilia, including T-shirts, jewelry, mugs.

Ocean Treasures: shark jewelry, shark T-shirts, other shark souvenirs.

Hawaiian Gift Shop: Hawaiian-style clothing, jewelry, and gifts.

HINTS FOR TRAVELING WITH CHILDREN, ELDERLY, HANDICAPPED

Diaper-changing areas are available in restrooms. All facilities and show areas provide wheelchair seating and are accessible by ramps. Shaded seating areas are located throughout the park, and the first aid station (located by Cap'n Kids Pavilion) is staffed by certified nurses and paramedics.

HELPFUL TIPS ON MAKING YOUR VISIT MORE ENJOYABLE

To enjoy Sea World completely, allow for at least eight hours in the park. Remember, shirts and shoes are required at all times.

SILVER SPRINGS AND WILD WATERS

Silver Springs covers more than 300 acres of heavily wooded land surrounding North America's largest springwater formation. The springs produce more than 750 million gallons of 99.7 percent pure springwater every 24 hours. Each year approximately 1 million visitors enjoy the park's major attraction, a 2½-mile Jungle Boat Safari along Silver Springs. From the boat guests can observe more than 100 species of wild animals that roam freely, including monkeys, llamas, giraffes, gazelles, and antelopes. Visitors can also cruise the springs in glass-bottom boats. Wild Waters, a water park with a pool, slides, and more, is located on the same site. The brand-new Dinamation Dinosaurs Alive! is located next to Silver Springs.

ADDRESS AND TELEPHONE

Silver Springs and Wild Waters
P. O. Box 370
Silver Springs, FL 32688

(904) 236-2121 or 1-800-234-7458

LOCATION

Silver Springs is located one mile east of Ocala, Florida, on State Road 40. Take I-75 to the State Road 40 East exit; continue east for approximately nine miles.

OPERATING SEASONS AND HOURS

Silver Springs is open daily year-round. Wild Waters is open from the end of March through the end of September. Hours: 9 A.M. to 5 P.M. Hours are extended in the summer.

ADMISSION FEES

For Silver Springs: Adults: $19.95. Children ages 3 to 10: $14.95. Children under 3: free.
For Wild Waters: Adults: $9.95. Children ages 3 to 10: $8.95.
Combination ticket to Silver Springs and Wild Waters: Adults: $22.95. Children ages 3 to 10: $16.95.
For Dinamation's Dinosaurs Alive!: Adults: $4.95. Children ages 3 to 10: $3.95.

TRANSPORTATION AND ACCOMMODATIONS WITHIN THE PARK

None.

GUEST SERVICES

Restrooms, telephones, information booth, first aid, kennels, lost and found, message center, stroller and wheelchair rental. Visa, MasterCard, and American Express cards accepted.

RIDES

Glass Bottom Boats: cruise over North America's largest natural springs formation.
Jeep Safari: ride in a zebra-striped open-air four-wheel-drive vehicle through forests centuries old that are home to more than 60 species of free-roaming native and exotic wildlife.
Jungle Cruise Boat Rides: glide silently along and see monkeys, apes, zebras, antelopes, and many more than 100 other species of wild animals.
Lost River Voyage: a 30-minute, mile-long voyage down the Silver River and into an untamed world of the past; see an area registered as a national natural landmark.

ATTRACTIONS

Doolittle's Deer Park: petting zoo where kids get a chance to pet a variety of tame animals.
Cypress Point: stroll through this semitropical forest, a five-acre island plaza suspended above a natural marsh.
Walk-a-Round Animals: handlers walk through the grounds carrying or leading animals from all corners of the earth.
Wild Waters: a full-fledged water park located on the same site, complete with a wave pool, slides, flumes, kiddie pool, gift shop, cafe, and snack bars. (Separate admission.)
Dinamation's Dinosaurs Alive!: an all new exhibit of moving, roaring, lifelike dinosaurs and hands-on exhibits such as

Dig-a-Fossil and Dino-Rub. (Separate admission.)

SHOWS

At Cypress Point.
Animal Antics: see ordinary house cats and dogs doing amazing tricks.
How to Train an Animal: learn the secrets from the pros on how easy it can be to have your pet do tricks for you at home.
Reptile Show: see snakes, alligators, snapping turtles, and other reptiles.

RESTAURANTS

The Outback: burgers, hot dogs, taco salads, cheese steaks, hot entrees, ice cream, cookies.
Springside Pizzeria: pizza, salads, beer.
Billy Bowlegs: cheese steaks, burgers, hot dogs, salads, cookies, ice cream.

SNACK BARS

Snack stands located throughout the park sell popcorn, hot dogs, ice cream, beer, soft drinks.

CATERING

Contact Robert Aagard at (904) 236-2121.

SOUVENIR SHOPS

Dockside Emporium: T-shirts, hats, glassware, jewelry, knickknacks, photography equipment and supplies, Silver Springs memorabilia.
Pavilion: T-shirts, hats, glassware, jewelry, knickknacks, video camera rentals.
The Nautilus: shell shop.
The Shirt Locker: T-shirts.
Treasure Chest: children's clothing.
Cypress Point Gift Shop: wooden figurines and more.
  Other stands located throughout the park sell T-shirts, hats, shorts, jewelry.

HELPFUL TIPS ON MAKING YOUR VISIT MORE ENJOYABLE

Plan to spend about five hours in the park. Early morning is the best time to see the animals at their most active.

UNIVERSAL STUDIOS FLORIDA

Universal Studios Florida is a combination motion picture/television production studio and entertainment attraction located on 444 acres in Orlando, Florida. Visitors to the studio step behind the scenes and experience what it's like to be in feature films via rides such as Kongfrontation, The FUNtastic World of Hanna-Barbera, E. T. Adventure, and Back to the Future . . . the Ride. The studio attraction also reveals the secrets of TV and motion picture production through many live and interactive shows including Ghostbusters, a Live-Action Spooktacular; "Murder She Wrote" Mystery Theatre; Alfred Hitchcock: The Art of Making Movies; and the Wild, Wild, Wild West Stunt Show. Visitors have the opportunity to star in their own home video adventure at the Screen Test Home Video Adventure. Other entertaining shows include the American Tail Show and the Blues Brothers Show. Park visitors also get to meet such costumed characters as Woody Woodpecker, Fred Flintstone, Popeye, and Harry from "Harry and the Hendersons" as well as celebrity look-alike characters such as Mae West, Groucho Marx, Marilyn Monroe, and Laurel and Hardy. A wide assortment of restaurants and shops are also located at Universal Studios Florida.

ADDRESS AND TELEPHONE

Universal Studios Florida
1000 Universal Studios Plaza
Orlando, FL 32819-7610

(407) 363-8000

LOCATION

Universal Studios Florida is located near the intersection of Interstate 4 and the Florida Turnpike, 10 miles southwest of downtown Orlando on Kirkman Road.

OPERATING SEASONS AND HOURS

Open daily year-round. Hours: from June to early September, 9 A.M. to 11 P.M. Check with the park for hours during the rest of the year.

ADMISSION FEES

One-day ticket: Adults: $31. Children ages 3 to 9: $25. Children under 3: free.
   Two-day ticket: Adults: $49. Children ages 3 to 9: $39. Children under 3: free.

TRANSPORTATION AND ACCOMMODATIONS WITHIN THE PARK

Shuttle service available from parking areas to front gate.

GUEST SERVICES

Restrooms, telephones, information booths, check cashing, ATM full-service banking, camera rental, first aid, kennels, lockers, lost and found, message center, strollers, wheelchairs. Visa, MasterCard, American Express, and Discover cards accepted.

RIDES

Back to the Future . . . the Ride: jump in a DeLorean automobile and experience your own time-travel adventure with the help of Doc Brown.
E.T. Adventure: mount a BMX bicycle to help E.T. save his planet.
Earthquake—the Big One: experience the sensation of an earthquake that measures 8.3 on the Richter scale.

The FUNtastic World of Hanna-Barbera: become part of a cartoon in a high-speed chase with Yogi Bear, the Flintstones, and others.
Kongfrontation: take a tram ride and meet the 30-foot, 13,000-pound King Kong in all his roaring glory.

ATTRACTIONS AND GAMES

Universal Studios Backlot: more than 50 set locations, ranging from Fisherman's Wharf in San Francisco to a brownstone street in New York City.
Screen Test Home Video Adventure: star in your own outrageous film and take home the video.
Fotozine: appear on the cover of your favorite magazine.
Trick Photography Photo Spot: create movie magic with your own camera.
MCA Recording Studios: cut your own hit single or music video.
The Boneyard: explore some of the most amazing film props.
Namco's Coney Island: Skee ball, basketball, and other games of skill.
Namco Space Station: more than 50 arcade games.
New Entertainment Technology: play space-age games and see the latest inventions.
Costumed Characters: see celebrities such as Woody Woodpecker, Frankenstein, W. C. Fields, Humphrey Bogart, and more.

SHOWS

Ghostbusters, a Live-Action Spooktacular: a live-action show based on the film hit.
The Gory, Gruesome & Grotesque Horror Makeup Show: experts demonstrate the craft of makeup and transform people into horrors right before your eyes.
"Murder, She Wrote" Mystery Theatre: as executive producer for one episode of this hit TV show, you choose the stars, capers, crooks, cops, and sound track.
Nickelodeon Tour: take a studio tour and participate in the filming for the only children's television network.

Alfred Hitchcock: The Art of Making Movies: play a part in the films of the master of suspense.

Production Tour: an in-depth, close-up look at how everything from comedies and drama to sci-fi is created.

Animal Actors Stage: Lassie and 50 other stars demonstrate their animal magnetism.

Wild, Wild, Wild West Stunt Show: recapture the thrill and adventure of some of cinema's most memorable classic Western films.

American Tail Theater: a song-and-dance show based on the animated movie.

Street Entertainment: includes the Blues Brothers Show, the Hollywood Hi-Tones, and the rollerskating hostess at Mel's Drive-In.

RESTAURANTS

The park has more than 40 restaurants and snack bars, each an authentic set for motion picture and television production, including the following:

Mel's Drive-In: burgers, chili, and other drive-in delights in the authentic set from *American Graffiti.* The real Wolfman Jack has been spotted here!

Schwab's Pharmacy: an ice-cream parlor based on the famous Hollywood Boulevard spot that also serves hot dogs, chili, and other favorites.

Cafe La Bamba: relive the glamour of Hollywood's golden age while enjoying tacos, tostados, and other Mexican delights.

San Francisco Pastry Company

Lombard's Landing: seafood.

Chez Alcatraz: shrimp cocktail, clam chowder, sourdough rolls, and more. They say it's so delicious, it's almost a crime.

Boardwalk Snacks: hot dogs, ice cream, cotton candy (including piña colada flavor), lemonade.

International Food Bazaar: Greek, German, American, Italian and Chinese specialties.

Animal Crackers: hot dogs, chicken fingers, beef brochettes, yogurt.

Hard Rock Cafe: the largest Hard Rock Cafe in America, built in the shape of a large guitar, serves burgers, salads, fresh desserts, and the famous pig sandwich.

Studio Stars Restaurant: a gourmet dining room serving California cuisine.

Finnegan's Bar and Grill: Irish delicacies, including corned beef and cabbage, fish and chips, stew, and shepherd's pie.

Louie's Italian Restaurant: pasta, pizza, antipasto, cappuccino.

The Fudge Shoppe

Beverly Hills Boulangerie: gourmet snacks for the rich and famished.

Specialty carts throughout the park serve hot dogs, ice cream, popcorn, juices, and soft drinks.

SOUVENIR SHOPS

Universal Studios Store: one-of-a-kind items to put on, play with, or give as gifts, including fashions, novelties, electronic toys, and more.

Studio Gifts: souvenirs, candy, hats, maps.

Lights-Camera-Action: Kodak film, still and video cameras, accessories, rentals.

Hanna-Barbera Store: cartoon clothing, toys, hats, videos, and more.

Bates Motel Gift Shop: macabre memorabilia, gruesome goodies, autographed pictures.

Ghostbusters Paranormal Merchandise: locaters, poppers, zappers, "exorcise" equipment.

Safari Outfitters Ltd.: jewelry, watches, pith helmets, safari clothes.

Doc's Candy

Second-Hand Rose: New York–style thrift shop.

Brown Derby Hat Shop

The Darkroom: film developing in an hour or less.

Silver Screen Collectibles: authentic one-of-a-kind originals.

It's a Wrap: hip fashions.

Hollywood Makeup and Masks: take home gruesome greasepaint and masks, or be made up on the spot.

Quint's Nautical Treasures: brassware, ship models, diver helmets, carvings.

Golden Gate Mercantile: souvenirs.

Bayfront Crafts: crystal, wood carvings, and more.

San Francisco Imports: silk screens, ginger jars, sake sets, and other gifts from the Orient.

Back to the Future Gifts: from the prehistoric to the twenty-fifth century.

E.T.'s Toy Closet and Photo Spot: cosmic creations.

Animal House: a wild and woolly collection of animal stars.

HINT FOR TRAVELING WITH CHILDREN, ELDERLY, HANDICAPPED

Universal Studios Florida is totally accessible to handicapped guests and visitors with special needs. Handicapped parking is located at the main entrance.

WALT DISNEY WORLD

At twice the size of Manhattan, Walt Disney World is a one-of-a-kind entertainment complex. Each year the 43-square-mile vacation resort hosts more than 20 million visitors of all ages. Repeat guests say it takes at least three to four days of touring to get the resort's flavor. Walt Disney World operates several theme parks within its borders. The Magic Kingdom, a park based on the Disneyland design, covers 100 acres and offers 45 rides, shows, and adventures in seven lands, including Main Street U.S.A., Adventureland, Frontierland, Liberty Square, Fantasyland, Tomorrowland, and Mickey's Starland. Epcot Center is a 260-acre international showplace in which Future World explores technologies of the future, and World Showcase presents the culture and entertainment of many nations.

One of the newest parks is the Disney–MGM Studios Theme Park, featuring shows, attractions, and a backstage tour of a working television and movie studio. Typhoon Lagoon, a 56-acre water theme park, boasts slides, tubing flumes, and a 2½-acre wave-making lagoon that lies at the base of a mountain. River Country is an 11-acre water park with water slides and rapids, and Discovery Island is a zoological park filled with a variety of bird species. Finally,

Pleasure Island showcases seven different nightclubs that present a wide variety of entertainment. Restaurants, shops, special attractions, and live performances dot all the theme parks, making Walt Disney World a world-renowned resort and entertainment center.

ADDRESS AND TELEPHONE

Walt Disney World
P. O. Box 10,000
Lake Buena Vista, FL 32830-1000

(407) 824-4321

LOCATION

Walt Disney World is located at Lake Buena Vista, 20 miles southwest of Orlando, off Interstate 4 and U.S. 192.

OPERATING SEASONS AND HOURS

Open daily year-round. Opens at 9 A.M. Operating hours and closings vary from season to season and park to park, so check with the park before arriving.

ADMISSION FEES

One-day, one-park ticket (to Magic Kingdom or Epcot Center or Disney–MGM Studios Theme Park): Adults: $33. Children ages 3 to 9: $26. Children under 3: free.

Four-day, all-three-parks passport: Adults: $111. Children ages 3 to 9: $88. Children under 3: free.

Five-day PLUS Super Pass (unlimited admission to Magic Kingdom, Epcot Center, and Studios Theme Park on any five days plus unlimited admission to River Country, Typhoon Lagoon, Discovery Island, and Pleasure Island for seven days): Adults: $145. Children ages 3 to 9: $116. Children under 3: free.

One-day River Country ticket: Adults: $12. Children ages 3 to 9: $9.50. Children under 3: free.

Discovery Island ticket: Adults: $8. Children ages 3 to 9: $4.50. Children under 3: free.

River Country/Discovery Island combination ticket: Adults: $15. Children ages 3 to 9: $11. Children under 3: free.

One-day Typhoon Lagoon ticket: Adults: $18.50. Children ages 3 to 9: $14.75. Children under 3: free.

Pleasure Island ticket: $11.93.

TRANSPORTATION AND ACCOMMODATIONS WITHIN THE PARK

Transportation: monorail trains, ferryboats, launches, and shuttle services carry visitors between all areas.

Accommodations (for reservations call 407-W-DISNEY):

Disney's Grand Floridian Beach Resort: turn-of-the-century grand hotel with pool, beach, health club, marina.

Disney's Caribbean Beach Resort: five island villages, each with its own pool, beach, laundry.

Disney's Village Resort: villas and suites in a village setting, all with room service and housekeeping.

The Disney Inn: comfortable inn, rustic on the outside, light and airy on the inside.

Disney's Contemporary Resort: an ultramodern hotel of tomorrow, with pool, beach, lake; the monorail glides in and out of its Grand Canyon concourse.

Disney's Polynesian Resort: tropical architecture and landscaping, with pool, marina, spacious accommodations.

Disney's Fort Wilderness Resort and Campground: rent an air-conditioned trailer home in the woods; campsites are available for your own camper or tent.

GUEST SERVICES

Restrooms, telephones, message center, lost and found, first aid, lockers, baby services (for feeding, changing, nursing), lost children center, stroller and wheelchair rental, camera rental, hospitality house (for show reservations), automated teller machine, check cashing. Visa, MasterCard, and American Express cards accepted.

RIDES

At Magic Kingdom:

Big Thunder Mountain Railroad: catch a runaway mine train for a coaster-style ride.

Cinderella's Golden Carousel: merry-go-round with 90 galloping horses.

Grand Prix Raceway: take the wheel of your own race car.

Haunted Mansion: come face-to-face with 999 happy ghosts.

Jungle Cruise: board an explorer's launch for a cruise on tropical rivers.

Liberty Square Riverboat: cruise on an authentic steam-powered stern-wheeler.

Mad Tea Party: whirl and twirl in a giant teacup.

Mike Fink Keelboats: a backwoods journey.

Mr. Toad's Wild Ride: a reckless ride through old London.

Pirates of the Caribbean: sail through pirate strongholds and treasure rooms.

Skyway: a glide-in-the-air journey over the Magic Kingdom.

Space Mountain: experience a winding, soaring race through space on a roller-coaster-type ride.

Star Jets: pilot your own spacecraft on an aerial adventure.

Tom Sawyer Island: ride a raft to this fun-filled island.

20,000 Leagues Under the Sea: sail under the sea in a submarine.

Walt Disney Railroad: tour the entire Magic Kingdom.

WEDway PeopleMover: travel around Tomorrowland aboard this revolutionary system.

At Epcot Center:

Body Wars: at Wonders of Life Pavilion—a thrill ride through the human body.

Caribbean Coral Reef Ride at the Living Seas: the world's largest man-made saltwater environment holds 5.7 million gallons of seawater and more than 80 species of tropical fish and mammals.

El Rio del Tiempo: sail the River of Time through Mexico.

Horizons: your vehicle takes you on an incredible journey through the life-styles of the twenty-first century.

Journey into Imagination: a romp through the creative process.

Listen to the Land: take a boat ride through the plants and animals that make up our food supply.

Maelstrom: encounter a three-headed troll during this high-seas adventure in Norway.

Spaceship Earth: journey through the history of communications.

World of Motion: a rib-tickling ride through the evolution of transportation.

At Disney–MGM Studios Theme Park:

The Great Movie Ride: a spectacular journey into the movies.

Star Tours: the ultimate thrill adventure: a high-speed race to the Moon of Endor.

At Typhoon Lagoon:

Castaway Creek: hop onto a raft or inner tube for a meandering water tour through a rain forest and hidden grotto.

Mt. Mayday: enjoy two speed slides, three curving body slides, and three white water rafting adventures.

Typhoon Lagoon: body-and raft-surf in the largest inland surfing lagoon in the world.

KIDDIE RIDES

At the Magic Kingdom:

Dumbo, the Flying Elephant: an aerial journey in a pint-sized pachyderm.

It's a Small World: hundreds of singing, dancing international dolls entertain on a happy cruise.

Peter Pan's Flight: board a pirate galleon to Never-Never Land.

Snow White's Adventures: a trip through the forest to meet the Seven Dwarfs and the Wicked Witch.

At Typhoon Lagoon:

Ketchakidee Creek: a water playground for kids ages 2 to 5 that features a scaled-down version of adult rides, including a pint-sized white water rafting adventure and an activity pool.

ATTRACTIONS AND GAMES

At Magic Kingdom:

Mickey's House: see Mickey's car, furniture, and memorabilia.

Grandma Duck's Farm: see barnyard babies.

Swiss Family Treehouse: climb winding stairways through a giant replica of the shipwrecked family's home.

Mission to Mars: visit Mission Control, then blast off to Mars.

Dreamflight: explore the history of aviation and experience hypersonic flight.

Carousel of Progress: trace 100 years of progress.

Penny Arcade: games for a penny, nickel, dime, or quarter.

Frontierland Shooting Arcade: test your shooting skills.

At Epcot Center:

Backstage Magic: a journey through the history of computers.

Universe of Energy: at Wonders of Life Pavilion—traveling theater cars powered by a rooftop array of solar cells take you back in time to the land of dinosaurs and on an exploration of the forces that fuel people's lives.

Wonders of China: discover the mysterious East in this presentation.

O Canada: experience Canada's grandeur.

The American Adventure: a dramatic and inspirational story of America presented through motion pictures and audio-animatronics.

Impressions de France: celebrate the French countryside.

At Disney–MGM Studios Theme Park:

Indiana Jones Epic Stunt Spectacular: death-defying feats recreated from movie adventures.

The Monster Sound Show: a comic show in which the audience adds sound to hilarious scenes starring famous actor-comedians.

Superstar Television: you may be cast in a live television special that re-creates the production of hit TV shows.

Backstage Studio Tour: an adventure behind the scenes of a real motion picture studio, featuring visits to Costuming, Scenic Shop, Residential Street, Catastrophe Canyon,

New York Street, Water Effects Tank, Special Effects Workshop, Sound Stages, and Postproduction Editing and Audio.

The Magic of Disney Animation: watch artists create the newest featurettes starring classic Disney characters.

At Pleasure Island:

XZFR Rock 'n' Roll Beach Club: dance in this multilevel gathering place with a beach theme and classic rock 'n' roll music.

Mannequins Dance Palace: a nightclub where animated mannequins dance with guests to the beat of the theatrical world.

Cage: a high-tech alternative dance club featuring 170 video screens.

SHOWS

At Magic Kingdom:

Adventures Club: The Mask Room, Treasure Room, and Library are filled with eccentric surprises.

Comedy Warehouse: stand-up comedy shticks and a troupe perform the "best of" edition of "Forbidden Disney."

Neon Armadillo Music Saloon: toe-tapping country and western bands.

The Walt Disney Story: film that follows Disney from his boyhood through the creation of Walt Disney World. Also rare film footage.

Tropical Serenade: sing along with birds, flowers, and tikis in a musical revue.

Country Bear Vacation Hoedown: audio-animatronic bears perform a hoedown.

The Diamond Horseshoe Jamboree: live musical floor show.

Magic Journeys: world of magic and wonder at this 3-D motion picture.

Tomorrowland Theatre: song and dance stage show starring Disney characters.

Disney Character Hit Parade: daily parade down Main Street featuring all the Disney characters.

Main Street Electrical Parade: electrifying nighttime light extravaganza during summer and holidays, featuring floats and Disney characters.

Surprise Celebration Parade: daytime celebration of Disney World's anniversary.

Spectra Magic Nighttime Parade: nighttime celebration of Disney World's anniversary.

At Epcot Center:

Captain EO: 3-D musical motion picture space adventure starring Michael Jackson.

Harvest Theater: motion picture that examines our relationship with the land.

Kitchen Kabaret: song and dance salute to nutrition.

America Gardens Theatre: performances by the Epcot Center World Dancers and special guest entertainment.

Surprise in the Skies: Disney characters and the world's largest daytime fireworks display.

At Disney–MGM Studios Theme Park:

Dick Tracy in Diamond Double Cross: the comic strip detective battles the overlords of the underworld nightly on the Theater of the Stars stage.

Hollywood, Hollywood!: a star-studded cast of Disney characters and performers sing and dance their way through movie history on the Theater of the Stars stage.

Teenage Mutant Ninja Turtles: the popular characters make appearances daily, with their reporter friend April singing "Heroes on a Half Shell."

Here Come the Muppets: a lively stage show featuring Kermit, Miss Piggy, and the lovable Muppet cast.

Muppets on Location

Muppet Vision 3-D

At Pleasure Island:

AMC Pleasure Island 10: the latest film releases are shown here.

Dinner Shows:

You can combine entertainment with eating at a variety of dinner shows (call 934-7639 for reservations).

Hoop-Dee-Doo: enjoy barbecued ribs, fried chicken, corn on the cob, and strawberry shortcake as you watch this whooping and hollering troupe of singers and dancers. At Pioneer Hall.

The Polynesian Review: authentic Polynesian dancers perform as you are served a full Polynesian-style meal. At the Polynesian Village (the Luau).

Mickey's Tropical Revue: a Polynesian show for the younger set features Disney characters alongside Polynesian performers; a full dinner is served. At the Polynesian Village Resort.

Broadway at the Top: take in a dazzling view of the Magic Kingdom as well as a revue of Broadway hits as you are served a four-course dinner. At the Contemporary Resort.

The Biergarten: a continuous show through the evening complete with traditional German musicians, yodelers, and dancers as you enjoy hearty fare. At Epcot Center's Germany Pavilion.

RESTAURANTS

At Magic Kingdom:

The Crystal Palace: salads, prime rib, chicken, fish, coffee.

Tony's Town Square Cafe: pasta, steak, seafood, burgers, salads.

Plaza Restaurant: burgers, sandwiches, ice cream.

King Stefan's Banquet Hall: prime rib, steak, fish, salads.

Liberty Tree Tavern: sandwiches, salads, beef, chicken, fish.

At Epcot Center:

Le Cellier: pork pie, rib roast, salads.

Restaurant Akershus: salmon, herring, meats, cheeses, beer, wine, spirits.

The Land Grille Room: sandwiches, pizza, steak, poultry, seafood.

Coral Reef Restaurant: seafood.

San Angel Inn Restaurante: Mexican food and beer, spirits.

Nine Dragons Restaurant: Chinese-style beef, chicken, shrimp, duck, wine, spirits.

Biergarten: German fare, sausage, schnitzel, beer, spirits.

L'Originale Alfredo di Roma Ristorante: Italian food, veal, chicken, seafood, pasta.

Mitsukoshi Restaurant: Japanese food, meat, seafood, beer, sake, spirits.

Marrakesh: Moroccan food, wine, spirits.

Chefs de France: French food, chicken, fish, meat, wine, champagne, spirits.

Rose & Crown Pub & Dining Room: United Kingdom fare, beef, fish and chips, drinks.

At Disney–MGM Studios Theme Park:

The Hollywood Brown Derby: veal, chicken, pork, beef, pasta, seafood, the original Cobb salad.

'50s Prime Time Cafe: cold and hot platters, sandwiches, soda fountain treats served in a sitcom setting.

Hollywood & Vine Cafeteria: chicken, ribs, seafood, steaks, prime ribs, salads.

Soundstage Restaurant: pizza, pasta, sandwiches, soups, salads.

Min & Bill's Dockside Diner: subs, ham and cheese sandwiches, seafood salads, fruit and cheese plates, drinks.

Studio Catering Co.: sandwiches, fruit and cheese plates, churros, ice cream, drinks.

At Pleasure Island:

The Portobello Yacht Club: pizza and many Italian specialties, including pasta and entrees.

Fireworks Factory: barbecued ribs, chicken, corn bread.

The Empress Lily: an "authentic" riverboat named after Walt Disney's wife and permanently moored at Pleasure Island; it is stacked with top-notch restaurants and lounges, including:

Fisherman's Deck and Steerman's Quarters: New Orleans–style items including a spicy Cajun egg roll; bayou gumbo with duck; shrimp creole; bouillabaisse; fresh fish prepared to order; prime ribs, filet mignon, and veal; bread pudding and caramel flan.

The Empress Room: hot and curried spinach and oyster soup, chilled avocado soup, salads, pâté, smoked duck, sautéed crabmeat, Dover sole, pheasant, venison, and more in this elegant Louis XV dining room.

SNACK BARS

At Magic Kingdom:

Main Street Wagons: fruit, hot dogs, baked goods, drinks.

Refreshment Corner: hot dogs, coffee, soft drinks.

Adventureland Veranda: Oriental entrees and sandwiches, burgers, hot dogs.
El Pirata y el Perico: hot dogs with toppings, including chili and cheese, drinks.
Pecos Bill Cafe: burgers, barbecued chicken.
Columbia Harbour House: shrimp, chicken, Monte Cristo sandwiches, cold sandwiches, fruit salad.
Pinocchio Village Haus: burgers, hot dogs, chicken, salads, drinks.
Tomorrowland Terrace: soups, salads, sandwiches, beverages.

At Epcot Center:
Stargate Restaurant: omelets, burgers, pizza, salads.
Sunrise Terrace Restaurant: fried seafood, chicken, salads.
Farmers Market: ice cream, soup, salad, cheese, and special desserts.
Odyssey Restaurant: burgers, chicken, hot dogs, salads, freshly baked pies.
Cantina de San Angel: tortillas, taquitos, tostadas, churros.
Kringla Bakeri og Kafe: Norwegian pastries, sandwiches, beer.
Lotus Blossom Cafe: stir-fried beef, sweet-and-sour pork, egg rolls.
Yakitori House: teriyaki chicken, beef.

At Disney–MGM Studios Theme Park:
Backlot Express: burgers, hot dogs, chicken, salads, desserts, drinks.
Dinosaur Gertie's: ice cream.
Starring Rolls: cookies, cakes, pastries, drinks.
Specialty Food Trucks: located throughout the park, trucks serve sausages, hot dogs, nachos, drinks.

At Typhoon Lagoon:
Typhoon Tilly's Galley and Grog: sandwiches, kebabs, seafood salads, ice cream, beer.

At Pleasure Island:
Merriweather's Market: a boutique of meats, fruits, vegetables.

CATERING

Contact Convention/Banquet Services at (407) 828-3200.

SOUVENIR SHOPS

At Magic Kingdom:
Emporium: Disney character merchandise, Magic Kingdom mementos.
Disney Clothiers: Disney character fashions.
The Chapeau: Disney character hats.
Frontier Trading Post: Western, Indian, and Mexican gifts, leather goods.
Bearly Country: plush bears, country crafts, clothing.
Big Al's: Davy Crockett coonskin caps, Big Al merchandise.
Ichabod's Landing: magic tricks, masks, gags.
Disneyana Shop: old and new Disney collectibles.
Tinkerbell's Toy Shop: toys, games, plush Disney merchandise.
Mickey's Christmas Carol: Christmas accessories and gifts.
Space Place: Florida T-shirts, sweatshirts, glow jewelry.
Mickey's Mart: Disney memorabilia.

At Epcot Center:
Future World Kiosk: Disney character merchandise and Epcot mementos.
Living Seas Shop: memorabilia from the Living Seas attraction.
Disney Traders: Disney character souvenirs, decorative gifts from around the world.
Port of Entry: gifts from many nations.
Plaza de los Amigos: baskets, clothing, hats, piñatas from Mexico.
The Puffin's Roost: porcelain, glass, pewter, wooden items, clothing from Norway.
Yong Feng Shangdian: authentic gifts from China.
Glas und Porzellan: ceramic collectibles from Germany.
Der Teddybar: German toys, teddy bears, dolls.
La Gemma Elegante: gold, sterling, Venetian bead and cameo jewelry.
Heritage Manor Gifts: handcrafted American items.
Mitsukoshi Department Store: dolls, kimonos, Japanese handicrafts.
Tangier Traders: Moroccan clothing, accessories, leather goods.
Plume et Palette: French art, crystal, Limoges porcelain, mementos.

The Magic of Wales: Welsh handicrafts, gifts, mementos.

Northwest Mercantile: Indian and Eskimo crafts, Canadian clothing, moccasins, gifts.

At Disney-MGM Studios Theme Park:

Movieland Memorabilia: movie souvenirs, sundries.

Mickey's of Hollywood: Disney character merchandise, including T-shirts and ready-to-wear.

Keystone Clothiers: Disney character clothing, jewelry, Hollywood-style accessories.

Golden Age Souvenirs: gifts from the golden age of radio and TV, plus Disney Channel logo products.

The Disney Studio Store: Walt Disney Studios and Touchstone Pictures clothing and accessories.

Animation Gallery: original Disney animation art, limited reproductions, books, figurines, collectibles.

At Typhoon Lagoon:

Singapore Sal's Souvenirs and Saleable Salvage: swimsuits, souvenirs, sundries.

At Pleasure Island:

Island Shop: art jewelry, tableware, posters, clothing, accessories.

Avigators Supply: adventurewear, souvenirs.

HINTS FOR TRAVELING WITH CHILDREN, ELDERLY, HANDICAPPED

Disabled guests are urged to stop by Magic Kingdom's City Hall to pick up the "Walt Disney World Disabled Guests Guidebook." For sight-impaired guests, tape cassettes and portable tape recorders are available at these locations, with a small deposit required. Also, a Telecommunications Device for the Deaf (TDD) is available at all parks and when calling 407-W-DISNEY for accommodations and/or dinner show reservations. These same service items are available at Epcot's Earth Station and at Disney–MGM Studios Theme Park Guest Services Building at the main entrance.

HELPFUL TIPS ON MAKING YOUR VISIT MORE ENJOYABLE

If possible, plan to spend at least one day per park when visiting Walt Disney World. To get the best value buy a four-or five-day passport upon arrival. Because Walt Disney World is so large, it is important to pace yourself carefully. Remember, there's lots to do at night, so make sure you have enough energy left at day's end to enjoy the festivities.

Guided tours of the Magic Kingdom and Epcot Center are available at a nominal charge. Check at City Hall (in the Magic Kingdom) or Earth Station (in Epcot Center) for more information.

WATER MANIA

Water Mania is a 24-acre family water theme park located less than two miles east of Walt Disney World. It features a range of water thrill rides, including the spiraling Looney Flumes and the curving Double Berserker. The park also offers such "dry" attractions as an 8,100-square-foot maze and the Big Chipper, an 18-hole miniature golf course. Visitors can tan on the white sand beach or cool off in hammocks nestled among oaks and pines. There's a three-acre wooded picnic area, a snack bar for refreshments, and a gift shop with swimwear fashions.

ADDRESS AND TELEPHONE

Water Mania
6073 W. Highway 192
Kissimmee, FL 34746

(407) 396-2626

LOCATION

Water Mania is located south of Orlando and 1½ miles east of Walt Disney World. Take Interstate 4 to Highway 192, exit 25A. From Orlando International Airport, take the Beeline Expressway to Interstate 4 West to exit 25A.

OPERATING SEASONS AND HOURS

Open daily from March to November. Hours: from March to May and from September to November: 10 A.M. to 5 P.M. From June to August: 9:30 A.M. to 8:30 P.M.

ADMISSION FEES

Adults: $16.95. Children ages 3 to 12: $14.95. Children under 3: free.

TRANSPORTATION AND ACCOMMODATIONS WITHIN THE PARK

None.

GUEST SERVICES

Restrooms, lockers, changing facilities, lost and found, first aid, raft rental. Visa, MasterCard, and American Express cards accepted.

RIDES

Anaconda: raft ride; four people to a raft.
Banana Peel: raft ride; two to a raft.
Double Berserker: streak down a slide with a double curve.
Looney Flumes: slide through 960 feet of crazy twists and turns.
The Screamer: jet down a 72-foot-high free-fall speed slide.

KIDDIE RIDES

The Squirt Pond: a two-foot-deep pool with kid-sized slides and colorful tubes.

ATTRACTIONS AND GAMES

The White Caps: frolic in one of the largest wave pools in Florida.
Rain Forest: a water playground just for kids.

The Big Chipper: an 18-hole miniature golf course.
Maze: find your way through this 8,100-square-foot maze to four different flags; try to exit with the fastest time.
Volleyball: play on the beach.
Midway: arcade games that range from pinball to batting cages.

SHOWS

Big-name concerts are featured throughout the year. Check with the park for its performance schedule and show times.

RESTAURANTS

None.

SNACK BARS

Sub Shop: submarine sandwiches.
Swirls: ice cream.
Snack Bar: burgers, hot dogs, soft drinks.

CATERING

Contact Lisa Murphy at (407) 396-2626.

SOUVENIR SHOP

Swimwear, apparel, park and Florida souvenirs.

HINT FOR TRAVELING WITH CHILDREN, ELDERLY, HANDICAPPED

Small children should have life vests or water wings.

WEEKI WACHEE SPRING AND BUCCANEER BAY

At Weeki Wachee Spring, the Mermaids of Weeki Wachee perform an underwater show in the world's only underwater spring theater. Included is their all new performance of Hans Christian Andersen's classic love story, *The Little Mermaid*. The 100-acre park also features river cruise boat rides during which visitors can see raccoons, osprey, alligators, and heron in their natural habitat. Children can make friends with a llama, pygmy deer, and emu in the Mermaids' Petting Park. Buccaneer Bay, located next to Weeki Wachee Spring, is a natural springwater park complete with a white sand beach and river flumes.

ADDRESS AND TELEPHONE

Weeki Wachee Spring
6131 Commercial Way
Spring Hill, FL 34606

(904) 596-2062 or 1-800-678-9335

LOCATION

The park is located 45 miles north of Tampa on U.S. 19 at State Road 50.

OPERATING SEASONS AND HOURS

Open daily year-round. Hours: 10 A.M. to 6 P.M. (Exception: from late March to mid-June Buccaneer Bay is open from 10 A.M. to 5 P.M.)

ADMISSION FEES

For Weeki Wachee Spring: Adults: $13.95. Children ages 3 to 11: $9.95. Children under 3: free.
   For Buccaneer Bay: Adults: $7.95. Children ages 3 to 11: $6.95. Children under 3: free.
   Combination ticket to Weeki Wachee Spring and Buccaneer Bay: Adults: $17.95. Children ages 3 to 11: $13.95. Children under 3: free.

TRANSPORTATION AND ACCOMMODATIONS WITHIN THE PARK

None.

GUEST SERVICES

Restrooms, telephones, information booth, first aid, kennels, lost and found, message center, stroller and wheelchair rental. Visa, MasterCard, and American Express cards accepted.

RIDES

At Weeki Wachee:
Wilderness River Cruise: wild raccoons, osprey, alligators, and herons come out to meet the boat as you cruise the springwater river.

At Buccaneer Bay:
Rocket Sleds: two water slides into a natural spring.
Turbo-Charged Thunderbolt: a tube water slide that lands you in a natural spring.

KIDDIE RIDES

At Buccaneer Bay:
Kiddie Slides

ATTRACTIONS AND GAMES

Animal Forest Petting Zoo: pet llamas, pygmy deer, and emus in this children's petting park.
Beach Volleyball: at Buccaneer Bay.
Video Game Arcade: at Buccaneer Bay.

SHOWS

Mermaids of Weeki Wachee: live "mermaids" perform in an underwater show. See the world's only live underwater performance of Hans Christian Andersen's childhood classic, *The Little Mermaid*.

Birds of the World Show: free-flying eagles, hawks, falcons, and owls swoop and dive on command in an awesome display of beauty, speed, and power.

Exotic Bird Show: a colorful exhibition of macaws, parrots, and other exotic birds performing stunts.

RESTAURANT

Mermaids' Galley: sandwiches, salads, nachos, hot dogs, ice cream, drinks.

SNACK BAR

Mermaids' Lagoon: burgers, hot dogs, chicken, fish, fries, drinks.

CATERING

Contact Kelly Gassaway at (904) 596-2062 or 1-800-678-9335.

SOUVENIR SHOPS

Treasure Chest: T-shirts, hats, collectibles, Weeki Wachee memorabilia.

Gift Locker: T-shirts, hats, jewelry, fudge.

WET'N WILD

Adding to the many entertainment attractions found in Orlando, Florida, Wet'n Wild is a 25-acre water theme park for adults and children. It features several thrill slides and water activities, including the 76-foot-high Der Stuka, The Blue Niagara, two intertwined looping tubes that send riders screaming down more than 300 feet of slide, and the all new Bubba Tub. For the less adventurous there is the Lazy River gentle float, and for very young guests there are pint-sized versions of the popular adult rides, such as the Wave Pool, Raging Rapids, and the Lazy River.

ADDRESS AND TELEPHONE

Wet'n Wild
6200 International Drive
Orlando, FL 32819

(407) 351-3200

LOCATION

Wet'n Wild is located 10 minutes south of downtown Orlando. Take I-4 west of Orlando to exit 30A, then turn onto International Drive.

OPERATING SEASONS AND HOURS

Open from mid-February to December. Opens at 9 A.M. Both opening and closing times vary, so check with the park before arriving.

ADMISSION FEES

Adults: $19.95. Children ages 3 to 12: $17.95.

TRANSPORTATION AND ACCOMMODATIONS WITHIN THE PARK

None.

GUEST SERVICES

Restrooms, lockers, showers, towels, life vest and inner tube rental, first aid. Visa and MasterCard accepted.

RIDES

The Black Hole: blast off into outer space through a dark tunnel complete with special music, lighting, and other effects that will make you feel as if you're soaring through the galaxy.

The Blue Niagara: go screaming down two intertwined, looping tubes from a starting platform 57 feet in the air and more than 300 feet of slide.

Bubba Tub: speed in a four-person inner tube from a six-story tower down a 300-foot triple dip slide to a splash landing pool below.

Der Stuka: towering 76 feet in the sky, this speed slide gives you the feeling of free-fall before letting you glide to a slippery landing.

Hydra-Maniac: two translucent tube slides plummet from a 30-foot high tower into a 360-degree turn before dropping you into a sparkling clear pool.

Kamikaze: try this chute that's as long as a football field and rises more than six stories above pool level.

Knee Ski: a cable-operated ski tow gives you the opportunity to knee-board around a half-mile, hexagon-shaped lake course at speeds up to 15 miles per hour.

The Mach 5: five state-of-the-art super flumes carry you down a twisting, dropping course nearly ½ mile in length.

Raging Rapids: bump and bounce through whirlpools and wave pools, then rush along the white rapids and over the waterfall for your final plunge.

KIDDIE RIDES

Kid's Water Playground: pint-sized versions of popular adult rides such as the Wave Pool, Raging Rapids, and the Lazy River.

ATTRACTIONS AND GAMES

Surf Lagoon: a 570,000-gallon pool where you can enjoy oceanlike waves.

The Bubble Up: a giant, colorful inflated bubble with a cascading water fountain, perfect for climbing, bouncing, and sliding for the youngest guests.

Mini-Golf

SPECIAL ANNUAL EVENTS

Summer Nights: from mid-June to mid-August, special live entertainment, contests, games, and prizes, and the Beach Club with music videos and dancing.

RESTAURANTS

None.

SNACK BARS

Main Snack Bar: burgers, hot dogs, gyros, salads, fries, barbecue sandwiches, chips, beer, wine, soft drinks.

Pizza Building: pizza, hot sub sandwiches, beer, wine, soft drinks.

Chicken 'n' Suds: chicken fingers, corn dogs.

Cookies 'n' Cones: ice cream.

CATERING

Contact Group Sales at (407) 351-1800.

SOUVENIR SHOP

Beach Connection Gift Shop: swimwear, sportswear, T-shirts, beach towels, sandals, park souvenirs, film, candy.

HINT FOR TRAVELING WITH CHILDREN, ELDERLY, HANDICAPPED

The park has a large variety of shaded seating areas that serve as good places to get small children and the elderly out of the direct Florida sun.

HELPFUL TIP ON MAKING YOUR VISIT MORE ENJOYABLE

Facilities are not available for pets at the park, and you are strongly urged *not* to leave pets in the car.

GEORGIA

SIX FLAGS OVER GEORGIA

Six Flags Over Georgia is considered by many to be Georgia's premier family theme park. Spread across 331 acres, the park offers guests a wide array of shows, sights, meals, and munchies. But the park is perhaps best known for its spectacular thrill rides, including Ragin' Rivers which allows guests to spill and splash down contoured water channels without changing into swimwear and the breathtaking Georgia Cyclone patterned after the legendary Coney Island Cyclone. Another favorite is The Great Gasp, the South's only parachute drop with a mind-boggling 20-story drop. For the smaller guests Bugs Bunny Land offers a charming area of "soft play" with Wile E. Coyote's Cave and Bugs Bunny's Carrot Patch. Entertainment, featuring musical, magical, and comedy shows, rounds out the park's attractions.

ADDRESS AND TELEPHONE

Six Flags Over Georgia
P. O. Box 43187
Atlanta, GA 30378

(404) 948-9290

LOCATION

Six Flags Over Georgia is located at I-20 West and Six Flags Parkway, approximately 12 miles west of Atlanta. The park is also accessible by mass transit. MARTA Rapid Rail runs from downtown Atlanta to the Hightower station, just six miles east of the park where MARTA bus travels to and from Six Flags every hour. For more information call (404) 848-4711 for the time schedule. Grayline Tours operates for groups of 30 or more with advance notice. Call (404) 767-0594.

OPERATING SEASONS AND HOURS

Open weekends from mid-March to May and September and October. Open daily from the end of May to the end of August. Opens at 10 A.M. Closing times vary, so check with the park upon arrival.

Also open during spring break. Check the park for a schedule.

ADMISSION FEES

Adults: $22. Children ages 3 to 9: $15.70. Children 2 and under: free. Seniors 55 and over: $11. Two-day Best Buy: $26.20.

TRANSPORTATION AND ACCOMMODATIONS WITHIN THE PARK

Six Flags Railroad tours the park.

GUEST SERVICES

Restrooms, telephones, coin-operated lockers, stroller rental, diapering and nursing center, wheelchairs, Guest Relations office, first aid, vending machines with international medications, lost parents area, kennels at Toll Plaza, gasoline and other auto needs in northeast corner of guest parking lot. Visa and MasterCard accepted.

RIDES

Dahlonega Mine Train: re-creates the thrill of a runaway mine train from the Georgia gold rush days.
Dodge City Bumper Cars: ride in miniature bumper cars designed like the Indy 500 race cars of the early 1900s.
The Flying Dutchman: a giant suspended swinging pirate ship creates a "sinking sensation."
Free Fall: see how it feels to fall off a 10-story building.
Georgia Cyclone: a replica of the legendary Coney Island Cyclone that plunges, twists, and races through high-banked turns.
The Great American Scream Machine: this roller coaster ride races through dips and plunges.
The Great Gasp: the South's only parachute ride features a breathtaking 20-story drop.
The Great Six Flags Air Racer: fly in an open-cockpit biplane reminiscent of 1930s barnstorming.
Hanson Cars: enjoy the touring grace of early roadsters.
Highland Swing: take a ride on a Maypole-style circular swing.
Lick Skillet and Confederate Skybuckets: sky-high cable cars offer a panoramic view of the park.
Log Flume: a log ride that gives a unique twist to a feature of Georgia's early logging camps.

Looping Starship: experience the feeling of space flight as the giant shuttle makes ever-widening arcs, eventually suspending you upside down before making several 360-degree turns.
Mind Bender: this triple-loop roller coaster catapults you through three loops, two of them vertical.
Monster Plantation: journey by boat through a tale of Southern mystery with animated monsters.
Ragin' Rivers: four water participatory rides that allow guests to spill and splash their way down various contoured water channels.
Riverview Carousel: an antique carousel featuring handcarved wooden horses and "lovers' chariots."
Splashwater Falls: a wet, wild adventure in which 20-passenger boats plunge over a 50-foot waterfall.
Thunder River: ride in 12-person rafts through roaring rapids.
Wheelie: gondola cars rotate to dizzying speeds, then move into vertical position.

KIDDIE RIDES

Buccaneer Boats: pirate ships fly through the air.
Road Runner's Convoy: a realistic trailer tractor rig drives cross-country in style.
Tweety's Swing: up and down, round and round on a miniature circular swing under a gaily colored canopy.

ATTRACTIONS

Yosemite Sam Playfort: featuring one-of-a-kind soft-play components such as Sylvester's Slide, the fort lets young children explore and meet Looney Tunes characters.

SHOWS

Southern Star Amphitheatre: shows feature top performers from rock and country to contemporary Christian.

Chevy Show: varying adventures shown on a 180-degree screen in the Chevy Show Theatre.

A variety of live shows are held in the Crystal Pistol and the Showcase Theatre as well as other outdoor locations.

RESTAURANTS

Tondee's Tavern: char-grilled hamburgers and chicken sandwiches, fries.
Contemporary Kitchen: gourmet half-pound burgers.
Plantation House: fried chicken, chicken breast fillet strips, fries, coleslaw, desserts.
Dixie Belles: char-grilled specialties.
Country Cookout: smoked barbecue specialty.

SNACK BARS

More than 40 portable stands sell burgers, hot dogs, fries, pizza, ice cream, popcorn, pretzels, cotton candy, drinks.

CATERING

Contact Group Sales at (404) 739-3430.

SOUVENIR SHOPS

Front Mall Bazaar: apparel, souvenirs, gifts, Looney Tunes toys and merchandise.
Thrillseekers: mementos of favorite thrill rides.
Gallery: giftware, posters, jewelry.
Miss Abigail's: gifts and collectibles.
Atlanta Gifts & Souvenirs: souvenirs of Atlanta.
Last Chance: T-shirts, gifts, memorabilia.

Souvenir stands located throughout the park sell Six Flags memorabilia.

HINTS FOR TRAVELING WITH CHILDREN, ELDERLY, HANDICAPPED

Special parking is available for handicapped guests in the main parking lot. Ask for directions from Toll Plaza hosts and hostesses. Re-duced admission will be granted to disabled guests based on individual limitations; inquire at Guest Relations office. Wheelchairs can be accommodated in most restaurants, gift shops, games, arcades, and restroom facilities. Theaters can provide special seating to accommodate disabled guests. Please arrive at least 20 minutes before showtime to secure assistance.

A diapering and nursing center is located in the Lost Parents Schoolhouse near the Great Gasp ride.

WHITE WATER AND AMERICAN ADVENTURES

White Water is a 35-acre water theme park featuring the Atlanta Ocean, a wave pool with four-foot waves, a lazy float down the Little Hooch, and a variety of water thrill rides. Among the most popular attractions is the Bahama Bob-Slide, a ride designed for up to six people. American Adventures, located on the same premises, is a dry amusement park with all-time favorite rides such as Go-Carts, bumper cars, and a carousel. There are also volleyball, an arcade, a children's pool area, activity pool, restaurants, and gift shops.

ADDRESS AND TELEPHONE

White Water and American Adventures
250 North Cobb Parkway
Marietta, GA 30062

(404) 424-WAVE

LOCATION

White Water and American Adventures are located northwest of Atlanta in Marietta. Take I-75 north to exit 113.

OPERATING SEASONS AND HOURS

White Water: Open daily from the first weekend in May to Labor Day. Hours: 10 A.M. to 9 P.M.

American Adventures: Open year-round. Hours: 10 A.M. to 9 P.M.

ADMISSION FEES

White Water: Adults: $14.99. Children under 48 inches: $9.99. Children under 4: free.

American Adventures: Free admission. Pay-as-you-play.

TRANSPORTATION AND ACCOMMODATIONS WITHIN THE PARK

None.

GUEST SERVICES

Restrooms, telephones, information booth, check cashing, locker rental, bathhouses, showers, free life vests, free lounge chairs. Visa, MasterCard, American Express, and Discover cards accepted.

RIDES

At White Water:

Bahama Bob-Slide: exciting new six-person ride.

Bermuda Triangle: ride a boat or double inner tube through a partly enclosed tunnel with high-banking curves.

Black River Falls: ride with a buddy in a double inner tube through a completely enclosed tunnel.

Caribbean Plunge: a free-falling 100-foot plunge, complete with a dip along the way.

Dragon's Tail Falls: a 250-foot triple drop that will send you flying at speeds up to 30 miles per hour.

Gulf Coast Screamer: a specially designed inner tube zips you down two twisting, turning water flumes.

Little Hooch: walk, swim, or float down a ⅓-mile water area.

Splashdown Body Flumes: three slides, each more than 300 feet long, propel you down twisting, turning fiberglass chutes.

Tidal Wave: plunge down a 250-foot slide into Little Hooch.

White Water Rapids: experience the thrill of white water rafting as you soar down two rapids carved from the natural hillside to create rushing pools.

At American Adventures:

Balloon Ride: spinning simulated hot air balloon ride.

Barnstormers: miniature airplane ride.

Circus Spin: the ringmaster of the circus leads you as you spin around.

The Great Race: motorcars that reach 22 miles per hour on an auto track.

Main Street Motorcars: bumper cars.

Merry-Go-Round: carousel complete with calliope music.

Ridgeline Racer: miniature-sized roller coaster.

Timberline Truckers: kids can drive while parents sit in the backseat.

KIDDIE RIDES

At White Water:

Little Squirt Island: huge activity pool only 1½ feet deep, with squirt guns, slides, swings, inner tube ride, sand beach area, and crawl-through maze.

ATTRACTIONS AND GAMES

At White Water:

Atlanta Ocean: largest wave pool in the area; you can bodysurf on four-foot waves.

Video Arcade

Games of Skill: games such as Skee ball are located in the park, and players can win prizes.

At American Adventures:

Professor Plinker's Laboratory: indoor play area for young children with ball crawls, nets, toys, a shadow room, and more.

Main Street Golf: play "through" buildings, down sidewalks, and across streets.

Hidden Harbor Miniature Golf: play through Foggy Reef and walk the plank to the shipwrecked U.S.S. *Marietta* where the course continues across the creaking deck and into the ship's eerie hold.

Penny Arcade: games of amusement and skill with prizes.

SHOWS

Dive-Ins: "dive-in movies" are shown after dark at White Water in July, every Wednesday and Friday night.

RESTAURANTS

At White Water:
Mainstreet: nachos, funnel cakes, fries.
Sternwheeler: chicken, corn dogs, fries.
Smokey's: burgers, hot dogs, barbecue.
Geno's: pizza.
Seaside Snacks: hot dogs, ice cream.
Lite-House Deli: cold sandwiches, salads, fruit.

At American Adventures:
Inventor's Club Restaurant: family-style restaurant.

SNACK BARS

At White Water:
Good Humor: ice cream on a stick.
Icee: ice treats.
Berries-N-Cream: soft-serve floats.

CATERING

Contact Carolyn Sadler at (404) 424-6683.

SOUVENIR SHOPS

At White Water:
Treasure Chest: suncare items, park mementos.
Surf-N-Swim: sunwear and suncare items, park mementos.

HINT FOR TRAVELING WITH CHILDREN, ELDERLY, HANDICAPPED

The park is wheelchair accessible, but most of the rides have lots of stairs.

HELPFUL TIPS ON MAKING YOUR VISIT MORE ENJOYABLE

All you need is a towel and a swimsuit; the park provides more than 2,000 lounge chairs, life vests, shade and deck areas. The least crowded days are Monday and Friday. No cutoff shorts, bottles, glass, or cans allowed. You cannot bring your own food into the park.

NORTH CAROLINA

CAROWINDS

Carowinds is an 83-acre world-class park featuring 10 themed areas, each depicting a different aspect of life in the Carolinas. For instance, Old World Market Place reflects the international heritage of the two Carolinas, Carolina R.F.D. salutes rural Carolina, while Pirate Island reminds visitors of the Carolina coast where colorful pirates once loomed. The park also offers rides ranging from the hair-raising to the serene, and a complete water play area, Rip Tide Reef. Also at Carowinds are shows spotlighting top-notch entertainment, shopping, and a wide assortment of eateries and games.

ADDRESS AND TELEPHONE

Carowinds
P. O. Box 410289
Charlotte, NC 28241-0289

(704) 588-2600 or 1-800-822-4428

LOCATION

Carowinds is located just off I-77 (exit 90) on the North Carolina/South Carolina state line, approximately 10 miles south of Charlotte, North Carolina, and 12 miles north of Rock Hill, South Carolina.

OPERATING SEASONS AND HOURS

Open weekends from mid-March to May and from mid-August to mid-October. Open daily except Friday from June to mid-August. Opens at 10 A.M. Closing times vary, so check with the park upon arrival.

ADMISSION FEES

Adults: $21.95. Children ages 4 to 6 and seniors: $10.95. Children 3 and under: free. Two-day admission: $26.95.

TRANSPORTATION AND ACCOMMODATIONS WITHIN THE PARK

A 207-site campground provides a pool, game room, miniature golf, volleyball, and softball facilities. Transportation to the adjacent theme park is available during the season. For reservations call (704) 588-2606 or (704) 588-3363.

GUEST SERVICES

Restrooms, telephones, first aid, lost and found, lost parents center, message center, lockers, free kennel (at Plantation Square Guest Relations Office), stroller rental, wheelchairs, baby care center, courtesy phones along parking lot fence for car assistance. Personal checks and Visa, MasterCard, American Express, and Discover cards accepted.

RIDES

Blackbeard's Revenge: experience a pirate ship battle as you step into a pivoted room that rotates to create an illusory swinging effect.

Carolina Cyclone: quadruple looping roller coaster with trains spinning through two 360-degree vertical loops, two 360-degree barrel rolls, and a 450-degree uphill helix.

Carolina Goldrusher: steel roller coaster that feels like a runaway mine train.

Carolina Pipeline: two 352-foot-long racing tube raft rides that take you through a series of curves, spirals, and drops.

Carolina Sternwheeler: paddle wheel boat ride around Smurf Island.

Carowinds Skytower: view the entire Carowinds complex and downtown Charlotte, North Carolina, in an air-conditioned cabin that travels up a 320-foot tower.

Dodgem's: ever-popular bumper cars.

Flintstone Express: a miniature train takes you through the woods.

Frenzoid: a giant ship that swings backward, forward, and then completes a series of 360-degree loops. You experience sudden speed changes, rocking motions, anticipation, and controlled free-fall.

The Gauntlet: this family thrill ride will take you around 360-degree loops and pause at the highest point for a spectacular park view.

Kaleidoscope: ride in whirling, spinning gondolas.

Meteorite: gondolas connected to a large wheel that starts spinning, then tilts and sends the gondolas into upside-down orbit.

Monorail: electric monorail train takes you on a two-mile ride through Carowinds complex.

Powder Keg Flume: flume ride with boats shaped like gunpowder kegs.

Racing Rivers: experience breathtaking drops down cascading waters in sleds that skip across a pool before gliding to a stop.

Rip Roarin' Rapids: a man-made river in which you ride in round boats through rapids, wave lakes, geysers, canyons, waterfalls, and a cavern.

Scooby Doo: wooden roller coaster with the theme of famous Hanna-Barbera characters.

Thunder Road: double wood out-and-back roller coaster drops 85 feet at a 50-degree angle.

Vortex: all new stand-up roller coaster that takes riders through a series of loops, spins, and drops.

Whirling Dervish: elevated whirling swings.

Whitewater Falls: 20-passenger boats plunge down a 45-foot waterfall through a 20-foot wave of water to a soaking wet splashdown.

Wild Bull: train speeds through a 360-degree curve to simulate thrills of bobsledding.

KIDDIE RIDES

Bamm Bamm's Boat Float: minirapids river ride designed for both children and adults.

Boo Boo's Ballon Race: a colorful balloon adventure for both children and adults. Ride in gondolas as they move up and in a circular motion.

Carousel: built in 1923, with 68 handcarved horses. (Located in kiddie area; adults ride too.)

Dastardly's Flying Circus: flying biplanes that kids can control.

Elroy's Skychase: miniature swing ride.

Judy's Jetliners: 10 planes that climb and dive in a circular path.

Scrappy's Skytower: a miniature version of the Carowinds skytower.

ATTRACTIONS AND GAMES

Riptide Reef: a six-acre area featuring slides, wave pool, and water play area for young guests.

Tidewater Bay: fan-shaped wave pool makes you feel as if you're in the ocean surf.

Plantation Square: the main park entrance is highlighted by a huge mansion and shopping area modeled after the Charleston waterfront.

Old World Market Place: reflects the international heritage of the two Carolinas.

Hanna-Barbera Land: activities that cater to little guests.

Carolina R.F.D.: a salute to rural Carolina.

County Fair: reminiscent of an old-fashioned country fair.

Pirate Island: a reminder of the Carolinas' beautiful coast and the colorful pirates that once sailed there.

Blue Ridge Junction: log cabins, mining towns, and crafts with all the hospitality of the Appalachian Mountains.

Carolina Showplace: features contemporary Carolina singing and dancing.

Smurf Island: a 1⅓-acre wooded island based on the Smurf theme and featuring a play area with a giant rope climb, two ball crawls, hilly exploring trails, slides, and a hidden Smurf village.

Video Arcades: two arcades featuring the latest video challenges.

Shooting Gallery

Games of Skill: located throughout the park.

SHOWS

Six theaters feature a variety of entertainment for all ages, from Broadway-style shows to popular and country music fests. Check with the park for its performance schedule and show times.

RESTAURANTS

Casey's Grill: burgers, barbecue, grilled chicken sandwiches, salads, stuffed potatoes, fresh-baked breads, special meals for children.

Country Kitchen: fried chicken, barbecued chicken and ribs, baked beans, fries, coleslaw, salads, desserts, drinks, special meals for children.

Village Tavern: turkey, ham, and roast beef sandwiches, hot dogs, soft drinks.

SNACK BARS

Blue Ridge Corn Dog: corn dogs, soft drinks.

Blue Ridge Yogurt

Grubsteak: burgers, corn dogs, fries, soft drinks.

Billy Bob's: burgers, hot dogs, fries, soft drinks.

White Water Shakes: nondairy shakes.

Pizza Snack

Country Fair Cotton Candy

Country Fair Corn Dogs

Dairy Dip: soft-serve ice cream.

Granny's Sweet Treats: ice cream.

Yogi's Picnic Basket: hot dogs, soft drinks.

Cafe Italiano: spaghetti, pizza, hoagies, Italian subs.

Jester's Sausage Haus: bratwurst, sauerkraut, Italian sausage, hot dogs.

Jester's Ice Cream

Sundae Isle: ice cream

Bakery

Dockside Deli: turkey, ham, and roast beef sandwiches, hot dogs.

Funnel Factory: funnel cakes.

Plantation Bar-b-que: barbecue, hot dogs, soft drinks.

The Oasis: frozen nonalcoholic drinks.

Castle Kitchen: ices, pretzels, drinks.

Assorted other stands throughout the park serve hot dogs, candy, ice cream, soft drinks.

CATERING

Contact Group Sales at (704) 588-2606, ext. 2630.

SOUVENIR SHOPS

Appalachian Trader: toys and souvenirs from the Wild West.

Magic: magic tricks.

Corner Candy Shop

Glass Blower Shop: hand-blown glass.

Buttons 'n Books: your child's name throughout a storybook, and buttons with his or her picture.

Picture Productions: wall calendars, T-shirts, and buttons with your own likeness.

Recording Studio: make and buy your own audiotape or music video.

Airbrush Factory: custom-designed T-shirts.

Closet Classics: T-shirts.

Hanna-Barbera Shop: Hanna-Barbera toys, games, stuffed animals, and other souvenirs.

Kids Clothing: clothing, hats, stuffed animals.

On-Shore: swimwear and accessories.

HINTS FOR TRAVELING WITH CHILDREN, ELDERLY, HANDICAPPED

The Baby Care Center provides facilities for diaper changing, warming bottles, feeding, and nursing. An attractions guide for physically impaired guests in wheelchairs is available by writing to the Public Relations Department of Carowinds.

HELPFUL TIPS ON MAKING YOUR VISIT MORE ENJOYABLE

If you visit on a weekend, Sunday is less crowded than Saturday. On busy days it's a good idea to board the most popular rides before 11 A.M. or after 4 P.M. to avoid lines. Midday is a great time to take in a show and cool down.

EMERALD POINTE

Emerald Pointe is the Carolinas' largest water park offering diverse activities for all ages. In a beautifully landscaped setting, guests will find both excitement and relaxation. Featured at the park are such rides as the Bonzie Pipeline water slide, the slow-moving Lazy River tube ride, and the rip-roaring Raging Rapids ride. There's also Thunder Bay, a giant wave pool, the Leisure Lagoon shallow pool, and Doodle's Nest, a kiddie play park area. For relaxing there is an abundance of lounge chairs.

ADDRESS AND TELEPHONE

Emerald Pointe
3910 South Holden Road
Greensboro, NC 27407

(919) 852-9721

LOCATION

Emerald Pointe is conveniently located south of Greensboro, North Carolina. Take I-85 to South Holden Road (exit 121).

OPERATING SEASONS AND HOURS

Open weekends from mid-May. Open daily June through August.

ADMISSION FEES

General: $13.50.

TRANSPORTATION AND ACCOMMODATIONS WITHIN THE PARK

None.

GUEST SERVICES

Restrooms, telephones, first aid, locker rental, changing rooms, showers, free life vests, lost and found, free parking. Visa and MasterCard accepted.

RIDES

Bonzie Pipeline: race down a water slide up to 40 miles per hour.

Lazy River: slow-moving cool stream carries riders leisurely on comfortable tubes.

Pirates Plunge: ride a cable trolley before splashing down into cool clear water.

Raging Rapids: realistic re-creation of a rip-roaring rapids ride.

White Water Run: three five-story water slides provide a quick plunge through tunnels, twists, turns, and loops into a shallow splashdown pool.

KIDDIE RIDES

Kiddie Kove: the magic mushroom and mini water slides end in water only 18 inches deep

ATTRACTIONS AND GAMES

Thunder Bay: giant wave pool with 1.9 million gallons of water that generate a six-foot wave every few minutes.
Leisure Lagoon: play in a large pool never deeper than 3½ feet.
Shipwreck Cove: swim to a sunken battleship in the middle of a large activity pool.
Doodle's Nest: a kiddie play park area with a softball pit, climbing ropes, a punching bag maze, and crawling tubes.
Crew's Quarters Arcade: the latest and most popular video games.

RESTAURANT

Surfer's Bay Cafe: hot dogs, hamburgers, chicken, pizza, fries, funnel cake.

SNACK BARS

Refreshment stands located conveniently throughout the park offer drinks, cotton candy, ice cream, nachos, frozen lemonade, and other snacks.

CATERING

Contact Dale Hawkins at (919) 852-9721.

SOUVENIR SHOP

Barefoot Surfer: suntan lotion, swimsuits, coverups, T-shirts, thongs, film, towels, souvenirs.

GHOST TOWN IN THE SKY

Ghost Town in the Sky is located atop a mountain in scenic western North Carolina, also known as the gateway to the Smoky Mountains. Visitors to the 275-acre theme park begin their day with a chairlift railway ride up Ghost Mountain. Once there they step back in time to streets, shops, and exhibits that replicate the Old West. The park features live gunfights, country music, Cherokee Indian dances, and an assortment of thrill rides. The park's newest attraction is the Red Devil Roller Coaster, a looping steel coaster built on top and over the side of a mile-high mountain.

ADDRESS AND TELEPHONE

Ghost Town in the Sky
P. O. Box 369
Maggie Valley, NC 28751

(704) 926-1140

LOCATION

Ghost Town in the Sky is located in Maggie Valley, about 35 miles west of Asheville, North Carolina.

OPERATING SEASONS AND HOURS

Open daily from the first Saturday in May to the last Sunday in October. Hours: 9:30 A.M. to 6 P.M. on Monday to Friday and Sunday; 9 A.M. to 7 P.M. on Saturday. After early June the park opens at 9 A.M. daily.

ADMISSION FEES

Adults: $13.95. Children ages 3 to 9: $10.95. Children under 3: free.

TRANSPORTATION AND ACCOMMODATIONS WITHIN THE PARK

Incline railway chairlift to the top of the mountain. Bus transportation is available within the park.

GUEST SERVICES

Restrooms, telephones, first aid. Visa, MasterCard, American Express, and Discover cards accepted.

RIDES

Bumper Cars: crash about on this park classic.
Globe Swings: swing into the air.
Merry-Go-Round: choose your prancing mount.
Paratrooper: daredevil thrill ride.
Red Devil Roller Coaster: soar through one loop and 2½ spirals at speeds up to 60 miles per hour on this steel coaster built on top and over the side of a mile-high mountain.
Round-Up: take a fast and furious whirl.
Scrambler: move in many directions all at once.
Sea Dragon: speed around on this thrill ride.
Tilt-a-Whirl: a motion-packed park staple.
Train: journey through the park.
Yo-Yo: swing up and down, round and round.

KIDDIE RIDES

Canoe Ride: ride the waters in a special canoe.
Kiddie Merry-Go-Round: pint-sized steeds.
Kiddie Swings: gentle swing ride.
Little Coaster: gentle inclines and slopes.
Log Ride: not-too-speedy log adventure.
Pony Ride: ponies around a track.
Sky Fighter: kids can fly up in the air.

GAMES

Games of Skill: tosses, pitches, water games, and other games are located throughout the park.

SHOWS

Gunfights: witness a live shoot-out in Ghost Town.
Country Music Show: a hand-clapping, foot-stomping jamboree.
Cherokee Indian Show
Silver Dollar Saloon Can-Can Dancers
Country Critter Jamboree: animated critters sing and dance.
Thriller Theater: see movie clips full of thrills and chills.

RESTAURANTS

None.

SNACK BARS

Stands located throughout the park serve hot dogs, meat loaf, mashed potatoes, ice cream, fudge, pretzels, yogurt, popcorn.

CATERING

Contact R. B. Coburn at (704) 926-1140.

SOUVENIR SHOPS

Stands located throughout the park sell mementos, jewelry, clothing, leatherware.

HINT FOR TRAVELING WITH CHILDREN, ELDERLY, HANDICAPPED

The many gravel streets make it difficult for strollers and wheelchairs.

HELPFUL TIPS ON MAKING YOUR VISIT MORE ENJOYABLE

Allow at least three or four hours to see all the shows, play the games, and enjoy the rides. Make sure to bring jackets and sweatshirts; it's often cooler than you expect in the mountains.

SANTA'S LAND

As the name suggests, Santa's Land has a Christmas theme. Covering 16 acres and drawing some 100,000 visitors annually, the park features such attractions as Santa's House, where children can see and talk with Santa, and several Christmas houses containing animated yuletide scenes and stories. The park also offers traditional rides, including a carousel and Ferris wheel.

ADDRESS AND TELEPHONE

Santa's Land
Route 1, Box 134A
Cherokee, NC 28719

(704) 497-9191

LOCATION

Santa's Land is located on Highway 19, three miles east of Cherokee in the Smoky Mountains.

OPERATING SEASONS AND HOURS

Open daily from May to early November. Hours: 9 A.M. to 6 P.M.

ADMISSION FEES

Adults: $8.95. Children ages 2 to 12: $7.95. Children under 2: free.

TRANSPORTATION AND ACCOMMODATIONS WITHIN THE PARK

None.

GUEST SERVICES

Restrooms, telephones, lost and found, first aid. Visa, MasterCard, and Discover cards accepted.

RIDES

Carousel: fun for visitors of all ages.
Ferris Wheel: a park classic.
Helicopter: a copter flies through the air.
Paddleboats: pedal your way through the water.
Rudy Coaster: Rudolph the Red-Nosed Reindeer pulls Santa's toy-filled sled on this roller coaster for both adults and children.
Train: journey on this brightly colored train that is a replica of a steam engine.

KIDDIE RIDES

Midget Racers: mini racing cars.
Wet Boats: a short but seaworthy journey.
Umbrella: motorcycles, buses, and cars.

ATTRACTIONS AND GAMES

Santa's House: children meet and speak with Santa, have their picture taken, and star in a Santa videotape.
Christmas Animation Houses: animated yuletide scenes and stories.
Zoo: one of the largest zoos in the Smoky Mountains; features lions, zebras, monkeys, and more.
Arcade: favorite amusement park games for all ages.

SHOW

Magic Show: entertaining illusions daily.

SPECIAL ANNUAL EVENT

Harvest Festival: on weekends in October see and hear antique equipment in operation, mountain songs, decorated pumpkins, country crafts folk at work, cider making, clogging.

RESTAURANTS

Shops serving sandwiches, ice cream, and candy are available.

SNACK BARS

Cabin: barbecue, homemade pork rinds, soft drinks.
Snack Bar: hot dogs, corn dogs, burgers, fries, ice cream, drinks.

CATERING

Not available.

SOUVENIR SHOP

Gift Shop: Christmas decorations, park souvenirs, T-shirts, other shirts.

HELPFUL TIPS ON MAKING YOUR VISIT MORE ENJOYABLE

Plan to spend at least four or five hours in the park in order to enjoy all the attractions. Children should be accompanied by an adult at all times.

TWEETSIE RAILROAD

For more than 30 years visitors to the northwestern Carolina Mountains have enjoyed the rides and attractions offered at Tweetsie Railroad, a park with a Western theme. The park's main feature is an entertaining three-mile ride on a coal-fired steam train during which visitors see a Wild West show, complete with cowboys and Indians, sheriff, and shoot-out. Visitors can also enjoy Tweetsie's shows, traditional amusement park rides, gift shops, and games.

ADDRESS AND TELEPHONE

Tweetsie Railroad
Highway 321
P. O. Box 388
Blowing Rock, NC 28605

(704) 264-9061 or 1-800-526-5740

LOCATION

Tweetsie Railroad is located on Highway 321 between Boone and Blowing Rock, two miles off the Blue Ridge Parkway.

OPERATING SEASONS AND HOURS

Open daily from Memorial Day to the end of October. Hours: 9 A.M. to 6 P.M. through Labor Day; 10 A.M. to 4 P.M. weekdays and 9 A.M. to 6 P.M. weekdays after Labor Day.

ADMISSION FEES

Adults: $12.95. Children ages 4 to 12: $10.95. Children 3 and under: free. Seniors 60 and over: $10.95.

TRANSPORTATION AND ACCOMODATIONS WITHIN THE PARK

None.

GUEST SERVICES

Restrooms, telephones, first aid, lost and found, stroller rental. Visa, MasterCard, and Discover cards accepted.

RIDES

Ferris Wheel: reach the stars in a traditional favorite.
Merry-Go-Round: choose your favorite mount on this park classic.
Tilt-a-Whirl: sit back as you swirl and whirl.
Turnpike Cruisers: drive your own gas-operated car on a track.
Tweetsie Railroad: take a three-mile ride on an authentic steam train. Keep your eyes peeled for a Wild West cowboys and Indians shoot-'em-up.

KIDDIE RIDES

Boats: ride a boat in the water.
Helicopters & Planes: kids can pilot their own colorful flyers.
Mouse Mine Train: a little train takes you on a minijourney and offers an animated show with a mine theme.

ATTRACTIONS AND GAMES

Animal Petting Farm
Panning for Gold: pan for gold in special troughs.
Games: carnival games are located throughout the park.
Shooting Gallery

SHOWS

Country Music Show: country music performed by the Tweetsie Band.
Tweetsie Railroad Jamboree: a tuneful show that's the top choice of most visitors.
Tweetsie's Palace Revue: a family musical extravaganza with singing, dancing, and comedy.
Clogging Show: Tweetsie Cloggers kick up a storm.
Rainmaker: kids join in as a rainmaker lets it pour.

SPECIAL ANNUAL EVENTS

Railroaders' Day: In mid-June, train fans peek into Tweetsie's past with a look at the East Tennessee and Western North Carolina Railroad. Guests listen to tales of old-time railroaders and see model train displays.
Fourth of July: fireworks and special entertainment.

RESTAURANTS

Feed 'n' Seed: burgers, hot dogs, fried chicken, barbecue, chicken fillets, fruit plate, chicken salad plate.
Sparkey's Barbecue: barbecue sandwiches, hot dogs.

SNACK BARS

Ice Cream Parlor
Mountain Top Ice Cream
Arcade Concession: popcorn, candy, soft drinks.
Miner's Diner: hot dogs, popcorn, soft drinks.

CATERING

Contact Tracey Ford at (704) 264-9061.

SOUVENIR SHOPS

Depot Souvenirs: tomahawks, children's toys, park mementos.
Kitchen Shop: kitchen gadgets and decorations with a country theme.
General Store: jewelry, Indian merchandise, T-shirts, books, posters, park mementos.
Western Shop: hats, belts, souvenirs.
Miners' Mountain Souvenirs: park mementos, children's toys.
Heritage Craft Shops: located in Craft Junction, includes blacksmith, leatherworker, doll maker, basket weaver, and woodcarver—all selling their wares.
Hat Shop

GREAT LAKES AND CENTRAL

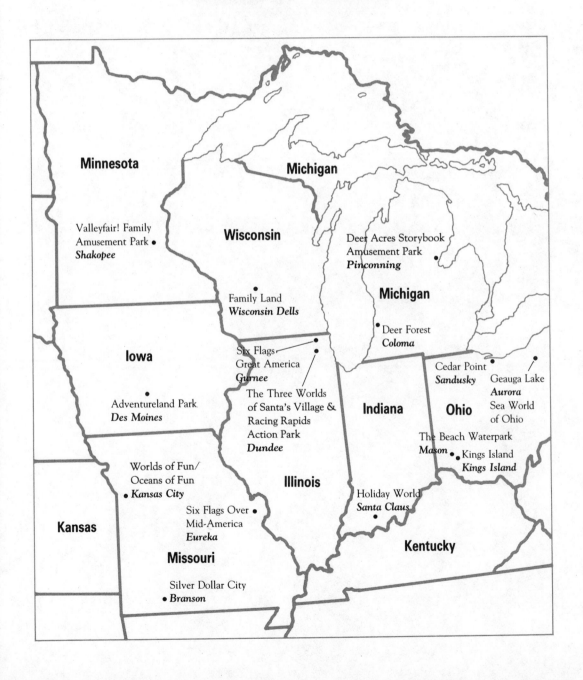

Minnesota

Michigan

Valleyfair! Family
Amusement Park •
Shakopee

Wisconsin

Deer Acres Storybook
Amusement Park •
Pinconning

•
Family Land
Wisconsin Dells

Michigan

• Deer Forest
Coloma

Iowa

Six Flags
Great America
Gurnee

Cedar Point
Sandusky

Geauga Lake
Aurora

•
Adventureland Park
Des Moines

The Three Worlds
of Santa's Village &
Racing Rapids
Action Park
Dundee

Indiana

Ohio

Sea World
of Ohio

The Beach Waterpark
Mason • • Kings Island
Kings Island

Worlds of Fun/
Oceans of Fun
• *Kansas City*

Illinois

Six Flags Over •
Mid-America
Eureka

Holiday World •
Santa Claus

Kansas

Kentucky

Missouri

Silver Dollar City
• *Branson*

ILLINOIS

SIX FLAGS GREAT AMERICA

Each year approximately 2.4 million guests visit Six Flags Great America in Gurnee, Illinois, a 200-acre entertainment center with a broad assortment of rides, shows, and other attractions. In addition to Carousel Plaza, the entrance area, the park is divided into five sections, each with a different theme: Hometown Square, rural America of the 1920s; County Fair, which combines a turn-of-the-century Midwest rural county fair with state-of-the-art rides; Yukon Territory, an authentically landscaped area recalling the days of the Klondike region during the Gold Rush; Yankee Harbor, Great America's own fishing village, resembling a late-nineteenth-century Eastern seaboard town; and Orleans Place, the New Orleans French Quarter circa 1850. A special attraction for the park's younger visitors is Bugs Bunny Land, a magical fantasy and activity area. And don't miss the six thrilling roller coasters.

ADDRESS AND TELEPHONE

Six Flags Great America
P. O. Box 1776
Gurnee, IL 60031

(708) 249-1776

LOCATION

Six Flags, located between Chicago and Milwaukee on I-94 at Route 132, can be reached by car. Transportation from Chicago is also available through Greyhound bus service.

OPERATING SEASONS AND HOURS

Open weekends from early May through October. Open daily from mid-May to late August. Opens at 10 A.M. Closing times vary, so check with the park upon arrival.

ADMISSION FEES

Adults: $21.50. Children ages 4 to 10: $18.50. Children 3 and under: free. Seniors 60 and over: $12.50. Two-day, best-buy ticket: $25.50.

TRANSPORTATION AND ACCOMMODATIONS WITHIN THE PARK

None.

GUEST SERVICES

Restrooms (most with diaper-changing tables), telephones, check cashing, first aid, lost and found, wheelchair and stroller rental, kennel (outside main entrance), camera loans, lost parents area. Visa, MasterCard, American Express, and Discover cards accepted.

RIDES

The American Eagle: enjoy the speeds and thrills on this double-tracked wooden roller coaster.

Ameri-Go-Round: a picturesque antique carousel.

Big Top: a catapulting challenge for thrill ride veterans.

Cajun Cliffhanger: feel the force when the floor drops from below you as you spin around at high speeds.

Columbia Carousel: ride this 10-story, old-fashioned, double grand carousel.

The Demon: be prepared for an 82-foot drop, double corkscrew, vertical loops, and display of light and sound on this roller coaster.

Fiddler's Fling: swirl and spin.

Great America Raceway: race against other riders in custom-designed cars.

Great America Scenic Railway: take a relaxing journey around the park.

Haybaler: whiz past bales of hay.

Hometown Fun Machine: high-speed thrills.

Iron Wolf: this fast stand-up looping coaster is the latest in roller coaster design.

The Lobster: ride this gigantic lobster for "spun in the fun."

Logger's Run: cool off on this thrilling flume ride.

The Orbit: watch your world turn upside down.

Power Dive: fly in a giant fighter plane as it soars through a 360-degree loop.

Roaring Rapids: take a real white water raft ride.

Rolling Thunder: experience 1,500 feet of simulated bobsled action with high banks and sharp turns.

Rue Le Dodge: enjoy bumper car action in Grand Prix cars.

Shock Wave: a steel looping roller coaster that turns you upside down seven times.

Sky Trek Tower: climb aboard an escalating cabin as it rises 285 feet in the air for a great park view.

The Sky Whirl: climb 120 feet in the air in this triple-arm Ferris wheel.

Splashwater Falls: boats that make a splash landing.

Triple Play: swing and sway on this park favorite.

Whirligig: based on the backyard swing, this ride whirls the fun right at you.

The Whizzer: try this white-knuckle coaster with its high speeds, banked turns, and free-fall.

Yankee Clipper: splashy fun with a 60-foot vertical drop.

KIDDIE RIDES

Bugs Bunny Carrot Patch: a maze of dangling, swinging carrots.

Bugs Bunny Hippity Hop: tumbling and jumping on an air mattress.

Ladybugs: bouncy fun on colorful ladybugs.

Petunia Pig Puddle: a romp on a water mattress.

Porky Pig Playpen: an ocean of colorful balls.

Red Baron: World War I biplanes.

Sylvester Cat Climb: a multilevel net climb.

Sylvester Scooters: spins on kid-propelled scooters.

Tot's Livery: beautiful little self-drive carriages.

Wile E. Coyote Hideaway: tunnel crawl.

ATTRACTIONS AND GAMES

Character Clubhouse: meet such costumed characters as Bugs Bunny, Sylvester the Cat, and Daffy Duck in Bugs Bunny Land.

Hometown Arcade: electronic, electric, and mechanical challenges.

Games Gallery Arcade: more than 80 video games.

Games of Skill: located around the park.

Northwest Shooting Gallery: 26 guns available to shoot at targets.

Remote Control Village: captain your own boat.
Cirque Electrique Games and Arcade: skill and video games.
Yukon Games Area

SHOWS

REFLECTIONS: the sights and sounds of the '60s, a song and dance tribute to the era featuring the Great America Singers.
Snowshoe Saloon Revue: revives old-time Western fun in a family song and dance presentation.
The Last Buffalo: a state-of-the-art 3-D phenomenon in the Pictorium IMAX theater.
All Night Party: a magical sight and sound spectacular featuring the entire Looney Tunes Gang and the Great America Singers.

There are also new shows every season in Theatre Royale, Wilderness Theater, and the Orleans Place Gazebo.

SPECIAL ANNUAL EVENT

Joyfest Christian Music Celebration: two weekends of Christian singing groups each season. (Check park for dates.)

RESTAURANTS

Hometown Boarding House: fried chicken, salads, corn on the cob, apple dumplings.
Hometown Grill: burgers, nachos, fries, drinks.
The Firehouse: milk shakes, ice cream, pizza.
Burgers on the Run
Pizza Luigi
Yukon-Do-It: hot dogs, roast beef, and ham and cheese sandwiches.
Klondike Cafe: barbecued ribs and chicken, burgers, cheesecake.
Snowshoe Saloon: snacks, beer, soft drinks.
Angelo's Italian Restaurant: spaghetti, bread, lemon ice.
Dockside Grill: hot dogs, fries.

Bourbon Street Cafe: family buffet with two types of meat, vegetables, potato salad, and roll.
Ala Burger: burgers, chicken fillet sandwiches.
Pizza Orleans
Sticky Fingers
Wolf's Den Snacks
Penny P. Patrick's

SNACK BARS

Kiosks and stands located throughout the park serve nachos, cotton candy, funnel cakes, popcorn, ice cream, soft drinks.

CATERING

Contact Group Sales at (708) 249-1776.

SOUVENIR SHOPS

Carousel Plaza Gifts: T-shirts, mementos, Looney Tunes plush toys, film, candy.
Carousel Hats and Balloons
Daffy Duck Duds: children's T-shirts, Looney Tunes character merchandise.
Bear Necessities: teddy bear merchandise and souvenirs.
County Fair Shirt Shop
County Fair Hats
Totem Post: souvenirs and kids' shirts.
Moosejaw Trading Post: wood products, wind chimes, pottery, shirts, sundries.
Happy Hatter
Tradewinds: nautical gifts.
Shoreline Gifts: glass, collectibles, musical carousels.
Karacter Korner: Looney Tunes merchandise and clothing.
Mardi Gras Emporium: gifts, apparel, mementos.
Lafitte's Treasure Chest of Toys: toys, souvenirs, shirts.
Simone's: jewelry, accessories.
Gateway Gifts
Hocus Pocus
Sweet Shop
The Dug Out: licensed athletic sportswear.
Hot Trax

Airbrush and Caricature Artists
Outrageous Threads
You Sing Recording
Freeze Frame Photo

HINTS FOR TRAVELING WITH CHILDREN, ELDERLY, HANDICAPPED

When traveling with children, visit Bugs Bunny Land first. It's located in the back portion of the park and usually isn't crowded in the morning hours. Free admission will be granted to visitors in wheelchairs. Special parking is available in the guest parking lot. Pick up a brochure at the information booth.

THE THREE WORLDS OF SANTA'S VILLAGE & RACING RAPIDS ACTION PARK

The Three Worlds of Santa's Village features 55 acres of family entertainment. Located among the oaks and pines of the scenic Fox River Valley of northern Illinois, this theme park has been in operation for more than 30 years. It offers a variety of rides, shows, and attractions in three themed areas, including the Snowball and Christmas Tree rides found in Santa's World, the eighteenth-century galleon pirate ship replica in the Coney Island area, and the more than 50 different animals roaming about Old MacDonald's Farm. The 10-acre water park, Racing Rapids Action Park, offers three giant water slides, refreshing Fiji Falls, plus Children's Fun Island where little ones can play among fountains, swings, water cannons, and the Wet Wilbur turtle slide.

ADDRESS AND TELEPHONE

The Three Worlds of Santa's Village &
  Racing Rapids Action Park
Routes 25 and 72
Dundee, IL 60118

(708) 426-6751

LOCATION

The Three Worlds of Santa's Village & Racing Rapids Action Park is located 45 minutes northwest of downtown Chicago. Take I-90 (Northwest Tollway) and exit at Route 25 near Elgin. Go north approximately two miles. The parks are located at the intersection of routes 25 and 72.

OPERATING SEASONS AND HOURS

Santa's Village: Open weekends only beginning Mother's Day in May and in September. Open daily from early June through Labor Day. Hours: weekdays from 10 A.M. to 6 P.M.; weekends and holidays from 11 A.M. to dusk.
  Racing Rapids: Open daily from Memorial Day to Labor Day. Hours: 11 A.M. to 8 P.M.

ADMISSION FEES

General admission to one park: $10.95. Seniors 62 and older: $8.95. Combined admission to Santa's Village and Racing Rapids: $15.95. Children under 3: free.

TRANSPORTATION AND ACCOMMODATIONS WITHIN THE PARK

None.

GUEST SERVICES

Restrooms, telephones, information booth, first aid, lost and found, lost children center, picnic tables, free parking, locker rentals, stroller rentals. Showers in Racing Rapids. Visa, MasterCard, American Express, and Discover cards accepted.

RIDES

At *Santa's Village:*
Candy Cane Sleigh: an old-fashioned, horse-pulled sleigh ride.

Carousel: this one is driven by a real horse.

Dundee Zizzler: classic bumper cars.

Express Train: all aboard for a minijourney.

Ferris Wheel: a park favorite.

Galaxi Roller Coaster: a thrilling six-story-high coaster.

Galleon Pirate Ship: an eighteenth-century replica takes you on a high seas adventure as you swing over 40 feet in the air.

Himalaya: zip around a circle in a car in this superfast ride.

Skyliner: take a ski-lift-style ride for great views of the park.

Tarantula: spin at the end of the spider's legs.

Tilt-a-Whirl: another classic.

Yoyo: individual swings that go up, down, and around, simulating free flight.

At Racing Rapids:

Bumper Boats: splashy boats you can bump about.

Giant Slidewinder: two 50-foot water slides.

Gran Prix Go-Karts: ride your own vehicle.

Lazy River Tube Ride: take an inner tube journey more than 450 feet as you soak up rays and pass through Fiji Falls.

Twister Tube Slide: super-slick slide whisks you down the chute with 4,000 gallons of water per minute.

KIDDIE RIDES

At Santa's Village:

Antique Cars: kids can drive their own antique cars.

Christmas Tree: ornaments ride around a Christmas tree.

The Convoy: vehicles in a circle.

The Dragon Coaster: a smaller coaster for kids and parents.

Fire Engines: minis for the kiddies.

Kiddie Cars: cars in a circle.

Li'l Stinger: bees in a circle.

Merry-Go-Round: a park favorite for kids and parents.

Rainbow Bounce: air bounce.

Rock-Spin 'n' Roll: a teacup-style ride.

Snowball: a teacup-style spin.

Space Ships: special minispaceship.

Star Jets: little jets in a circle.

At Racing Rapids:

Auto Kid Wash: just like a car wash, only for kids.

Duck Slide: slippery water slide for the pint-sized.

Wet Wilbur: turtle slide.

ATTRACTIONS AND GAMES

At Santa's Village:

Santa's Home: visit the house where Santa Claus lives.

The North Pole: Santa's "hometown."

Playport Play Arena: children's activity area.

Santa Statue: in honor of St. Nick himself.

Petting Zoo: pet more than 50 barnyard animals.

Polar Dome Ice Arena: 16,000 square feet of indoor ice surface for skating pleasure. Skate rentals are available. (Open October through March.)

Games of Skill/Video Arcade: try more than a dozen games of skill and more than 30 of the latest video games.

At Racing Rapids:

Children's Fun Island: little ones can play among mushroom fountains, a giant gorilla statue holding swings, and water cannons.

SHOWS

The Evergreen Theatre: music and variety shows are performed four times daily.

RESTAURANTS

Alpine Dining Room: burgers, hot dogs, fries, sloppy joes, pizza, beer, soft drinks.

Pixie Pantry Restaurant: burgers, hot dogs, fries, chili dogs, fish sandwiches, soft drinks.

Ice Cream Parlor

Three Worlds Carryout: pizza, hot dogs, burgers.

Igloo Italian Ice

Coney Island Foods: hot dogs.

SNACK BARS

At Santa's Village:
Popcorn Wagon
Pepe's Place: tacos, burritos.
Hofbrau House Beer Garden: bratwurst, polish sausage, sauerkraut, soft pretzels, beer, soft drinks.
Gingerbread House: hot dogs, corn dogs, sodas.
Soft Drink Wagon
Rainbow Stand: funnel cakes.

At Racing Rapids:
Snack Bar: burgers, hot dogs, fries, nachos, ice cream, drinks.

CATERING

Contact Maynard Catering at (312) 426-6753.

SOUVENIR SHOPS

At Santa's Village:
Ye Old Gift Shop: T-shirts, sweatshirts, pennants, jewelry, Christmas ornaments, park mementos.

Exit Gift Shop: T-shirts, pennants, souvenirs, toys.
Tee Shirt Shop: T-shirts, sweatshirts, apparel.
The Mad Hatter: hats, caps, visors, tote bags.
The Carousel Shop: shorts, sweatshirts, T-shirts.
The Coney Island Souvenir Shop: park mementos, novelties.

At Racing Rapids:
Gift Shop: water paraphernalia, Racing Rapids mementos.

HELPFUL TIPS ON MAKING YOUR VISIT MORE ENJOYABLE

Plan on spending at least five hours in Santa's Village and more time if you're also visiting Racing Rapids. Feel free to pack a picnic lunch.

INDIANA

HOLIDAY WORLD

Holiday World, originally called Santa Claus Land, was one of the first theme parks in the United States. The park, which welcomes approximately 7,500 visitors each day, features such thrill rides as the fast and furious Firecracker Coaster and Frightful Falls splashdown, as well as white water rafting. It also offers musical entertainment, Indiana's only wax museum, and exciting action shows such as the U. S. High-Diving Team.

ADDRESS AND TELEPHONE

Holiday World
P. O. Box 179
Santa Claus, IN 47579

(812) 937-4401 or 1-800-46-SANTA

LOCATION

Holiday World is located seven miles off I-64 at exit 63 in southwestern Indiana.

OPERATING SEASONS AND HOURS

Open weekends from early to mid-May and selected weekends from September to December. November and December hours: 11 A.M. to 4:30 P.M. Open daily from Memorial Day to late August. Opens at 10 A.M. Closing times vary, so check with the park upon arrival.

ADMISSION FEES

Adults: $11.95. Children 2 and under: free. Seniors 60 and over: $9.95. Season pass: $34.95.

TRANSPORTATION AND ACCOMMODATIONS WITHIN THE PARK

A tram takes guests between the parking lot and the main entrance.

GUEST SERVICES

Restrooms, telephones, information booth, check cashing, lost and found, lost parents area, first aid, wheelchairs, strollers, camera and video recorder rental, kennels.

RIDES

Banshee: a free-falling ride from over 66 feet in the air that swings you clockwise and counterclockwise.
Eagle's Flight: swoop above the treetops.
Firecracker Roller Coaster: experience quick drops and a corkscrew loop.
Frightful Falls Log Flume: speed through a mysterious tunnel and down a long chute.
Lewis & Clark Trail: drive your own antique cars.
Paul Revere's Midnight Ride: spin and twirl.
Raging Rapids: white water rafting.
Rough Riders: classic bumper cars.
Roundhouse: a whirling force of gravity ride.
Scarecrows Scrambler: move in too many directions at once.
Thunder Bumpers: bumper boats.
Virginia Reel: a tilt-a-whirl.

KIDDIE RIDES

Indian Dance: a mini whip ride.
Indian River: a mini canoe ride.
Rudolf's Reindeer Ranch: features a merry-go-round, airplanes, rockets, sea horses, and junior bumper boats.
Salmon Run: adorable floating fish.

ATTRACTIONS AND GAMES

Wax Museum: Indiana's first and only.
Frontier Farm: pet tame barnyard animals.
Dollhouse: features more than 2,000 dolls.
Santa Claus: appears at popular Kringle Haus.
Toyland: see antique toys, Lincoln memorabilia, toy trains.
Avenue of Flags: 20 historic U.S. flags.
Games: games of skill as well as an electronic arcade game room.
Outdoor Air Conditioning: you have to feel it to believe it, 20 degrees cooler.

SHOWS

Musical Shows: musical revues and performances are featured each season. Check with the park for its performance schedule and show times.

SPECIAL ANNUAL EVENTS

Santa Fest: in November and December.

RESTAURANTS

Alamo: tacos, burritos, and other Mexican foods.
Mrs. Klaus' Kitchen: homemade fudge, desserts.
The All-American Hot Dog
Pumpkin Plantation: barbecued chicken, fried chicken, fish.
Kringle's Kafe: burgers, chicken, fries, pizza, salad.

SNACK BARS

Kringle's Ice Cream: hand-dipped, frozen yogurt.
Santa's Snacks: hot dogs, cotton candy.
Sweet Stuff: chocolate-covered waffles on a stick, ices, fruit.
Funnel Cake and Ice Cream Factory
Stands located throughout the park sell popcorn, cotton candy, and fruit juice drinks.

CATERING

Contact Group Sales at (812) 937-4401, ext. 271.

SOUVENIR SHOPS

St. Nick's Nacks
Bavarian Glassblower: glass gifts.
Liberty Bell Shoppe: Holiday World
   mementos.
Toyshop
Boulder Canyon Gift Shop
Spooky's Woodshop
Front Porch Airbrush Shop

HELPFUL TIP ON MAKING YOUR VISIT MORE ENJOYABLE

When bringing a group of 15 or more, call ahead for reservations.

IOWA

ADVENTURELAND PARK

One of Iowa's premier attractions, Adventureland Park features a charming replica of a turn-of-the-century town square with shops and restaurants at the park entrance. Throughout the park there are rides for all ages from hair-raising roller coasters to a scenic train ride. A variety of shows and a wide assortment of eateries and games in themed areas throughout the park provide fun and entertainment for all.

ADDRESS AND TELEPHONE

Adventureland Park
P. O. Box 3355
Des Moines, IA 50316

(515) 266-2121 or 1-800-532-1286

LOCATION

Adventureland Park is located at the intersection of Interstate 80 and Highway 65, exit 142, just outside Des Moines.

OPERATING SEASONS AND HOURS

Open weekends from the end of April to Memorial Day and in September. Open daily from the end of May to late August. Opens at 10 A.M. Closing times vary, so check with the park upon arrival.

ADMISSION FEES

Adults: $15.95. Children ages 4 to 9: $14.95. Children 3 and under: free. Seniors 65 and over: $11.95.

TRANSPORTATION AND ACCOMMODATIONS WITHIN THE PARK

For reservations and information call (515) 266-2121 or 1-800-532-1286.

The Adventureland Inn: located adjacent to the park. Offers rooms, restaurants, indoor pool, and meeting and banquet facilities. Shuttle bus to the park. (Open year-round.)

Campground: complete with RV hookups, showers, restrooms, tent sites, swimming pool. Shuttle bus to the park. (Open year-round.)

GUEST SERVICES

Restrooms, telephones, bank machine, check cashing, first aid, stroller rental, wheelchair rental, lost and found, package check, lost parent center. Visa, MasterCard, American Express, and Discover cards accepted.

RIDES

Balloon Race: up and around in balloon gondolas.
Der Flinger: this popular ride takes you up, around, and down.
Dodge 'em Cars: classic bumper cars.
The Dragon: take off on this hair-raising, upside-down double loop roller coaster.
Falling Star: travel at speeds up to 33.7 feet per second, nearly 100 feet in the air, and then . . . drop.
Galleon: climb aboard a swinging, rocking boat.
Giant Skywheel: gondola-type sky wheel offering a panoramic view of the park.
Lady Luck: twist and turn.
Lighthouse: fly fast, in, out, and around.
Raging River: shoot the rapids in a six-person raft on this raging river.
River Rapids: ride a log on a roller-coaster-like path and be prepared to get wet.
Round Up: spin fast in many directions.
Silly Silo: spin at high speeds while the floor drops out.
Sky Rides: ski-lift-type ride over the park.
Super Screamer: twist and turn on this thrilling coaster.
Tea Cups: whirl in teacups.
The Tornado: you'll reach speeds up to 60 miles per hour on this wooden coaster.
Train: scenic ride through the park.

KIDDIE RIDES

Carousel: old-fashioned fun.
The Convoy: a ride in a mini 18-wheeler.
Infant Ocean: little ones captain their own boats.
Kiddie Cars: drive around in cars and motorcycles.
Lady Bugs: ride around on a ladybug.
Puff the Dragon: fly up and around in miniature dragons.
Red Baron: kids pilot their own planes up and around.

GAMES

Test your skill and win prizes at more than 50 games located throughout the park, including three arcades, a shooting gallery, boat races, and more.
Bingo Parlor: located on Main Street.

SHOWS

Four theaters offer a variety of live shows featuring music, magic, and more. Check the park for information on shows and schedules

SPECIAL ANNUAL EVENT

Fourth of July: fireworks display.

RESTAURANTS

Iowa Cafe: fried chicken with all the fixings.
Soda 'N Sounds: hamburgers and fries.
The Rathskellar: pizza, funnel cakes.
River City: barbecue beef, tacos, burritos.
The Old-Fashioned Ice Cream Shop: from cones to banana splits.
The Bakery: donuts, pastries, cookies.

SNACK BARS

Stands located throughout the park feature ice cream, funnel cakes, and malteds.

CATERING

Contact Bill Fisher at (515) 266-2121.

SOUVENIR SHOPS

The Clothing Store: T-shirts, key chains, park mementos.
Old Time Post Office: postcards.
Toy Store: Adventureland toys, hats.
Replica of Old Hotel: souvenirs, key chains, pens, toys.
Farm House: Adventureland T-shirts, hats.
Raging River Stand: T-shirts, hats.

MICHIGAN

DEER ACRES STORYBOOK AMUSEMENT PARK

Deer Acres Storybook Amusement Park is a 25-acre petting zoo and park with a storybook theme. Guests can hand-feed and photograph deer, and can see other animals, including a live bear, llama, monkeys, and buffaloes. As visitors walk around the grounds or take the train ride, they will also see sculptures of favorite storybook characters such as Peter Pan, Tom Sawyer, and Hansel and Gretel. All the characters are designed, sculpted, and constructed by the park's owner and his family, making Deer Acres an unusual entertainment attraction.

ADDRESS AND TELEPHONE

Deer Acres Storybook Amusement Park
2346 M-13
Pinconning, MI 48650

(517) 879-2849

LOCATION

Deer Acres Storybook Amusement Park is located 100 miles north of Detroit. Going north on I-75, take exit 164 and go straight ahead for 15 minutes; or take exit 173 east to M-13, then go north for five minutes. Going south on I-75, take exit 181 east to M-13, then go south for five minutes.

OPERATING SEASONS AND HOURS

Open weekends from Labor Day to mid-October. Hours: 10 A.M. to 6 P.M. Open daily from mid-May to Labor Day. Hours: 9 A.M. to 7 P.M.

ADMISSION FEES

Adults: $5.75. Children ages 3 to 12: $3.75. Children under 3: free. Seniors 62 and over: $4.75.

TRANSPORTATION AND ACCOMMODATIONS WITHIN THE PARK

None.

GUEST SERVICES

Restrooms, telephones, lost and found, baby strollers, wheelchairs. Visa and MasterCard accepted.

RIDES

Antique Cars: drive your own antique car.
Carousel: a classic.
Safari Ride: ride in canopied cars for a
narrated tour of the jungle area. See a
bear, cattle, buffaloes, and deer.
Train Ride: journey on a train for a narrated
look at sculptures of Hiawatha, Peter Pan,
Captain Hook, Hansel and Gretel, Tom
Sawyer, and more.

ATTRACTIONS

Deer Park: hand-feed, pet, and photograph
deer.
Storybook Sculptures: the park's owner and
his family designed and executed these
lifelike sculptures of favorite storybook
characters, including Jack and the
Beanstalk, Old Mother Hubbard, and Jack
and Jill.
Moonwalk: a giant balloon to jump around
in.
Play Area: swings, slides, and more for the
kids.

RESTAURANTS

None.

SNACK BAR

Stacey's Sip & Snack: cotton candy, slush,
pizza, popcorn, chips, hot dogs, soft drinks.

CATERING

Not available.

SOUVENIR SHOP

Moccasins and park souvenirs.

HELPFUL TIPS ON MAKING YOUR VISIT MORE ENJOYABLE

There is a large picnic and play area for families.
Don't forget to bring a camera since photo op-
portunites abound.

DEER FOREST

Deer Forest is a magical animal wonderland
geared to children. Visitors can pet and feed
Mama Llama, deer, goats, and exotic and tame
animals. See white elk, monkeys, rheas, aou-
dad, a 14-foot Burmese python, and many varieties of birds. Kids can see and hear their favorite
nursery rhymes when they wander down Story
Book Lane and can take a ride on the Deer
Forest Train or on a live pony or camel. Deer
Forest's 30 acres of scenic woodland and picnic
areas all add up to a fun-filled experience.

ADDRESS AND TELEPHONE

Deer Forest
P. O. Box 817
Coloma, MI 49038

1-800-752-DEER

LOCATION

Take I-94 north of Benton Harbor to exit 39,
Coloma. Turn right off the highway and follow
the green Deer Forest signs to the park.

OPERATING SEASONS AND HOURS

Open daily from Memorial Day to Labor Day.
Hours: 10 A.M. to 6 P.M.

ADMISSION FEES

Adults: $5. Children ages 3 to 11: $3.50.

TRANSPORTATION AND ACCOMMODATIONS WITHIN THE PARK

None.

GUEST SERVICES

Restrooms, first aid, lost and found, baby strollers, wagons.

RIDES

Deer Forest Train: a journey through the park to see deer, llamas, and other animals.
Ferris Wheel: a classic favorite.

KIDDIE RIDES

Swamp Buggy
Motorcycle Jump
Antique Cars

ATTRACTIONS

Animal Park: 25 acres of parkland with 650 animals to pet or feed.
Nursey Rhyme Lane: nursery rhymes such as Little Bo Peep, the Three Bears, and Mary Had a Little Lamb come to life.

SHOWS

Variety of live shows every year. Check with the park for schedules and show times.

RESTAURANTS

None.

SNACK BARS

Santa Claus's Sweet Shop: Mrs. Claus prepares Mackinac-style fudge and assorted candies here daily.
  Two concession stands serve burgers, hot dogs, corn dogs, chili dogs, fries, nachos, popcorn, cotton candy, soft drinks.

CATERING

Not available.

SOUVENIR SHOP

Michigan memorabilia, Deer Forest souvenirs.

HINTS FOR TRAVELING WITH CHILDREN, ELDERLY, HANDICAPPED

Call ahead to arrange for any required special services. There are several rest areas throughout the park.

MINNESOTA

VALLEYFAIR!
FAMILY AMUSEMENT PARK

Valleyfair is a 68-acre amusement park border-
ing the Minnesota River. Visitors can choose
from more than two dozen classic and thrill
rides, including a hand-built antique carousel,
a roller coaster boasting one of the steepest
grades in the world, and a white water river-
raft ride through a five-acre, man-made river.
Games, attractions, a large campground, a variety of entertainment, and the refreshing Liquid
Lightning Waterpark add to the park's popular-
ity.

ADDRESS AND TELEPHONE

Valleyfair! Family Amusement Park
One Valleyfair Drive
Shakopee, MN 55379

(612) 445-7600

LOCATION

Valleyfair is located in Shakopee, Minnesota,
20 miles southwest of Minneapolis/St. Paul on
Highway 101, nine miles west of the intersection of highways 13 and 35W.

OPERATING SEASONS AND HOURS

Open daily from May to Labor Day and weekends in September. Opens at 10 A.M. Closing
times vary, so check with the park upon arrival.

ADMISSION FEES

Adults: $16.50. Children over 4 and under 48
inches: $9.50. Children 3 and under: free. Se-
niors 62 and over: $9.50. Season pass: $47.50.
Starlight admission (after 5 P.M.): $9.50.

TRANSPORTATION AND ACCOMMODATIONS
WITHIN THE PARK

Valleyfair's campground offers 100 wooded
campsites nestled next to the Minnesota River.
Sites can accommodate RVs and trailers, tents,
and pull-through campers. The campground
features picnic tables, campfire rings, barbecue
grills, shower facilities, telephones, laundry,
and more. Valleyfair campers are eligible for a
special day-and-a-half ticket for the park.

GUEST SERVICES

Restrooms, telephones, first aid, lost and found,
lost parents area, stroller and wagon rental,
rental bins, information, cash machine, check

cashing. Swimsuit, towel, and locker rental available at Liquid Lightning. Visa, Master-Card, American Express, Diners Club, Carte Blanche, and major oil company credit cards accepted.

RIDES

Antique Carousel: this 1925 classic is illustrative of the handcarved artistry of American carousel building.

Corkscrew: a roller coaster takes you to a height of 85 feet, drops into a 360-degree vertical loop, follows two giant coil-like spirals, and ends with a 360-degree horizontal loop.

Enterprise: this giant wheel turns upside down as it spins in a circle.

Excalibur: carved out of steel and wood, this coaster boasts one of the steepest grades in the world, challenging you with its 60-degree drop and towering 10-story peak.

Ferris Wheel: the first of its size to be operated in the United States, it lets you enjoy great views of the Minnesota River Valley.

High Roller: a wooden roller coaster that reaches speeds close to 60 miles per hour.

Log Flume: hollowed-out logs move through a cave, along swirling rapids and water-filled chutes.

Looping Starship: a boat-shaped ride that rocks you back and forth, higher and higher, until it reaches a peak of 70 feet and swings in a full circle.

Minnesota River Valley Railroad: a trip around the park for the whole family.

Thunder Canyon: more than 100,000 gallons of water per minute rush through this five-acre man-made river that you can raft along.

Wild Rails: a steel coaster that lets you soar.

At Liquid Lightning Waterpark (separate admission):
Speed Slides: travel fast on two speed slides.
Tube Ride
Waterslides: enjoy three water slides.

KIDDIE RIDES

At Half Pint Park:
Children's Train: a pint-sized journey.
Kiddie Roller Coaster: little hills, gentle thrills.
Mini Hot Air Balloon
Roadsters: old-fashioned hot rods in miniature.
Twirling Seaplanes

At New Kiddie Area:
Kiddie Carousel
Kiddie U-Turns
Moon Buggy: moon cars ride around in a circle.
At Tot Town: walk across a swinging suspension bridge to a special little island just for tots.
Ball Crawl
Bike Race: pop a balloon and win a prize.
Ferris Wheel
Moon Walk: bounce around on a giant air-filled mattress.
Rub-a-dub Tubs: float on a calm stream in a large tub.

ATTRACTIONS AND GAMES

Challenge Park: a thrilling go-cart track and an all new 36-hole adventure golf course. (Separate admission.)
Games Arcade: the most popular games of skill, including Speed Pitch, Long Range Basketball, and more.
Shooting Gallery

SHOWS

Imax Theater: offers a new high-fidelity film each season that is both educational and entertaining.
Shows Arena: a different show every year.
Variety Entertainment: variety shows are featured on the stages of Red Garter Saloon, Gazebo, and Vignette.

SPECIAL ANNUAL EVENTS

Memorial Day Weekend: grand opening and ice cream social.
Fourth of July: fireworks display.
Labor Day Weekend: corn feast.

RESTAURANTS

Red Garter Saloon: sandwiches, drinks.
Palatable Palace: burgers, hot dogs, sandwiches.
The Eatery: southern-fried chicken, burgers, hot dogs.
Pizza Parlour: pizza, sausage sandwiches.
Herr Ziegfried's/Senor Pepes: German and Mexican delicacies.
Chicken & Pizza Patio: southern-fried chicken, pizza.
Grandma's Bake 'n' Sweet: homemade fudge, minidonuts, pies, cookies, fresh fudge apples.
Beer Caboose: soft pretzels, 3.2 beer.
Twister Pizza: pizza and frozen yogurt.
Northwoods Grill: grilled sandwiches.
Fryar Tuck's: homemade fries.

SNACK BARS

Stands located around the park serve ice cream, cotton candy, Sno cones, funnel cakes, caramel apples, Pronto pups, and soft drinks.

CATERING

Contact Group Sales at (612) 445-7600.

SOUVENIR SHOPS

Souvenir shops and carts located throughout the park sell T-shirts, visors, park maps, and other Valleyfair souvenirs.

HINT FOR TRAVELING WITH CHILDREN, ELDERLY, HANDICAPPED

Handicapped parking areas are located at the front of the main parking lot. All walkways, shows, and attractions are accessible to guests with physical impairments; most restrooms are wheelchair accessible.

Guests with mobile impairments should approach rides via the exit gate. Impaired visitors may be accompanied by two guests and may ride twice before exiting. On rides that can accommodate guests in wheelchairs, guests will have to leave their wheelchairs to be seated. While park hosts and hostesses can help, management recommends bringing an assistant when visiting the park.

HELPFUL TIPS ON MAKING YOUR VISIT MORE ENJOYABLE

The average visit lasts 7½ hours. Wear clothes that dry easily (guests get soaked on Thunder Canyon).

MISSOURI

SILVER DOLLAR CITY

Silver Dollar City is a 50-acre entertainment and crafts center with a theme of Ozarks of the 1800s. Visitors can browse among 40 different craft shops, including the blacksmith, glass-blowing, and wood carving shops, and see crafts people re-create the life-style of a century gone by. Among the most unusual of Silver Dollar City's attractions is the Marvel Cave, the largest cavern in Ozark Mountain country. The park also features a variety of rides, including Tom Sawyer's Skychase balloon ride and Becky's Carousel. Shows feature Dixieland jazz as well as country music. The park entertains 1.6 million visitors a year.

ADDRESS AND TELEPHONE

Silver Dollar City
Branson, MO 65616

(417) 338-2611

LOCATION

Silver Dollar City is located nine miles west of Branson on Missouri 76. Branson is 25 miles south of Springfield.

OPERATING SEASONS AND HOURS

Open from mid-April to October. Hours: 9:30 A.M. to 6 P.M. Closing times vary, so check with the park upon arrival. The park is often open during weekends in November and December; again, call the park for specific dates and hours.

ADMISSION FEES

Adults: $20. Children: $12.

TRANSPORTATION AND ACCOMMODATIONS WITHIN THE PARK

Free shuttle transportation from major motels in the area to the park.

GUEST SERVICES

Restrooms, telephones, information booth, check cashing, first aid, lost and found, locker rental, stroller and wheelchair rental, lost persons area. Visa, MasterCard, and Discover cards accepted.

RIDES

American Plunge: splash down a refreshing flume ride.
Fire in the Hole: an indoor coaster that speeds through a burning town.
Flooded Mine: an ore barge journeys through the mine's inundated passageways.
Frisco-Silver Dollar Line: a train excursion through deep woods.
Great Shootout in the Flooded Mine: a ride through a mine in an ore cart along a water tunnel. Shoot at animated targets and receive a score at the end of the ride.
Lost River: ride a river in a doughnut-shaped float.
Water Boggan: soar down a speed slide.

KIDDIE RIDES

Becky's Carousel: fun for little ones and the rest of the family.
Tom Sawyer's Landing: an activity area that includes a net climb and Huckleberry Ball Room (ball crawl).
Tom Sawyer Skychase: the whole family can whirl through the air in a balloon ride.
Tom's Runaway Ore Car: an ore car on a track.

ATTRACTIONS

Silver Dollar "City": see a working community of 100 years ago in which men and women in period dress take you into the past through their crafts, their music, their cooking, and their dedication to preserving Pioneer America. On any day there are at least 40 demonstrating crafts people making everything from brooms to wooden rockers.
Marvel Cave: tour the largest cavern in the Ozarks and the third largest cave in America, located beneath Silver Dollar City. Be sure to visit the Cathedral Room, which has a 20-story-high ceiling.
Pioneer Homestead: watch a pioneer family in its daily activities.

Heartland Furniture Showroom: handcrafted furniture showroom.

SHOWS

Silver Dollar Saloon Show: comedy antics. There is also a variety of musical shows ranging from country favorites to Dixieland jazz.

SPECIAL ANNUAL EVENTS

Flower and Garden Festival: in April and early May.
American Folk Music Festival: in June musicians from all over the United States come and perform.
National Quilt Festival: quilt show and sale in September.
National Crafts Festival: From September through November view displays of 100 rare and historic crafts.
Old-Time Country Christmas: in November and December.

RESTAURANTS

Molly's Mill: all-you-can-eat breakfast with eggs, biscuits, fruit; also salad bar, ham steak, fried chicken, fried catfish.
The Mine: beef stew, salads, corn on the cob.
The Garden Restaurant: steaks, beef, ham, salmon.
Riverside Rib House: barbecued ribs, vegetables, drinks.
The Lumbercamp Steak House: steaks, burgers.
Jack & Mary's Restaurant: sandwiches, salads, desserts.

SNACK BARS

Berries & Cream: strawberries, blueberries, blackberries with ice cream.
Funnel Cakes

Fried Fancies: fried pork rinds.

Other stands located throughout the park serve popcorn, peanuts, and lemonade.

CATERING

Contact Group Sales at (417) 338-2611.

SOUVENIR SHOPS

Ozark Market Place: T-shirts, cookbooks, toys, candy, mountain dulcimers.

Hospitality House: film, batteries, suntan lotion, sundries.

Craft Shops: 40 different craft shops run by crafts folk who re-create life 100 years ago. Shops include a blacksmith, glassblowing, wood carving, basketry, pottery, coppersmith, jewelry, leather, brooms, buggy factory, furniture, candles, bakery/gristmill, quilt, needlework, cut glass, chair maker, knife maker, gunsmith, boot maker.

HINTS FOR TRAVELING WITH CHILDREN, ELDERLY, HANDICAPPED

Pick up a special map for handicapped patrons at the information booth. Electric cart and wheelchair rentals are available.

SIX FLAGS OVER MID-AMERICA

Six Flags Over Mid-America, located 30 minutes west of St. Louis in the Ozark foothills, is a 200-acre theme park that draws over 1.5 million guests each year. The park offers many rides, from the state-of-the-art Ninja, a super roller coaster featuring over 2,000 feet of high-speed spirals, a double corkscrew, and a 360-degree loop, to the more traditional 77-year-old Grand Ole Carousel. Six Flags also offers a variety of entertaining shows, shops, and assorted eateries to round out the attractions.

ADDRESS AND TELEPHONE

Six Flags Over Mid-America
P. O. Box 60
Allenton-Six Flags Road
Eureka, MO 63025

(314) 938-4800

LOCATION

Six Flags Over Mid-America is located 30 minutes southwest of St. Louis. Take I-44 to exit 264 in Eureka.

OPERATING SEASONS AND HOURS

Open weekends from April to mid-May and from Labor Day to October. Open daily from mid-May to Labor Day. Opens at 10 A.M. Closing times vary, so check with the park upon arrival.

ADMISSION FEES

Adults: $19.95. Children ages 3 to 11: $14.50. Children 2 and under: free. Seniors 55 and over: $9.95.

TRANSPORTATION AND ACCOMMODATIONS WITHIN THE PARK

Tram service from the parking lot to the front gate.

GUEST SERVICES

Restrooms, telephones, first aid, baby nursing and changing station, lost parents area, kennels, lost and found, message center, post office, lockers, stroller and wheelchair rental, gas station and convenience center, check cashing. Visa, MasterCard, and Discover cards accepted.

RIDES

Aero Flyer: swing to the stars on this speedy ride.
Colossus: ride a Ferris wheel that is over 18 stories high.
Dodge City: bumper cars.
El Toro Bravo: move in several directions simultaneously.
Grand Ole Carousel: try this 77-year-old beauty.
Hannibarrels: oversized barrels spin you around.
Highland Fling: rotate, swing, and spin until you're perpendicular to the ground.
MoMo: twirl around on this spider ride.
The Moon: drive your own antique car.
Ninja: soar through 2,330 feet of spirals, a double corkscrew, sidewinder, and 360-degree loop, while reaching speeds up to 60 miles per hour.
The Plunge: a speeding log flume.
River King Mine Train: twist and turn in coaster craziness.
Rush Street Flyer: a platform swings you up and down.
Screamin' Eagle: an enormous snaking, turning wooden coaster.
Thunder River: experience the thrill of white water rapids.
Tunel del Tiempo: dare to journey aboard this dark ride.
Yankee Clipper: board a swinging, swaying ship.

KIDDIE RIDES

Acme Gravity-Powered Roller Ride: a smaller coaster.
Bugs Bunny Burrow: tunnel crawl.
Daffy Duck Airways: self-piloting planes.
Ferris Wheel: a perennial favorite.
Foghorn Leghorn Funasium: a crawl through an ocean of balls.
Porky Pig Ball Park: a ball crawl.
Sylvester Cat Climb: net climb, slides.
Tasmanian Devil Taxi Company: self-propelled scooters.
Yosemite Sam Summit: a ball crawl.

GAMES

Games of Skill: located throughout the park.
Video Arcades: two arcades, each with your favorite video challenges.

SHOWS

U.S. High-Diving Team: divers demonstrate springboard precision and stunt diving.
Splash Dance: dolphins perform their aquatic antics.
Each summer the park also offers an assortment of musical and variety shows.

SPECIAL ANNUAL EVENTS

Annual Country Fair: crafts, exhibits, foods, truck and tractor pulls, country music, dancing—in September and October.
Fright Nights: haunted house, costumed characters—on Halloween and on October weekends.

RESTAURANTS

D. J.'s Diner: steak, chicken, shrimp dinners, burgers, sandwiches.
Wascal's: burgers, fries, shakes.
Calico's Kitchen: chicken, fish.
Casa Meramec: tacos, taco salads, burritos.
Stockyards: barbecued beef and pork.
Stagecoach Inn: submarine sandwiches.
Colonnade's: burgers.
Angelo's: pizza.
Cicero's: pizza.

SNACK BARS

Hot Dog Stand
Arctic Frozen Lemonade
King Arthur's: burgers.
First Cone: ice cream.
Franny's Frozen Desserts: ice cream, drinks.
Funnel Cakes

CATERING

Contact Dennis Woerner at (314) 938-5300, ext. 287.

SOUVENIR SHOPS

The Hangar: clothing, monogramming.
Looney Tunes Boutique: Looney Tunes plush toys, T-shirts, hats, visors.
Chateau's Gifts & Collectibles: mugs, glassware, figurines, park mementos.
Soulard's Candy Cabin
Fiesta Gifts: piñatas, T-shirts, mementos with a Mexican theme.
J.M. Harveys: mugs, glassware, rocking chairs, crafts, figurines.
Glass Shop
Toy Circus
Computer Portraits: your face, by computer design.
Old-Time Photos: you in an old-fashioned picture.

HINTS FOR TRAVELING WITH CHILDREN, ELDERLY, HANDICAPPED

Guests restricted to wheelchairs are admitted to the park free. Wheelchair ramps are available at rides and shows.

HELPFUL TIPS ON MAKING YOUR VISIT MORE ENJOYABLE

Plan to spend the entire day at the park in order to take in all the rides, shows, and attractions. For concert and special events information, call the information office at (314) 938-4800.

WORLDS OF FUN/OCEANS OF FUN

Worlds of Fun has been in operation for 20 years. Each year over 1 million visitors participate in this 170-acre family-oriented amusement park's many attractions, including its live shows and rides. The theme of the park is based on Jules Verne's book, *Around the World in Eighty Days,* and is divided into five areas: the Orient, Scandinavia, Europa, Africa, and Americana. Among the guests' favorite rides are the roaring Timber Wolf wooden roller coaster and the Fury of the Nile million-gallon white water raft ride. The park also offers 13 kiddie rides, such as Crashem Bashem mini bumper cars and Bounce-a-Roos bouncing kangaroos. Oceans of Fun, a water park with a tropical theme, has more than 35 water-related attractions and fun for all ages on 60 acres of surf and sand.

ADDRESS AND TELEPHONE

Worlds of Fun/Oceans of Fun
4545 Worlds of Fun Avenue
Kansas City, MO 64161

(816) 454-4545

LOCATION

Worlds of Fun/Oceans of Fun is located 15 miles northeast of downtown Kansas City. The park can be reached via exit 54 off I-435.

OPERATING SEASONS AND HOURS

Worlds of Fun is open weekends in April, May, September, and October. Both parks are open daily from Memorial Day to Labor Day. Opens at 10:30 A.M. Monday through Friday, and Sunday and at 10 A.M. on Saturday. Closing times vary, so check with the park upon arrival.

ADMISSION FEES

Worlds of Fun: Adults: $19.95. Children ages 4 to 11: $14.95. Children 3 and under: free. Seniors 60 and over: $14.95.
  Oceans of Fun: Adults: $13.95. Children ages 4 to 11: $11.95. Children 3 and under: free. Seniors 60 and over: $11.95.

TRANSPORTATION AND ACCOMMODATIONS WITHIN THE PARK

Trams take guests to and from the parking lots.

GUEST SERVICES

Restrooms, telephones, guest relations booth, first aid, lost parents area, kennels, stroller and wheelchair rental, CIRRUS and Bankmate ATMs. Life jacket and inner tube rental and changing areas at Oceans of Fun. Visa, MasterCard, American Express, and Discover cards accepted.

RIDES

At Worlds of Fun:
Bamboozler: a favorite centrifugal force ride.
Der Fender Bender: bumper cars.
Finnish Fling: ride in a barrel, then experience the bottom dropping out.
Flying Dutchman: Dutch-style boats whirl and rise.
Fury of the Nile: bounce and splash down this million-gallon water raft ride.
Le Carrousel: a classic.
Le Grand Prix: mini motorized race cars.
Le Taxi Tour: drive a battery-powered taxi through a course.
Octopus: eight arms spin and speed.
Omegatron: swing back and forth, then over the top.
Orient Express: hold on tight as you plunge down the 115-foot drop and soar through two upside-down loops.
Python Plunge: four lightning-fast hydroflumes.
River City Rampage: whirls around, then lifts up.
Rockin' Reeler: fast-moving circular ride with tunnel covering.
Scandia Scrambler: move in several directions at once.
SkyLiner: 60-foot, open-cage Ferris wheel.
Timber Wolf: speed on a 4,230-foot-long wooden coaster.
Viking Voyager: a treetop water flume ride.
Whobble Wheel: speeds up and down in a circle.

Zambezi Zinger: a steel speed-racer roller coaster zips through the jungle.
Zulu: whirl along, then beware: the center lifts and tilts.

At Oceans of Fun:
Caribbean Cooler: tropical splendor as you float or swin through 800 feet of gently rushing water.
Diamond Head: three twisting, turning water slides.
The Typhoon: the world's longest dual water slide with over 400 feet of action at speeds up to 30 miles per hour.

KIDDIE RIDES

At Worlds of Fun:
Beetle Bumps: self-driven little cars.
Bounce-a-Roos: kangaroos bounce passengers as the ride turns around.
Crashem Bashem: small-sized bumper cars.
Habitot: a ball crawl.
Head-over-Wheels: a down-sized Ferris wheel.
Kiddie-Opolis: an activity area with net climbs, ladders, slides.
Micro Moto Bahn: kids can drive their own electric cars.
PandAm Airlines: little airplanes.
Pony Promenade: a mini merry-go-round.
Swing-a-Ling: little swings whirl around.
Too Too Train: a miniature electric train rides on a track.
Tots Yachts: boats move in a circular channel.
Turn Tyke: little motorcycles and cars.

At Oceans of Fun:
Crocodile Isle: featuring a 2,000-square-foot kiddie pool, three new 50-foot water slides, and soft animal slides.

ATTRACTIONS AND GAMES

At Worlds of Fun:
Video Arcade
Games of Skill: located throughout the park.

At Oceans of Fun:

Surf City Wave Pool: a million-gallon wave pool designed for body surfing and rafting.

Castaway Cove: a water rendezvous for adults only, featuring the Belly-Up refreshment cabana, Jacuzzi jets, and sun decks.

Neptune's Lagoon: an old-fashioned swimming hole.

SHOWS

Puppet Show: amusing show geared to young children.

Fins & Flippers Dolphin Show: diving, leaping, performing dolphins.

Stax of Wax: '50s and '60s musical revue.

P. J. Panda's Plan for the Planet: musical, fun-filled show starring the Worlds of Fun costumed characters.

Tivoli Music Hall: a Broadway-style show.

SPECIAL ANNUAL EVENTS

Big Thrill: a nostalgic celebration of the Sock Hop era, complete with DJ, music, and entertainment—on September weekends.

Octoberfest: music, German foods, cloggers, and more—on October weekends.

Kids Fest: activities geared specifically for children, throughout June.

Celebrate America: week-long Independence Day celebration.

Westward Ho Days: an array of Western entertainment during the month of July.

RESTAURANTS

At Worlds of Fun:

Inn of the Four Winds: hot and cold sandwiches, croissants, salad bar, chicken/brisket buffet.

At Oceans of Fun:

Belly-Up Bar: adults-only area that serves soft drinks and spirits.

There are also more than 10 eating and drinking facilities throughout Oceans of Fun.

SNACK BARS

More than 30 stands located throughout Worlds of Fun serve pizza, barbecue, chicken fingers, hot dogs, ice cream, candy, snacks.

CATERING

Contact Group Sales at (816) 454-4545, ext. 8200.

SOUVENIR SHOPS

Front Street Dry Goods: games, mugs, T-shirts.

Orient Expressions: logo merchandise from the Orient Express ride.

Trading Post: logo merchandise from the Timber Wolf roller coaster.

More than 25 souvenir stands located throughout the park sell souvenirs, T-shirts, balloons, postcards, paper flowers, Glo necklaces, gifts.

HINT FOR TRAVELING WITH CHILDREN, ELDERLY, HANDICAPPED

The parks are accessible to all guests; handicapped visitors should pick up a special guide at the Guest Relations booth.

OHIO

THE BEACH WATERPARK

The Beach Waterpark is the largest water theme park in Ohio. Set on 35 acres of rolling hills and wooded valleys, The Beach offers its visitors an unusually broad assortment of water rides and activities. Featured attractions include the Banzai's twin triple-drop body slides, the Typhoon's twisting, turning serpentine slides, the five-story free-fall water slide called The Cliff, as well as Emerald Bay, a 6,000-foot activity pool. Child-sized attractions include Penguin Bay activity pool, with its water slide, fountains, and jungle gyms.

ADDRESS AND TELEPHONE

The Beach Waterpark
2590 Waterpark Drive
Mason, OH 45040

(513) 398-7946

LOCATION

The Beach Waterpark is located 25 miles north of Cincinnati. The park can be reached via I-71 at exit 25.

OPERATING SEASONS AND HOURS

Open daily from Memorial Day to Labor Day. Hours: 10 A.M. to 7 P.M.; to 9 P.M. beginning early June. Closing times vary, so check with the park upon arrival.

ADMISSION FEES

Adults: $13.95. Children ages 3 to 9: $10.95. Children 2 and under: free.

TRANSPORTATION AND ACCOMMODATIONS WITHIN THE PARK

None.

GUEST SERVICES

Restrooms, telephones, guest relations area, first aid, showers, changing rooms, lost and found, locker and raft rental, arcade, life jackets. Visa, MasterCard, American Express, Discover, and Diners Club cards accepted.

RIDES

Banzai: soar down twin, triple-drop body slides while reaching speeds up to 35 miles per hour.

The Cliff: a five-story free-fall water slide.

Emerald Bay: enjoy an activity pool with two translucent hydrotubes, cable pulley rides, shoot tubes, diving platform, lily pads, and swinging rope bridge.

Hidden Rapids: an inner tube rapid ride that makes you feel as if you're shooting white water rapids.

Lazy River: take a relaxing float down a 1,200-foot river.

Riptide: multirider inner tube slide.

Snake River Rapids: float through the woods in an inner tube.

Typhoon: twist and turn down serpentine body slides.

Watusi: enclosed hydrotube that takes its riders through a 450-degree helix curve.

KIDDIE RIDES

Dolphin Bay: a special kid-sized tube ride with two body flumes and 60-foot-long otter slide.

Penguin Bay: a kiddie activity pool featuring a mini water slide, water fountains, and jungle gyms.

ATTRACTIONS AND GAMES

Thunder Beach Wavepool: ride four-foot-high, white-capped waves in this 25,000-square-foot pool.

Volleyball: four sand courts.

Pirate's Den: video games arcade.

SHOWS

Live Reggae Shows: on selected Sunday afternoons.

Polynesian Revue & Luau

RESTAURANTS

Thunder Beach Grill: bratwurst, hot dogs, barbecued rib sandwiches.

Captain Cook's: burgers, hot dogs, fries, drinks.

Lighthouse Pizza: pizza, hoagies.

SNACK BARS

Sandbar: ice cream, soft serve.

Cotton Candy: cotton candy, ice cream, slush puppies, soft drinks.

KoKoMo Kove Beer and Wine Garden

CATERING

Contact Doug Martin at (513) 398-7946 or (513) 398-4356.

SOUVENIR SHOP

Tradewinds: park souvenirs, swimsuits, beach apparel, T-shirts.

HINTS FOR TRAVELING WITH CHILDREN, ELDERLY, HANDICAPPED

Children under 9 must be accompanied by someone 16 or older. Life jackets are available free of charge to nonswimmers.

HELPFUL TIPS ON MAKING YOUR VISIT MORE ENJOYABLE

Plan to spend the entire day; raft and tube rentals are available throughout your visit. Changing rooms and showers are offered free of charge. Cutoff shorts are not allowed.

CEDAR POINT

Cedar Point has more roller coasters than any park in North America. Its unique location on a 364-acre Lake Erie peninsula has helped make this traditional park a popular vacation destination for 122 years. Cedar Point's combination of rides, live musical shows, themed areas, children's attractions, white sandy beach, Soak City water park (which includes a five-acre water slide complex), full-service marina, and RV campground draws about 3 million guests each summer. A recent expansion program is responsible for many new and exciting park features. Some of these are the 160-foot-tall Mean Streak, the tallest wooden roller coaster in the world; Tadpole Town, a children's water playground; and the Breakwater Cafe restaurant.

ADDRESS AND TELEPHONE

Cedar Point
P. O. Box 5006
Sandusky, OH 44871-8006

(419) 626-0830

LOCATION

Cedar Point can be reached by taking U. S. 250, Ohio routes 2, 4, or 6, or the Ohio Turnpike to exit 7 into Sandusky; follow signs to the park.

OPERATING SEASONS AND HOURS

Open daily from May to Labor Day. Hours: 10 A.M. to 10 PM. Closing times vary, so check with the park upon arrival.

ADMISSION FEES

Adults: $21.95. Children under 48 inches: $11.95. Children 3 and under: free. Seniors 60 and over: $12.75. Starlight admission (after 5 P.M. or after 4 P.M. when the park closes at 8 P.M.): $11.95. Check with the park for two-day pass rates, season passes, and admission to Soak City only.

TRANSPORTATION AND ACCOMMODATIONS WITHIN THE PARK

A shuttle takes guests from Causeway A-frames and condominiums to the park. For reservations and information call (419) 626-0830.

Hotel Breakers: a 400-room, turn-of-the-century resort hotel.

Sandcastle Suites: a new 96-unit, all-suites hotel, located on the northern tip of Cedar Point Peninsula.

Camper Village: a full-service, 400-site RV campground.

Cedar Point Marina: approximately 190 guest slips are available every day the park is open.

A-Frame Chalets and Condominiums: private accommodations are available to rent.

GUEST SERVICES

Restrooms, telephones, check cashing, first aid, kennels, message center, lost persons area, lost and found, stroller rental, wheelchairs, picnic shelters, CIRRUS automated teller machine. Visa, MasterCard, American Express, and Discover cards accepted.

RIDES

Antique Cars: ride your own old-style auto.
Blue Streak: soar to 78 feet in this exciting roller coaster.
Cadillac Cars: drive your own.
Calypso: climb aboard for island-style fun.
Carousels: four antique merry-go-rounds.
Cedar Downs: saddle up for a speedy horse ride.
Corkscrew: flip upside down three times in this 2,050-foot coaster thriller.
Demon Drop: a 131-foot tower falls more than 60 feet in two seconds.
Disaster Transport: on this futuristic space adventure featuring an enclosed roller coaster you travel through space and encounter pirates and asteroids.
Dodgem: two bumper car rides.
Gemini: climb 125 feet up, then drop to the ground on this coaster.

Giant Wheel: 36 colorful cars soar 15 stories in the air.

Iron Dragon: zoom around if you dare.

Magnum XL-200: at 205 feet, this is the tallest roller coaster in the world, and it speeds you along at 72 miles per hour.

Main Stream: ride along this 1,200-foot inner tube river in Soak City.

Matterhorn: speedy ups and downs.

Mean Streak: at 160 feet, this all new coaster is the tallest wooden roller coaster in the world.

Mill Race: a 1,242-foot water race.

Mine Ride: an unforgettable train trip.

Monster: board one of 24 cars for a monster of a ride.

Ocean Motion: ride the waves.

Paddlewheel Excursions: cruise on one of eight big boats.

Pirate Ride: shiver your timbers.

Railroad: an authentic coal-fired train journey.

Schwabinchen: a spinning ride on the edge of a giant woman's skirt.

Scrambler: move in many directions at once.

Sky Ride: see the park from high above.

Space Spiral: a cabin spirals 285 feet up.

Super Himalaya: a speedy, thrilling ride with 20 cars.

Thunder Canyon: splash down this thundering white water raft ride.

Troika: a colorful three-pronged "Scrambler" in the air.

Turnpike Cars: motor your own car.

Wave Swinger: swing and soar.

White Water Landing: descend 4½ stories at a 40-degree angle.

Wildcat: for the brave-hearted.

Witches' Wheel: a spinning wheel that starts out on the ground and is lifted upright while still spinning.

KIDDIE RIDES

Dune Buggies: individual little buggies.

4 × 4 Truck Ride: a miniature truck rides along a kiddieland roadway.

Helicopters: self-piloted colorful copters.

Hot Rods: jazzy little cars.

Junior Gemini: a pint-sized version of the adult thrill ride.

Krazy Kars: super-silly autos.

Moon Buggies: lunar-styled vehicles.

Motorcycles: small-sized cycles.

Mustangs: special cars for little ones.

Old-Time Cars: old-fashioned little autos.

Police Cars: official little autos.

Rock, Spin, Turn: a not-too-speedy thrill ride.

Roto Whip: whips around in a circle.

Sir Rub-a-Dub's Tubs: tubs circle.

Sky Fighters: for feisty, if pint-sized, pilots.

Space Age: a futuristic journey.

ATTRACTIONS AND GAMES

Tadpole Town: a children's water playground.

Oceana: a dolphin and sea lion stadium and aquarium.

Jungle Larry's Safari: wildlife shows and exhibits and educational wildlife encounters that bring baby animals within petting distance.

Cedar Point Beach: white sandy beach on Lake Erie.

Frontier Trail: a tree-lined area with shops, handicraft demonstrations, and a petting zoo with farm animals.

Town Hall Museum: artifacts and photos from the park's history.

Cedar Point Cinema: this seven-story-high cinema envelops guests in large-format IMAX feature films.

King Arthur's Court: five different play areas with a medieval theme.

Berenstain Bear Country: children can meet all the bears in their storybook forest home.

Arcades: five arcades contain nearly 500 machines, including electronic games and antique machines. Games of skill are located throughout the park.

SHOWS

Cedar Point Cinema: a featured IMAX film is shown daily.

Jungle Larry's Safari: the largest leopard show in the United States as well as a tiger act with performing Royal Bengal tigers.

Oceana: shows starring dolphins and sea lions.

Cedar Point's four live show theaters offer nine different original shows featuring music from big bands and Dixieland to rock and pop.

SPECIAL ANNUAL EVENT

The North American Sail and Power Boat Show: the largest in-water boat show on Lake Erie. Usually the second weekend in September.

RESTAURANTS

Breakwater Cafe: breakfast, hamburgers, sandwiches, steak, seafood.
Bay Harbor Inn: seafood, prime rib, steaks, chops, pasta, desserts, wines.
Marina Steak House: steaks, chops, chicken, ribs, fish, salad bar.
Dominic's: pizza, pasta, Italian specialty sandwiches.

SNACK BARS

Hofbrau: knockwurst, bratwurst, mettwurst, potato salad, soft pretzels, draft beer.
Los Gatos: Mexican foods, hot dogs, fries.
Happy Frier, Hot Potato, Mr. Potato: fries.
Old-Fashioned Chicken BBQ: chicken, corn on the cob.
Sweets 'n' Treats: taffy, fudge.
Burger Patio: burgers, chicken sandwiches, fries.
White Water Landing Refreshments: Sno cones, cotton candy.
Silver Dollar Cafe: breakfast and sandwich platters.
Chuck Wagon Inn: barbecued chicken, ribs.

CATERING

Contact Deb Hessler at (419) 627-2217.

SOUVENIR SHOPS

The Pagoda Gift Shop: T-shirts, sweatshirts, cups, park mementos, mini carousel horses.
The Emporium: toys, gifts with a Western theme, park souvenirs.
Safari Gifts: T-shirts and other souvenirs with a jungle, African, and wild animal theme.
Frontier Trail Crafts: several shops in one area featuring candles, glass, toys, pottery, wood carvings, china, and leather goods.
Park Plaza: fine giftware, sportswear, souvenirs.
Cedar Creek Trading Company: giftware with a Western theme, Mean Streak souvenirs, T-shirts, sweatshirts, toys, park mementos.

Other gift shops, carts, and stands located throughout the park sell merchandise and souvenirs ranging from handcrafted pottery to T-shirts and toys.

HINTS FOR TRAVELING WITH CHILDREN, ELDERLY, HANDICAPPED

Diapers, baby oil, baby powder, lotion, and infant shirts are available at Stroller Rental at the front of the park. Diaper-changing facilities are located in all ladies' rooms. First-aid stations will warm bottles and supply private quarters for nursing mothers. Bottles will also be warmed at all full-service restaurants.

The park is generally wheelchair accessible. Braille menus are available at Marina Steak House, Bay Harbor Inn, and Silver Dollar Cafe.

HELPFUL TIPS ON MAKING YOUR VISIT MORE ENJOYABLE

To avoid the largest crowds, the best time to visit the park is from opening day in early May through the end of June.

GEAUGA LAKE

Geauga Lake is a combination amusement and water park that hosts some 1.2 million visitors each year. The park features both classic and thrill rides, including the historic Big Dipper wooden coaster and Corkscrew twin-helix looping coaster. Boardwalk Shores water park offers The Wave, a 2-million-gallon pool with oceanlike six-foot waves. Geauga Lake also emphasizes kids' attractions. The highlight is the newly expanded Turtle Beach, a colorful water playground for kids, and Rad Reef, a "kid-kontrolled multistation aquatic playground." Kids can also see Butch Hightide and other Fun Bunch characters in shows around the park. Restaurants, games, and shops complete the Geauga Lake experience.

ADDRESS AND TELEPHONE

Geauga Lake
1060 North Aurora Road
Aurora, OH 44202

1-800-THE-WAVE, or 216-562-7131 outside the region

LOCATION

Take the Ohio Turnpike to exit 13 and go about 9 miles north. Geauga Lake is on Route 43 (North Aurora Road), 30 miles southeast of Cleveland.

OPERATING SEASONS AND HOURS

Open weekends in May and September. Hours: 12 A.M. to 8 P.M. Open daily from Memorial Day to Labor Day. Hours: 10 A.M. to 10 P.M.
   Opening and closing hours vary, so check with the park before arriving.

ADMISSION FEES

Adults: $14.95. Children under 3: free. Seniors: $8.50. After 5 P.M. weekdays: $9.50.

TRANSPORTATION AND ACCOMMODATIONS WITHIN THE PARK

None.

GUEST SERVICES

Restrooms, telephones, guest relations area, lost and found, first aid, lockers, baby care center, stroller and wheelchair rental, ATM bank machine, camera loans. Visa, MasterCard, American Express, and Discover cards accepted.

RIDES

Big Dipper: experience the special thrill of a historic wooden coaster.
Carousel: a historic 64-horse carousel.
Casino: roulette wheel.
The Corkscrew: the twin-helix loops of this coaster make it a real daredevil's ride.
Dodgems: bumper cars.
Double Loop: zoom through loops on a super coaster.
Enterprise: defy gravity as you spin upside down.
Euroracers: drive miniature race cars on a raceway.
Ferris Wheel: a park staple.
The Gold Rush: splash down this action-packed water log ride.
Matterhorn: experience the thrills of bobsledding.
Merry Olds Oldies: drive-yourself antique cars.
Mirage: giant "magic carpet" ride.
Musik Express: ride to rock music.
Neptune's Falls: soar down this four-flumed 1,600-foot water slide with 360-degree turns and 45-degree drops.
Parkview Express: a monorail trip around the park.
Raging Wolf Bobs: race at rip-roaring speeds on this coaster-style ride.
Rampage Slide: prepare to drop fast, then skid across water.
Rocket Ships: soar through space.
Rotor: centrifugal force holds you when the floor disappears.

Scrambler: spins you in all directions.
Sky Glide: a ski-lift ride to the clouds.
Skyscraper: rise above the park for a
  panoramic view.
Spider: your car swings around and around.
Stingray Slides: speed straight down.
Tilt-a-Whirl: spinning cups.
Yo-Yo: swing around in the air.

KIDDIE RIDES

At Rainbow Island:
Century Cycles: tyke-sized motorcycles go
  around a track.
Critter Express: a ride with favorite circus
  animals.
Flying Jumbos: fly high above the sky.
Junior Carousel: a pint-sized version of an
  amusement park favorite.
Rainbow Racers: small race cars ride a
  circular track.
Salt Water Tugs: kids can pilot their own
  little boats.
Space Patrol: planes swing around on a
  chain.
Star Shooters: cheerful hydraulic planes that
  go up and down.
Toddling Turtles: turtles in a circle.

At Turtle Beach:
Coconut Cave Canal: a tot-sized tube ride.
Lazy River: drifting in an inner tube.
Rad Reef: kids run the show in this colorful
  "kid-kontrolled multistation aquatic
  playground."

ATTRACTIONS AND GAMES

Wave: ride huge tsunami waves in this 2½-
  acre pool.
Turtle Beach: a water play area for children
  featuring mini water slides, fountain
  activity pools, and play areas.
Fun Bunch Characters: be sure to greet
  Butch Hightide, the park's radically cool
  spokesturtle, Geauga Do, and other Fun
  Bunch characters in your travels around
  the park.
Games of Skill: located throughout the park.

SHOWS

Live entertainment is featured in the Palace and
Gold Rush theaters.
Country Connections: a country and western
  show.
Sing Our Songs, America: tunes from our
  heritage.
Abracadazzle: an astounding magic act.
Rock It in the '90s: see the Fun Bunch
  characters perform.

SPECIAL ANNUAL EVENTS

Fourth of July: fireworks display.
Beach Party: live music and contests—in
  July.
Oktoberfest: amusement with a German flair;
  lots of German music and food—in late
  September.

RESTAURANTS

Funtime Cafe: steak, seafood, sandwiches,
  salads.
The Wharf: fish, chicken dinners.
Rainbow Station: burgers, hot dogs, fries,
  drinks.
Ala Burger: burgers, fries, hot dogs, chicken
  sandwiches, soft drinks.
The Engine House: Mexican-American
  specialties, beer, soft drinks.

SNACK BARS

Goldrush Saloon: nachos, hot dogs,
  barbecued beef sandwiches, beer, wine.
Paradise Pizza: pizza, ice cream.
Potato Factory: fries.
Sub Station: submarine sandwiches, salads,
  fruit.
Kountry Kitchen: funnel cakes, waffles.
Stop & Munch: sausages, kielbasi, rib
  sandwiches, hot dogs, breaded vegetables.
Terrace Lounge: hot dogs, beer, wine.
Arcade Refreshments: pizza, nachos, funnel
  cakes, waffles, beer.
Ruggles Ice Cream Parlor: hand-dipped ice
  cream.

Additional snack carts and stands located throughout the park serve hot dogs, burgers, ice cream, cotton candy, funnel cakes, candy apples, lemonade.

CATERING

Contact Catering at 1-800-THE-WAVE.

SOUVENIR SHOPS

Gift Shop: park mementos, plush animals.
Lovable Critter Shop: plush animals.
Bathhouse Boutique: swimwear, sundries.
Portrait Shop: art caricatures, color portraits.
Antique Photo: have your picture taken in costume.
Lighthouse Landing: collectibles, apparel, jewelry, novelties.
Stagecoach: collectibles, apparel, jewelry, novelties.

HELPFUL TIPS ON MAKING YOUR VISIT MORE ENJOYABLE

To beat the crowds, visit Thursday or Friday or, as a second choice, Monday or Tuesday. Come prepared with appropriate clothing to enjoy wet and dry attractions.

KINGS ISLAND

Kings Island, a 300-acre theme park, is part of the 1,600-acre family entertainment center that includes the Jack Nicklaus Sports Center, the College Football Hall of Fame, the Kings Island Inn and Conference Center, and campground. Kings Island itself contains seven theme areas: International Street, a colorful European boulevard of shops and restaurants; Wild Animal Habitat, a 100-acre wildlife preserve; Oktoberfest, a festive place with a German theme; Coney Mall, with old-fashioned amusements; Rivertown, a scenic spot that depicts life in the Ohio riverboat days; Hanna-Barbera Land, a storybook kingdom for children and their families; and Water Works, a 15-acre water park. The theme park also features original live shows, games, and a wide array of rides.

ADDRESS AND TELEPHONE

Kings Island
Kings Island, OH 45034

(513) 398-5600

LOCATION

Kings Island is located 24 miles north of Cincinnati on I-71.

OPERATING SEASONS AND HOURS

Open selected weekends in April, May, September, and October. (Call the park for details.) Open daily from Memorial Day to Labor Day. Hours: 9 A.M. to 10 P.M., Saturday until 11 P.M.

ADMISSION FEES

Adults: $21.95. Children ages 3 to 6: $10.95. Children 2 and under: free. Seniors 60 and over: $10.95. (Admission fee includes access to the water park.)

TRANSPORTATION AND ACCOMMODATIONS WITHIN THE PARK

Trams carry visitors between the parking lot and the main gate.

GUEST SERVICES

Restrooms, telephones, Guest Relations Department, first aid, kennel, lockers, lost and found, message center, baby care center, lost parents area, wheelchairs, baby stroller rental.

RIDES

Adventure Express: mine train roller coaster.

Amazon Falls: prepare to get soaked in boats that climb high before plunging into the lake below.

Beast: ride the world's longest roller coaster (7,400 feet).

Bonzai Pipeline: drop 35 feet through one of three enclosed tubes.

Carousel: one of the antiques still in operation.

Dodg'em: cars that bump and crash.

Ferris Wheel: you ride high above the crowds in this classic ride.

Flight Commander: make your own two-person space pod dive, climb, and perform barrel rolls.

Flying Eagles: white and blue airplanes propel you into the air and back again.

The Helix: four body slides snake their way down, rocking you right and left.

Kenton's Cover Keelboat Canal: plunge down a slide in a log float.

KI & MVRR: an old-time steam engine.

King Cobra: this green-and-yellow snake plunges you into a loop, then tosses you into a helix.

Kings Mill Log Flume: a smaller version of Kenton's Cover Keelboat Canal.

Kings Mill Run: a refreshing ride in an inner tube that meanders alongside waterfalls.

Les Taxis & Ohio Overland Livery: drive your own antique car around the island.

Monster: this black monster twists all around.

Phantom Theatre: the re-creation of an old theater once inhabited by performing greats.

The Plunge: prepare to drop 70 feet in this free-fall water slide.

Racer: ride a twin-track wooden coaster.

Rushing River: five-person inner tube careens through a 750-foot trough and drops 55 feet during descent.

Scrambler: this ride turns one way while your seat turns another.

Shake, Rattle & Roll: twists you in circles.

Sidewinder: speed down one of two troughs of rushing water.

The Streak and Thunder Run: try these two multibump slides.

Turnpike: practice your driving skills on scaled-down race cars.

Ultra Twister: twist through a 250-foot coil of intertwining tubes.

Viking Fury: board a vessel that flies up in the air and back down again.

Vortex: a steel coaster that turns you upside down six times.

White Lightning: slide 55 feet before plunging through a cushion of water.

White Water Canyon: rafts ride perilously close to boulders and under geysers.

Zephyr: a swinglike seat spins until it is parallel to the ground.

KIDDIE RIDES

Beastie: a small version of the Beast for younger coaster riders.

Boo Boo's Buggies & Pee Wee Raceway: kids pretend they're really driving.

Boulder Bumpers: pint-sized version of Dodg'em cars.

Flintstone's Flyboys: scaled-down copters propel youngsters into the air.

HB Carousel: Dino, Fred, Scooby, Yogi, and Jabber Jaws take young riders up, down, around and around.

Jabber Jaws Tubs: smaller version of the classic Tumble Bug.

Jelly Bean Bowl: a ball crawl.

Mr. Jinx Jalopies: scaled-down version of the Turnpike ride.

Rawhides Railways: kids actually propel themselves in handcars.

Scooby Choo: pint-sized trains carry little riders through scenes of Kings Island.

Screecher: riders whip around in circles.

Splash Island: water fun for little ones, with little slides and gentle wading curtain.

Witch's Cauldrons: Winsome Winnie delights in spinning hostages around and around.

ATTRACTIONS AND GAMES

Eiffel Tower: located in the park's center, it's a 332-foot scale model of the Paris original.

International Street: a colorful European boulevard of shops and restaurants.

Wild Animal Habitat: more than 350 wild animals from Africa, Asia, and North America roam freely on this 100-acre preserve.

Rivertown: a scenic area depicting life in the Ohio riverboat days.

Rivertown Games: electronic games and Skee ball.

Hanna-Barbera Games: kids can win prizes at pint-sized games.

Games of Skill: located throughout the park, including Dragon's Flight (roll a ball and win a prize).

SHOWS

Ice Adventure: professional figure skating show.

Several other original live shows are performed daily.

SPECIAL ANNUAL EVENT

Winterfest: an old-fashioned celebration of Christmas, complete with ice skating, live shows, Santa, and the world's tallest Christmas tree—from Thanksgiving to New Year's Eve.

RESTAURANTS

International Restaurant: soups, salads, prime ribs, and more.

The Deli: eggs, pancakes, bacon, sausage, soups, salads, deli sandwiches, potatoes, desserts, beer, soft drinks.

Burger Bistro: burgers, fries, fish sandwiches, soft drinks.

Bamm Bamm's Bon Bons: hot dogs, soft drinks.

Quick Draw's Cafe: hot dogs, popcorn, soft drinks.

Columbia Palace: fried chicken, baked fish, barbecued chicken, ribs, corn, salads, desserts.

Canyon Canteen: tacos, nachos, drinks.

Rib Pit: barbecued ribs, sausages, beer, soft drinks.

Lunch Basket: chili, beer, soft drinks.

Coney Cafe: burgers, hot dogs, fries, beer.

Thrillburger: burgers, fries, soft drinks.

The Festhaus: bratwurst, schnitzel, and other German treats.

Der Bier Garten: hot dogs, bratwurst, potato salad, beer, wine coolers.

Kafe Kilimanjaro: burgers, hot dogs, fries, beer, soft drinks.

SNACK BARS

Munchen Tower: soft pretzels, beer, soft drinks.

Cafe Parisienne: nachos, popcorn, cotton candy, soft drinks.

Tower Drinks: beer, soft drinks, pretzels.

Fried and True: fried mushrooms, onion rings, shrimp, fries.

Chiquita Tropical Fruit Island: fruit cups, fruit drinks.

Smurf Goodies: soft-serve cones.

Rivertown Pizza

Rivertown Potato Works: fries.

Frankfurter Factory: hot dogs, soft drinks.

Rivertown Lemon Quench: soft-frozen lemonade.

Depot Sundae: ice cream.

Antique Treats: shaved ice, pretzels, popcorn, soft drinks.

Sweet Tooth: cotton candy, sundaes, ice cream.

Coney Waffle: waffles, funnel cakes, corn dogs.

Oktoberfest Corn Dogs: corn dogs, Swiss-cheese-on-a-stick, soft drinks.

Snack Stop: hot dogs, pretzels, soft drinks.

CATERING

Contact Sonny Mancini at (513) 398-5600.

SOUVENIR SHOPS

The German Building: Kings Island and Hanna-Barbera souvenirs, handbags, scarves, jewelry.

Munchen Gifts: T-shirts, hats.

Kid's Clothing and Keepsakes: clothing, mementos, Hanna-Barbera souvenirs.

International Gift Shop: stuffed animals, T-shirts, collectibles.

Front Gate Shops: assorted Kings Island souvenirs.

Hanna-Barbera Fun Shop: hats, toys, T-shirts for tiny tots.

Beast Canyon Supplies: Beast T-shirts, hats, and more.

Grand Coaster Station: coaster and Kings Island memorabilia.

Coney Emporium: T-shirts, hats.

Vortex Gear: Vortex T-shirts, mugs, hats.

Congo Curio: Wild Animal Habitat T-shirts, hats, and other souvenirs.

HINTS FOR TRAVELING WITH CHILDREN, ELDERLY, HANDICAPPED

Much of the park is wheelchair accessible. Persons in wheelchairs should inform the ride operators or park hostesses before entering the attractions.

HELPFUL TIP ON MAKING YOUR VISIT MORE ENJOYABLE

To avoid the biggest crowds, visit the park on Monday or Friday.

SEA WORLD OF OHIO

More than 1 million visitors each year take in the sights and sounds of Sea World of Ohio. The marine life park, located in Aurora, Ohio, equidistant from Akron and Cleveland, encompasses 90 landscaped acres. Renowned for its family-oriented entertainment and educational value, Sea World's major attractions are its 20 exhibits, two aquariums, and lively shows that star such seaworthy celebrities as Shamu the killer whale, sea lions Clyde and Seamore, and performing bottlenose dolphins. Visitors will also enjoy the three-acre Shamu's Play Area, a creative playland, Penguin Encounter with more than 100 penguins, dolphin community pool, and sea lion community pool.

ADDRESS AND TELEPHONE

Sea World of Ohio
1100 Sea World Drive
Aurora, OH 44202

(216) 562-8101 or 1-800-63-SHAMU

LOCATION

Sea World is 25 miles southeast of Cleveland on Route 43 in Aurora. Take the Ohio Turnpike north to exit 13. Sea World is 14 miles north.

OPERATING SEASONS AND HOURS

Open daily from mid-May to early September. Opens at 10 A.M. Closing times vary, so check with the park upon arrival.

ADMISSION FEES

Adults: $19.50. Children ages 3 to 11: $15.50. Children under 3: free. Discount for seniors over 60.

TRANSPORTATION AND ACCOMMODATIONS WITHIN THE PARK

None.

GUEST SERVICES

Restrooms, telephones, first aid, infant nursing station, information booth, lost child booth, stroller and wheelchair rental, locker rental, PLUS System automated teller machine. Visa and MasterCard accepted.

RIDES

None.

ATTRACTIONS

Shamu's Play Area: three-acre playland for children with a nautical theme. Features Cap'n Kid's Fun Ship, a 60-foot pirate galleon perfect for climbing, and plenty of water activities.

Penguin Encounter: home to more than 100 penguins, it's Sea World's slice of the Antarctic, featuring daily snowfall, light changes, and icy sea pools.

Sea Lion and Seal Community Pool: feed the California sea lions and harbor seals.

World of the Sea Aquarium: a close-up look at the undersea world.

Trout Fishing Pond: catch and keep your own rainbow trout.

SHOWS

Shared World: the skill and grace of Shamu and Namu, the majestic killer whale stars, and bottlenose dolphins are highlighted in this exciting presentation. A renovated stadium featuring a natural-looking set and spirited music creates a breathtaking backdrop for these awe-inspiring animals.

International High-Dive Show: divers from around the world plunge into a fast-paced, high-energy show of athletic talent. Towering platforms, springboards and an octagonal pool become the stage for these daring divers.

Pirates of Pinniped: the comical sea lion duo, Clyde and Seamore, set sail on a whimsical mission to become pirates. They are joined by Pacific walrus, otters, and Sea World's mime as they attempt to find the lost treasure of the Pirate King.

Water Ski Show: a new show every season featuring Sea World's water-skiers.

Summer Nights: stay late at the park and take advantage of special evening prices, mid-June through late August and Labor Day weekend. Be dazzled at dusk as brilliant lasers light the sky with fabulous images, special effects, and graphics during an all new laser and fireworks show.

SPECIAL ANNUAL EVENT

Fourth of July: fireworks display.

Budweiser Clydesdales: check with the park for dates.

Arts & Crafts Festival: check with the park for dates.

RESTAURANTS

Platters: fried chicken, mashed potatoes, biscuits, apple pie.

Lakeside Cafe: corned beef and turkey sandwich platters, burgers, fries, salads, desserts, drinks.

Sandwich Works: alpine sandwich platter, California lite sandwich platter, ham and cheese platter, drinks.

All-American Sandwiches: steak and cheese sandwiches, knockwurst and bratwurst sandwiches, hot dogs, drinks.

Mama Rosa's: spaghetti, lasagna, Italian subs, and more.

Philly Steak Sandwiches: steak and cheese sandwiches, ham and cheese, fries.

Ice Cream Parlour

Smokehouse Ribs 'n' Chicken: ribs, chicken, or pork sandwich dinners.

SNACK BARS

Snack stands located throughout the park serve soft ice cream, pretzels, fries, hot dogs, burgers, popcorn, nachos, pizza.

CATERING

Not available.

SOUVENIR SHOPS

Emporium: collectibles, jewelry, T-shirts, stuffed animals, Sea World souvenirs.

Whales Tail: whales on hats, jewelry, posters, and more.

Hidden Cove: Sea World souvenirs, Christmas merchandise, fudge.

Friends of the Wild: distinctive gifts for the animal lover.

Faceball: create your own baseball card. Also large collection of sports merchandise.

Seaport Village: have an ama diver search for your very own oyster, guaranteed to contain a cultured pearl. Fine pearl rings and necklaces, and shell gifts.

Label Stable: Anheuser-Busch–brand merchandise including T-shirts, steins, collectibles.

Other shops and carts throughout the park sell Shamu plush toys, souvenir photos, candy, T-shirts, hats, jewelry, and other Sea World mementos.

HINTS FOR TRAVELING WITH CHILDREN, ELDERLY, HANDICAPPED

Sea World is handicapped accessible; be sure to pick up a brochure at the information booth.

Attendants are available at each stadium to assist handicapped guests.

If you're traveling with an infant, feel free to use the infant nursing station. Changing tables and diapers are available in most restrooms. Strollers must be left outside stadiums for safety reasons.

HELPFUL TIPS ON MAKING YOUR VISIT MORE ENJOYABLE

Most have preshow entertainment, and the majority of stadiums are weather protected.

WISCONSIN

FAMILY LAND

As its name implies, Family Land is a family-oriented water theme park located in the Wisconsin Dells. The park offers several styles of water activities, from an enormous wave pool and the super-steep Demon's Drop speed slide to tyke-sized kiddie rides. The 40-acre park also offers bumper boats, bumper cars, go-carts, and Cam-Am racers, as well as a miniature golf course. A nearby attraction is Storybook Gardens, a landscaped fantasy world with animated displays.

ADDRESS AND TELEPHONE

Family Land
Highway 12
Wisconsin Dells, WI 53965

(608) 254-7766 or (608) 254-8560

LOCATION

Family Land is located on Highway 12. Take exit 87 off Highway 190-94. Stay on Highway 12 for about two miles to the park.

OPERATING SEASONS AND HOURS

Open daily from mid-May to early September. Hours: 10 A.M. to 5 P.M. until June 15 and the last week of August; 9 A.M. to 8 P.M. for the rest of the summer.

ADMISSION FEES

All-day pass (includes all motorized rides, wave pool, water slides, and miniature golf, but excludes Skeeter Boats, which are $4 per ride): $13.95. All-water-park-activities pass (excludes motorized rides): $11.95.

Admission to Storybook Gardens: Adults: $6.50. Children: $5.

TRANSPORTATION AND ACCOMMODATIONS WITHIN THE PARK

None.

GUEST SERVICES

Restrooms, telephones, information booth, check cashing, first aid, lockers, changing rooms, lost and found, picnic areas. Visa, MasterCard, American Express, and Discover cards accepted.

RIDES

Blue Magnum: twist, turn, and tunnel down 2,000 feet of wetness. Actually four slides in one.
Bumper Boats: bump and splash.
Bumper Cars: the park classic.
Can-Am Racers: get behind the wheel of these racing vehicles.
Demon's Drop: slide fast down an 85-foot plunge.
Deuces Wild: zoom through turns and drops as you maneuver your two-person raft.
Double Barrel: two riders climb aboard a big inflatable tube and sail through 400 feet of an enclosed slide that twists and turns.
Double Rampage: speed down these wet slides.
Double Trouble: grab a buddy and hang on as you whistle down a spiraling double-rider slideway.
Dragon's Tail: travel over 300 feet through a double-hump tower that is more than seven stories high.
Go-Karts: drive your own.
Lazy River: a leisurely tube ride.
Pirate Ship: a 70-foot free-fall ride in a big ship.
Raging River: a slip-sliding tube slide.
Skeeter Boats: scoot around a water race course.

KIDDIE RIDES

Kiddie Antique Carousel: a pint-sized favorite.
Kiddie Bumper Boats: tyke-sized.
Kiddie Can-Am Racers: mini versions.
Kiddie Motorcycles: a circle of cycles.
Kiddie Roller Coaster: coaster with gentle slopes and dips.

ATTRACTIONS AND GAMES

Tidal Wave: this wave pool has oceanlike waves.
Fountain of Youth: kiddie activity pool.
Storybook Gardens: a landscaped fantasy world complete with animated displays (not included in all-day pass).
Surfside Mini-Golf: an 18-hole obstacled course.
Video Games: kids' favorites (not included in all-day pass).

SHOWS

The Beach Bears: cartoon bears come to life as they play and sing five times daily.

RESTAURANT

Huckleberry's Restaurant: deli sandwiches.

SNACK BARS

Stands located throughout the park serve burgers, hot dogs, cotton candy, popcorn, snacks.

CATERING

Contact Group Sales at (608) 254-7766.

SOUVENIR SHOPS

Suntamer Boutique: beach-oriented apparel.
Gift Shops: two shops offer souvenirs, film, suntan lotion, and sundries.

SOUTH CENTRAL

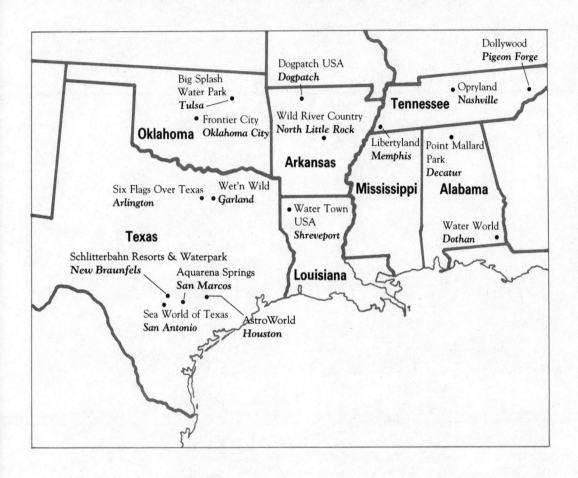

Big Splash
Water Park
Tulsa

Dogpatch USA
Dogpatch

Dollywood
Pigeon Forge

Tennessee

Oryland
Nashville

Frontier City
Oklahoma City

Oklahoma

Wild River Country
North Little Rock

Arkansas

Libertyland
Memphis

Point Mallard
Park
Decatur

Alabama

Six Flags Over Texas
Arlington

Wet'n Wild
Garland

Mississippi

Water Town
USA
Shreveport

Water World
Dothan

Texas

Schlitterbahn Resorts & Waterpark
New Braunfels

Aquarena Springs
San Marcos

Louisiana

Sea World of Texas
San Antonio

AstroWorld
Houston

ALABAMA

POINT MALLARD PARK

Point Mallard Park is a 750-acre family fun park with an emphasis on water activities. It features America's first wave pool as well as an Olympic-sized pool, a three-flume inner tube ride, the new Squirt Factory water play area, the new 43-foot-tall Sky Pond zoom flume, the Duck Pond Kiddie pool, and a beach. Visitors may also play a 200-acre 18-hole championship golf course, camp in the 25-acre, 175-site campground, bike, play miniature golf, or skate during winter months in the Deep South's only open-air regulation-sized ice rink.

ADDRESS AND TELEPHONE

Point Mallard Park
1800 Point Mallard Drive, S. E.
Decatur, AL 35601

(205) 350-3000 or 1-800-669-WAVE

LOCATION

Point Mallard is located in Decatur. From I-65 north take exit 340, turn on Point Mallard Drive, S. E. From I-65 south take exit 334, turn on U.S. Highway 31 north, take 8th Street, S. E.

OPERATING SEASONS AND HOURS

The Aquatic Center is open daily from mid-May through Labor Day. Hours: 10 A.M. to 6 P.M. on Wednesday, Friday, Saturday, and Sunday; 10 A.M. to 9 P.M. on Monday, Tuesday, and Thursday.

The championship golf course, campground, and hiking/biking trails are open daily year-round.

The ice skating rink is open weekends from mid-November to mid-March.

ADMISSION FEES

Aquatic Center: Adults: $10. Children under 48 inches: $5. Children 4 and under: free.

Specials: $10 per family on Monday nights, half price on Tuesday and Thursday nights.

Championship Golf Course: 9 holes: $8 to $10. 18 holes: $11 to $15.

Ice Skating Rink: $4.

Hiking/Biking trail: free.

TRANSPORTATION AND ACCOMMODATIONS WITHIN THE PARK

175-site campground. For information call (205) 351-7772.

GUEST SERVICES

Restrooms, telephones, information booth, lost and found, message center, paging system. Visa and MasterCard accepted.

RIDES

Inner Tube Slide: three fiberglass flumes wind 1,100 feet down a 50-foot hill into a 1,200-square-foot pool.
Sky Pond: 43-foot-tall double-wide flume shoots riders in inner tubes 166 feet into a splashdown pool.

KIDDIE RIDES

Duck Pond: 4,600-square-foot, 11-inch-deep children's pool featuring six miniature water slides, fountains, rocking figures on springs, and tire swings.

ATTRACTIONS AND GAMES

Wave Pool: the nation's first wave pool, it's 180 feet long with rushing waves rolling in at heights of three feet.
Olympic Pool: swim where many Olympic diving gold medalists trained.
Squirt Factory: wading pool for young swimmers packed with gushing water spouts, climbing areas, spray nozzles, and waterfalls.
Nature Trail: walk, hike, bike, or jog along the river.
Golf: test your swing, pitch, and putting skills on this 18-hole, 200-acre championship course.
Miniature Golf: this picturesque course overlooks pretty Flint Creek.
Tennis Courts: six lighted courts.
Ball Fields: play softball and baseball.
Recreation Center: basketball court, racquetball court, game room, meeting room, weight room, and showers.
Ice Rink: skate in the only open-air, regulation-sized ice rink in the Deep South.

SPECIAL ANNUAL EVENTS

Alabama Jubilee Hot Air Balloon Races: over 65 hot air balloons race each Memorial Day weekend.
Spirit of America Festival: one of the state's largest free celebrations of America's birthday. Includes the Miss Point Mallard Pageant.
September Skirmish: Civil War battle reenactment and living history camp.

RESTAURANTS

None.

SNACK BARS

Concession Stand: burgers, hot dogs, fries, chicken, tuna and steak sandwiches, chips, candy, soft drinks.
Hot Hut: tacos, nachos, chili dogs, chili, burritos, pizza.
Ice Cream Parlor: yogurt and a wide variety of ice cream flavors.

CATERING

Contact (205) 350-3000.

SOUVENIR SHOP

Gift Shop: T-shirts, swimsuits, beach towels, suntan products, park souvenirs.
Pro Shop: at the golf course.

HINT FOR TRAVELING WITH CHILDREN, ELDERLY, HANDICAPPED

Ramps and parking areas are available for the handicapped.

WATER WORLD

Water World is a 12-acre municipal water theme park. Its main attractions are a wave pool that features three-foot waves and three racing water flumes. The park also offers a kiddie pool with elephant and turtle slides, a video arcade, picnic area, gift shop, and bathhouses.

ADDRESS AND TELEPHONE

Water World
P. O. Box 2128
Dothan, AL 36302

(205) 793-0297

LOCATION

Water World is located one block off the Dothan Ross Clark traffic circle on Westgate Parkway between U. S. Highway 84 north and Highway 84 west.

OPERATING SEASONS AND HOURS

Open weekends in May. Open daily from June to Labor Day. Opens at 10 A.M. Closing times vary, so check with the park upon arrival.

ADMISSION FEES

Adults: $5. Children ages 3 to 12: $3.50. Children under 3 and seniors 60 and over: free.

TRANSPORTATION AND ACCOMMODATIONS WITHIN THE PARK

None.

GUEST SERVICES

Restrooms, telephones, first aid, locker rental, raft and inner tube rental, bathhouses. Visa and MasterCard accepted.

RIDES

Thrill Hill: three curving, twisting water flumes carry you from the top of the hill to a splashdown landing in the pool below.

KIDDIE RIDES

Kiddie Pool: kids 8 and under can slide on a turtle slide, climb and slide a smiling elephant, shower under the rain tree, or crawl through a four-foot tunnel.

ATTRACTIONS AND GAMES

Wave Pool: ride three-foot waves that alternate with 10 minutes of calm waters.
Video Arcade: features 18 video games.

RESTAURANTS

None.

SNACK BARS

Concession stands located throughout the park serve burgers, hot dogs, nachos, popcorn, chips, candies, ice cream, soft drinks.

CATERING

Not available.

SOUVENIR SHOP

Water World souvenirs, T-shirts, sunglasses, thermal mugs, key chains, suntan products, postcards.

ARKANSAS

DOGPATCH USA

Dogpatch USA, situated in the scenic Ozark Mountains of Arkansas, offers something for all ages, including native crafts people showcasing their skills, rides that range from mild to wild, a variety of shops, and beautiful scenery. Guests can catch their own trout at the park and either take it home or have down-home chefs fix it for lunch. Youngsters will especially like Kidventure Land, a recent park addition where kids can enjoy a ball crawl, net climb, and canoe float trip.

ADDRESS AND TELEPHONE

Dogpatch USA
P. O. Box 20
Dogpatch, AR 72648

(501) 743-1111

LOCATION

Dogpatch USA is located nine miles south of Harrison, Arkansas, on scenic Highway 7.

OPERATING SEASONS AND HOURS

Open daily from May through October. Hours: park: 9 A.M. to 6 P.M.; rides: 10 A.M. to 6 P.M.

ADMISSION FEES

None. (The rides have individual fees.)

TRANSPORTATION AND ACCOMMODATIONS WITHIN THE PARK

None.

GUEST SERVICES

Restrooms, telephones, information booth, first aid, lockers, lost and found, message center, baby strollers, wheelchairs, check cashing. Visa, MasterCard, American Express, and Discover cards accepted.

RIDES

Bumper Boats: you control the speed on your own bumper boat.
Impendin' Disaster Machine: a scrambler full of twists and turns.

Merry-Go-Round: a park mainstay.
Paddleboats: paddle around Wolf Island mountain lake.
Wes Pok Chop Spechul: a scenic train ride through Dogpatch over majestic Marble Falls, one of the largest waterfalls in the Ozarks.
Wild Water Rampage: sled down a flume and off a 35-foot-high tower, then skim across 80 feet of water.

KIDDIE RIDE

Air Rider: little biplanes.

ATTRACTIONS AND GAMES

Kidventure Land: children's play area with slides, rope climbs, ball crawls, kiddie canoes, sandboxes, punching bags.
Ozarks Crafts People: native crafts people showcase their skills.
Dogpatch Citizens' Cabin: learn how Dogpatch citizens live.
Kissin' Rocks: a rock formation that's great for pictures.
Barney Barnsmells Skunkworks: see animated skunks in action at this perfume factory.
Trout Farm: catch your own rainbow trout.
Arcade: video games, pinball games, Skee ball.
Remote-a-Boats: remote-control boats.
Diamond Mine: dig through bins for diamonds and fool's gold.

SHOWS

Dogpatch Mountaineers: an educational and entertaining show featuring authentic mountain-style music.

RESTAURANTS

Tyson's Chicken House: chicken strips and nuggets, fries, potato salad, coleslaw, nachos.
Hillbilly Burgers: burgers.

Rainbow Hollow Restaurant: rainbow trout, daily specials.

SNACK BARS

Daisy Mae's Ice Cream Parlor: ice cream, fudge, funnel cakes.
Coca Cola Canteen: cotton candy, Sno cones, soft drinks.

CATERING

Contact Jan Strother at (501) 743-1111.

SOUVENIR SHOPS

The General Store: cameras, film, mugs, cups, banners, Dogpatch mementos.
T-Shirt and Hat Shop
Other stands located throughout the park sell crafts, old-style photos, gifts, and Dogpatch souvenirs.

WILD RIVER COUNTRY

Wild River Country is a 23-acre water theme park featuring activities that range from the thrilling Lightning Bolt free-fall slide to the calm and gentle Driftin' River float ride. The park's 200,000 annual visitors can also enjoy a wave pool, flumes, adult and children's activity pools, river rapids ride, restaurant, arcade, and gift shop.

ADDRESS AND TELEPHONE

Wild River Country
6801 Crystal Hill Road
P. O. Box 1740
North Little Rock, AR 72115

(501) 753-8600

LOCATION

Wild River Country is located at the junction of Interstates 40 and 430, northwest of North Little Rock.

OPERATING SEASONS AND HOURS

Open weekends in May. Hours: 10:30 A.M. to 6 P.M. Open daily from June to the end of August. Hours: 10:30 A.M. to 8 P.M.

ADMISSION FEES

General: $10.95. Enter after 4 P.M.: $7.95.

TRANSPORTATION AND ACCOMMODATIONS WITHIN THE PARK

None.

GUEST SERVICES

Restrooms, telephones, information booth, check cashing, first aid, lockers, lost and found, message centers, picnic area, life jackets (no charge for use). Visa, MasterCard, and American Express cards accepted.

RIDES

Barratuba: whip through a completely enclosed slide.
Driftin' River: soak up the sun on this lazy river float ride.
Lightning Bolt: a free-fall speed slide.
Thunder Alley: twist and turn down these wild flumes.
Wild River Rapids: experience the thrills of white water rafting in this speeding tube ride.

KIDDIE RIDES

Tadpool: pint-sized slides, rides in shapes of animals, waterfall, and water fort.

ATTRACTIONS AND GAMES

Breaker Bay: ride the surf in a 17,000-square-foot wave pool.
Ole Swimming Hole: an adult activity area. Try the cable ride and lily pad crossing, and splash under the fountains.
Games Arcade

RESTAURANT

Cookhouse: burgers, hot dogs, pizza, nachos, fries, drinks.

SNACK BARS

Sidewalk Snacks: candy, chips, snacks, drinks.
Sip-n-Surf: ice cream, yogurt, drinks.

CATERING

Contact Sheila Peters at (501) 753-8600.

SOUVENIR SHOP

The Wearhouse: swimwear, apparel, sundries, park mementos.

HELPFUL TIPS ON MAKING YOUR VISIT MORE ENJOYABLE

Bring towels for every member of the family. Cutoffs are not allowed. To beat the crowds visit in the evening.

LOUISIANA

WATER TOWN USA

Nicknamed "Louisiana's Beach Within Reach," Water Town USA is a 20-acre water park and playground. The giant wave pool, with its surflike waves, headlines the park. Other attractions include four huge fiberglass slides, tubular flumes, and speed drops. For little ones there's a pint-sized pool and a sand-filled playground. Visitors can sunbathe on the sun deck, cool down in shaded areas, or take a break with an assortment of video games at The Gallery. Group picnics are welcome.

ADDRESS AND TELEPHONE

Water Town USA
P. O. Box 29009
Shreveport, LA 71149-9009

(318) 938-5475

LOCATION

To get to Water Town USA, take Interstate 20 to Industrial Loop exit and go west on West 70th Street (first light after you exit I-20) for approximately one mile. Water Town USA will be on your right.

OPERATING SEASONS AND HOURS

Open weekends in May and daily from June to Labor Day. Hours vary so check with the park before arrival.

ADMISSION FEES

Adults: $9.95 (discounts after 4 P.M.). Children 2 and under and seniors 62 and over: free. Wheelchair guests: free.

TRANSPORTATION AND ACCOMMODATIONS WITHIN THE PARK

None.

GUEST SERVICES

Restrooms, telephones, first aid, lockers, lost and found, message center, raft rental, picnic tables. Visa and MasterCard accepted.

RIDES

Big Bends: zoom through these four huge fiberglass slides that twist down a 40-foot tower to a splash landing.

The Bonzai: speed down dual slides that drop 40 feet to a splashdown pool.

Cannon Ball: double-barrel fun in a pair of tubular flumes that shoot into a pool below.

The Flash Flood: a 200-gallon wave will carry you around a big bend.

ATTRACTIONS AND GAMES

The Wave: giant wave pool with four-foot oceanlike waves and absolutely no seaweed or jellyfish!

Adventure Pool: kiddie play activity area, including rope crawls, waterfalls, and cable rides.

Silly Sand City: a sand-filled playground that offers swings, slides, and more for younger guests.

Tad Puddle: pint-sized fun in a supervised water playground.

The Gallery: a galaxy of video games.

Recreation Area: acres for sand volleyball, horseshoes, basketball, and softball, plus covered picnic tables.

RESTAURANTS

None.

SNACK BARS

Snack Shops: two snack shops serve pizza, chicken nuggets, burgers, hot dogs, corn dogs, yogurt, ice cream, fries, funnel cakes.

CATERING

Contact Melody Doucet at (318) 938-5475.

SOUVENIR SHOP

Trader Gift Shop: Water Town USA souvenirs and T-shirts, children's toys and games, adults' and children's apparel, candy, cigarettes, suntan lotion, sunglasses.

HELPFUL TIPS ON MAKING YOUR VISIT MORE ENJOYABLE

If you're coming with a group of 15 or more, be sure to call one week in advance to reserve a group shelter on the picnic grounds.

OKLAHOMA

BIG SPLASH WATER PARK

Big Splash Water Park is an amusement park with a water theme geared to both children and adults. The park features Motion Ocean, Oklahoma's largest wave pool, where four-foot waves crest like the ocean, as well as a variety of water slides, a huge activity pool, inner tube ride and lazy river, and Mazzio's Land kiddie water play pool. Approximately 300,000 guests visit the Big Splash every year.

ADDRESS AND TELEPHONE

Big Splash Water Park
P. O. Box 14156
Tulsa, OK 74159

(918) 749-7385

LOCATION

Big Splash is located at 21st Street and Yale Avenue on the Tulsa State Fairgrounds.

OPERATING SEASONS AND HOURS

Open weekends in May. Hours: 10 A.M. to 6 P.M. on Saturday; noon to 6 P.M. on Sunday.

Open daily from June to Labor Day. Hours: 10 A.M. to 8 P.M; noon to 8 P.M. on Sunday.

ADMISSION FEES

General: $13.55. Children 3 and under and seniors 60 and over: free. After 4 P.M.: $7.30.

TRANSPORTATION AND ACCOMMODATIONS WITHIN THE PARK

None.

GUEST SERVICES

Restrooms, telephones, first aid, changing facilities, lost and found, locker rentals, tube rentals. Visa, MasterCard, American Express, and Discover cards accepted.

RIDES

Schlitterbahn: float down this lazy river in an inner tube.
Speed Slides: two-story fast-paced slides.
Water Slides: three exciting, curving slides.

ATTRACTIONS AND GAMES

Motion Ocean Wave Pool: largest wave pool in Oklahoma.
Mazzio's Land Kiddie Water Play Pool: play area and pool for kids 9 and under.
Activity Pool: also offers recreation area.
Volleyball
Video Game Arcade

SPECIAL ANNUAL EVENTS

Christian Family Day: in June.
Fourth of July: discount admission during certain hours.

RESTAURANTS

None.

SNACK BARS

Shark Tooth Grill: burgers, fries, hot dogs, corn dogs, pretzels, soft drinks.
Surf Club: pizza, funnel cakes, salads.
Polar Bear Point: ice cream and yogurt.
Calypso Cafe: beer and snacks.
Buccaneer Bay: ice cream novelties, popcorn, pizza, drinks.

CATERING

Contact Barbara McMahon, Group Sales manager, at (918) 749-7385.

SOUVENIR SHOPS

None.

HELPFUL TIP ON MAKING YOUR VISIT MORE ENJOYABLE

No food or coolers may be brought into the park.

FRONTIER CITY

Frontier City is a park with a Western theme situated on 40 acres in Oklahoma City. The park offers both water and mechanical rides, including The Wildcat, Oklahoma's largest wooden roller coaster; Renegade Rapids; The Kiddie Korral, a hands-on play area for children 8 and under; several live entertainment shows; and a nightly fireworks display. The park's centerpiece is its authentic replica of an 1880s frontier town where visitors will find a variety of games, souvenirs, and craft shops.

ADDRESS AND TELEPHONE

Frontier City
11601 N. E. Expressway
Oklahoma City, OK 73131

(405) 478-2412

LOCATION

Frontier City is located on the west side of I-35, off the northeast 122nd Street exit.

OPERATING SEASONS AND HOURS

Open weekends in April, May, September, and October. Open daily except Monday in June, July, and August. Hours: Opens at noon, except Saturday when it opens at 10 A.M. Closing times vary so check with the park before arriving.

ADMISSION FEES

Adults: $17.99. Children 48 inches and under: $12.99. Children 2 and under: free.

TRANSPORTATION AND ACCOMMODATIONS WITHIN THE PARK

None.

GUEST SERVICES

Restrooms, telephones, information booth, check cashing, first aid, lost and found, stroller rental, wheelchairs, paging system. Visa, MasterCard, and American Express cards accepted.

RIDES

Blue Lightnin': try this speed slide.
Dodge City Bumper Cars: a park favorite.
Frontier City Express: climb aboard a train for a journey around the park.
Mystery River Log Ride: journey in a speeding log.
Nightmare Mine: swoop and soar on a totally enclosed roller coaster.
Prairie Schooner: swing up and back on a boat.
Raging Riptide: swoosh along this water ride.
Renegade Rapids: a circular raft ride through tunnels, lakes, waterfalls, and rapids.
Shoot the Chute: gather speed until you splash down.
Silver Bullet: speed around a one-loop coaster.
Thunder Falls: high speed, wet thrills.
The Wildcat: Oklahoma's largest wooden roller coaster.

KIDDIE RIDES

In the Kiddie Korral:
Ball Crawl: a crawl through thousands of colorful balls.
Bumper Boats: for splashing and bumping about.
Indian Canoes: paddle through a make-believe river.
Merry-Go-Round: a favorite of the youngest set.
The Wild Kitty: a smaller version of the Wildcat roller coaster.

ATTRACTIONS AND GAMES

Games of Skill: located throughout the park, including Skee ball, Gun Ball, and Crossbow.

Shooting Gallery
Penny Arcade

SHOWS

Fantasy of Fire: nightly fireworks extravaganza, from Memorial Day to Labor Day.
Magic Show: magicians perform in the Opera House.
Gunfight Stunt Show: live-action shoot-'em-up in the OK Corral.
Saloon Show: female dance hall performers dance, sing, and play the piano.
How the West Was Sung: musical of the West.

RESTAURANTS

Mazzio's Pizzeria: pizza and Italian subs.
Santa Fe Grill: brisket, sausage, hot links, potato salad, baked beans, coleslaw, rolls, beer, soft drinks.
Saddlerock Cafe: burgers, fries, drinks.
Best of the West: flame-broiled ½-pound burgers and breast of chicken sandwiches.

SNACK BARS

Pink Garter Ice Cream Parlor
Sweet Sioux's: ice cream.
Two John's Saloon: popcorn, pretzels, beer, soft drinks.
Buckhorn: ice cream, snacks, fries, corn dogs, soft drinks.
Opera House: snacks, soft drinks.
Mustard's Last Stand: hot dogs, chips, soft drinks.
Reloading Station
Jessie's Hideout

CATERING

Contact David Wright at (405) 478-2140.

SOUVENIR SHOPS

Murphy's Mercantile: toys, gifts for kids, stuffed animals.

Hardware Store: toys.

General Store: Western apparel, film, park mementos.

Trapper's Trading: T-shirts, hats, souvenirs, Disney character fashions.

Territorial Bank: glassware, porcelain dolls, park souvenirs.

Huckins Hotel: postcards, film.

Bon-Ton: candy.

Emporium: T-shirts, German mugs and ceramics.

Indian Trading Post: Indian jewelry, belts, moccasins, pottery.

The Woodcarver's Shop: wooden gifts.

Landrush Mercantile: gag gifts, posters, T-shirts, magic tricks.

Frontier Photography: a photo of you in Western gear.

TENNESSEE

DOLLYWOOD

Dollywood is nestled in the Smoky Mountains, not far from where its founder and namesake, country star Dolly Parton, was born and raised. The entertainment park showcases the fun and traditions of the Smokies through its many rides, shops, shows, and eateries. Among the park's unique attractions are its Parton Back Porch Theatre, a tribute to Dolly Parton's music; the Robert F. Thomas Chapel, named in honor of the country doctor who delivered Dolly and in which services are held each Sunday during the operating season; the Dolly Parton Museum, spotlighting the life of the rags-to-riches celebrity; and Dolly's Tennessee Mountain Home, a replica of Dolly's childhood home.

ADDRESS AND TELEPHONE

Dollywood
1020 Dollywood Lane
Pigeon Forge, TN 37863-4101

(615) 428-9488

LOCATION

Dollywood is located 35 miles southeast of Knoxville, Tennessee, on Highway 441 in Pigeon Forge. Trolley systems run to the front gate of the park from all motels and campgrounds in Gatlinburg and the Pigeon Forge area.

OPERATING SEASONS AND HOURS

Open daily from late April to October (except Thursday in May and October). Opens at 10 A.M. Closing times vary between 6 P.M. and 9 P.M., so check with the park upon arrival.

Open for the Smoky Mountain Christmas Festival from mid-November to December. Check with the park for times and days.

ADMISSION FEES

Adults: $19.99. Children ages 4 to 11: $14.99. Children 3 and under: free. Seniors 60 and over: $17.99. Arrive after 3 P.M. and the next day is free.

TRANSPORTATION AND ACCOMMODATIONS WITHIN THE PARK

Trams are available from the parking lots to the front gate. Visitors can rent electronic convenience vehicles inside the park.

GUEST SERVICES

Restrooms, telephones, information booth, first aid, lost and found, message center, electronic convenience vehicles, wheelchair and stroller rental, video camera rental, free camera loans, check cashing. Visa, MasterCard, American Express, and Discover cards accepted.

RIDES

Blazing Fury: race through a burning town to a fast-paced finish.
Carousel: an original handcarved Dentzel carousel.
Dollywood Express: a five-mile journey on an authentic coal-burning steam train.
Flooded Mine: board an ore boat for an excursion through a flooded prison mine.
Malfunction Junction: classic bumper cars.
Mountain Slidewinder: a mountainside toboggan ride.
Mountain Swinger: swing on this old-fashioned ride with a new twist.
Smoky Mountain Rampage: a white water rafting adventure.
Thunder Express: a runaway mine train in a unique backwoods setting.
Timber Mountain Log Run: soar down this log flume ride to a splashdown ending.

KIDDIE RIDES

Balloon Race: suspended hot air balloons.
Convoy: big rigs for little folks.
Little Swinger: a smaller swing ride for kids.
Red Baron: planes for a barnstorming adventure.
Road Rally: classic cars built for the pint-sized.

ATTRACTIONS AND GAMES

Critter Creek Playground: a play area for kids that has a cable slide, play tower, and maze.
Gold Panning: strike it rich for a minimal extra charge.
Dolly's Tennessee Mountain Home: replica of Dolly Parton's childhood home.
Rags to Riches Museum: the life of Dolly Parton, with over 2,000 items from her childhood, life, and career.
Robert F. Thomas Chapel: named in honor of the country doctor who delivered Dolly; services are held each Sunday at 11:30 A.M. during the park's operating season.
Craftsmen's Valley: see crafts people demonstrate their skills at soap making, candle making, lathing, blacksmithing, wagon making, glass cutting, quilting, leathercrafting, wood carving, broom making, and basket weaving. Crafts are for sale at each shop and demonstration area.
Thunder Express Games: assorted amusement games and games of skill.
Arcade
Farmer's Market Games: games of skill and amusement with prizes for winners.

SHOWS

Dollywood's Celebrity Theatre: top country music artists appear live in concert.
Parton Back Porch Theatre: a tribute to Dolly's kind of music, featuring her kinfolk and friends.
New Valley Theatre: southern gospel harmonies, country and mountain melodies.
Rainmaker Show: zany one-man show.
Smoky Mountain Song: daytime musical productions performed in Barnwood Theatre.
Dollywood Jamboree: a musical variety show with clogging, country, and gospel.
Gaslight Theatre: James Rogers performs in an electrifying combination of style and charisma. Randy Parton stars in a musical showcase of American life and values.

Bird of Prey Show: entertaining and educational show offering an intimate view of numerous birds.

SPECIAL ANNUAL EVENTS

National Crafts Festival: crafts people from all over America showcase their wares in October.

Smoky Mountain Christmas: Dollywood gets turned into an old-fashioned Christmas fest with over 500,000 lights, shows, gift shops, and holiday feasts from mid-November to December.

RESTAURANTS

Aunt Granny's Restaurant: "all you care to eat" country breakfast buffet with eggs, sausage, hash browns, fruit, biscuits; lunch and dinner buffets with country-fried chicken, ham, vegetables.

Apple Jack's Mill: deli-style sandwiches.

Miss Lillian's Chicken House: southern-fried chicken, country-fried steak, barbecued ribs, vegetables, desserts, drinks.

Granny Ogle's Ham 'n Beans: ham, beans, sausage, red beans and rice, beef stew, cobbler.

Whistle Stop Steakhouse: barbecued chicken, smoked beef brisket, chef salad.

Hickory House BBQ: smoked ribs, pork, beef brisket, chicken.

Mountain Dan's Burgers: burgers, fries, onion rings, desserts, drinks.

SNACK BARS

Popcorn Wagon: popcorn, drinks.
Crossroads Funnel Cakes
Grist Mill Bakery
Wainwright's Concessions: popcorn, pork rinds, drinks.
Signal Light Snack Shack: popcorn, nachos, drinks.
Ice Cream Parlor
Depot Snacks: popcorn, nachos, drinks.
Strawberries & Cream: frozen yogurt, strawberries, peaches, and cream.

Barnwood Refreshments: popcorn, nachos, drinks.
Boardwalk Hotdogs: chili dogs, hot dogs, drinks.

CATERING

Contact Group Sales at (615) 428-9487.

SOUVENIR SHOPS

9 to 5 & Dime Valley Mercantile: Dolly souvenirs, apparel, Dollywood mementos, film.

Hillside General Store: jams, jellies, cookware, candy.

Rivertown Trading Co.: T-shirts, gifts, Dollywood memorabilia.

Mountain Laurel Mercantile: apparel, toys, gifts, and Dollywood souvenirs.

HELPFUL TIPS ON MAKING YOUR VISIT MORE ENJOYABLE

Use the park's "arrive after three, next day free" program for maximum value and flexibility. To beat the crowds, keep in mind that lines for rides, shows, and attractions are shortest after 3 P.M. and in the evening.

LIBERTYLAND

Libertyland is a 25-acre park with a patriotic theme. Featured at the park are live musical shows, rides, games, miniature golf, and two areas for kids: a children's playground on Tom Sawyer Island and Kids Corner, which has a tropical theme. Among the most popular rides are the Revolution, a 360-degree-loop double-corkscrew coaster, and Zippin Pippin, a wooden roller coaster with a 70-foot drop. The park also offers several historical attractions, including a 1909 Dentzel carousel, and scale models of Philadelphia's Independence Station and Liberty Bell, and New York's Statue of Liberty.

ADDRESS AND TELEPHONE

Libertyland
940 Early Maxwell Boulevard
Memphis, TN 38104

(901) 274-1776

LOCATION

Libertyland is located within the Memphis city limits at Mid-South Fairgrounds, at the intersection of Central Avenue and Airways Boulevard. When traveling to Memphis on I-240, exit at Airways Boulevard and go north to the fairgrounds.

OPERATING SEASONS AND HOURS

Open weekends from mid-April to mid-June. Hours: 10 A.M. to 9 P.M. on Saturday; noon to 9 P.M. on Sunday. Open Tuesday to Sunday from mid-June to August. Hours: 10 A.M. to 9 P.M.; noon to 9 P.M. on Sunday.

Open daily during the Mid-South Fair, from the end of September to early October.

ADMISSION FEES

General (includes kiddie rides, shows and events, train ride, and Grand Carousel): $6. Thrill ride ticket (includes most action rides): $6 additional. Children under 3: free. Seniors 55 and over: $2. Twilight (enter after 4 P.M.): $3.

TRANSPORTATION AND ACCOMMODATIONS WITHIN THE PARK

None.

GUEST SERVICES

Restrooms, telephones, information booth, first aid, lost and found, message center, baby strollers, wheelchairs. Visa, MasterCard, and American Express cards accepted.

RIDES

Bumper Boats: enjoy an excursion on motorized bumper boats for two.
Casey's Cannonball: board this train at Independence Station or Southern Station for a scenic trip through the park.
Fender Bender: take off in these dodge 'em cars.
Grand Carousel: mount any one of 48 handcarved wooden horses on this famed Dentzel carousel.
Group Bumper Boats: glide through the "lost lagoon" in four-to six-passenger fiberglass bumper boats.
Old Hickory: ride through a dark 300-foot concrete tunnel before plunging into a giant splash of water from a 45-foot peak.
Ozark Ridge Runner: hear top rock songs while whirling clockwise.
Revolution: a 360-degree loop turns you topsy-turvy on this sense-scrambling, double-corkscrew coaster.
River Roundup: turn from horizontal to vertical in the wink of an eye.
Spinning Spider: far-reaching spider legs take you up, down, and around for a spinning experience.
Surf City: a brand-new double water slide.
Tennessee Tilt: spin clockwise and counterclockwise in teacup-type seats.
Turnpike: drive along a track in Tin Lizzies.
Twain's Twister: get scrambled in a ride filled with unexpected turns.
Whirl-a-Wheel: Ferris wheel.
Zippin Pippin: a wooden coaster with a 70-foot drop.

KIDDIE RIDES

Bawl Crawl: a pool of 36,000 brightly colored balls.
Big Top: fire trucks, police cars, spaceships, motorcycles, and buses carry little passengers.
Junior Pirate Ship: board an 18-by-7-foot vessel that rocks side to side while soaring 16 feet in the air.
Kiddie Kar Carousel: miniature cars turn inside the carousel.

Little Fender Bender: a smaller version of bumper cars.

Little Tot Bumper Boats: kids steer their own motorized boats.

Mini Scrambler: a miniversion of the adult thrill ride.

Racing Turtle: scooters are self-propelled to lively music.

Red Baron: pint-sized airplanes circle the enemy.

Round-About: a kiddie carousel.

Sky Fighter: streamlined jets.

ATTRACTIONS AND GAMES

Miniature Golf

Independence Station: a replica of Independence Hall tower in Philadelphia, Pennsylvania.

Liberty Bell: a scale model of the original ringer.

Statue of Liberty: a 12-foot scale model of the renowned lady.

Water Wheel: a replica of a nineteenth-century impulse turbine water wheel.

Frisco Caboose: built in 1924, this wood-sheeted steel-frame model operated on trains in Memphis for many years before being restored.

Waddey Cabin: built in 1820 by pioneer farmer Hames Waddey of Tennessee.

Gotten Cabin: replica of a late-nineteenth-century log cabin.

Arcade

Games of Skill: located throughout the park, including six-lane bowler roller and 24-lane Skee ball.

SHOWS

Shenanigans: a fun-and-games show for little ones that includes lots of audience participation and performances by costumed characters. Performed four times daily in the Bell Tavern Theatre from Tuesday to Saturday.

Heartbeat: a live onstage music video featuring what's hot in pop music. Performed four times daily in the W. C. Handy Theatre from Tuesday to Saturday.

How the West Was . . . Fun: music from Broadway Western shows performed four times daily in the Liberty Dance Hall Theatre.

SPECIAL ANNUAL EVENTS

Children's International Festival: the park celebrates kids from all over the world in May.

Fourth of July: special festivities.

Libertyland Remembers Elvis: music and memorabilia of the King in August.

Muscular Dystrophy Weekend: a local telethon with Libertyland open 30 straight hours on Labor Day weekend.

Bluegrass Festival: featuring name and local acts on an early July weekend.

Christian Appreciation Day: features a well-known contemporary Christian act in July.

RESTAURANTS

Huckleberry's: fish 'n' chips, burgers, hot dogs, roast beef sandwiches, ham sandwiches, fried chicken, fries, salads, nachos, desserts, tea, coffee, soft drinks.

Becky Thatcher's Country Kitchen: catfish, barbecued ribs, fried chicken, baked ham and yams, vegetables, salads, desserts.

SNACK BARS

Food stands located throughout the park sell ice cream, candy apples, chocolate-covered frozen bananas, funnel cakes, popcorn, cotton candy, watermelon, hot dogs, milk shakes.

CATERING

Contact Angela McCullough at (901) 274-1776.

SOUVENIR SHOPS

Stands located throughout the park sell Libertyland memorabilia, stuffed animals, T-shirts, hats, toys, candy, film, old-time photographs, and other items.

OPRYLAND

Opryland, a 120-acre "showpark," is part of the larger entertainment complex known as Opryland USA that is also home to the famous Grand Ole Opry and The Nashville Network. The theme park emphasizes musical entertainment in numerous formal venues and with impromptu performances throughout the park. Opryland auditions thousands of talented entertainers nationwide every year to select 450 who will perform in Music City USA. There can be more than a dozen fully staged shows in simultaneous production at the park, including those at the Celebrity Theatre, the site of more than 200 concerts a year. The park is known as "the home of American music" and presents country, bluegrass, gospel, rock 'n' roll, Broadway, Hollywood, Western, and other styles of music. A full complement of rides including a white water rafting ride, an innovative indoor roller coaster, restaurants, shops, games, artists, and crafts people add to the enjoyment of the approximately 2 million guests each year.

ADDRESS AND TELEPHONE

Opryland
2802 Opryland Drive
Nashville, TN 37214

(615) 889-6600

LOCATION

Opryland is located nine miles northeast of downtown Nashville. Take exit 11 north on Briley Parkway between I-40 and I-65.

OPERATING SEASONS AND HOURS

Open selected weekends in March, April, May, September, and October. Open daily from the end of May to early September. Opens at 10 A.M. Closing times vary with the season, so check with the park upon arrival.

ADMISSION FEES

Adults: $21.95. Children ages 4 to 11: $12.95. Children 3 and under: free.

TRANSPORTATION AND ACCOMMODATIONS WITHIN THE PARK

Opryland Hotel: a luxury hotel with 1,891 rooms located within the larger entertainment complex called Opryland USA, of which the theme park is only one part. For hotel information call (615) 889-1000.

GUEST SERVICES

Restrooms, telephones, first aid, kennel service ($1), wheelchair and stroller rental, postal and photo services. Visa, MasterCard, American Express, and Discover cards accepted.

RIDES

The Barnstormer: Waldo Pepper–style biplanes are pulled up a 100-foot tower. Planes rotate, and as the speed increases you experience a free-fall effect.

Chaos: combines traditional coaster thrills with state-of-the-art audio and visual technology for a ride that touches all the senses.

Country Bumpkin: bumper cars that look like Model A Fords.

Flume Zoom: hollow log boats climb, then float through a treetop flume chute.

Grizzly River Rampage: circular rafts free-float down Opryland's own white water river designed to resemble a raging river in the Great Smoky Mountains.

Little Deuce Coupe: a spinning ride in a geodesic dome with flashing lights and rock and roll music.

Old Mill Scream: board 20-passenger boats for a double-dipped ride off a 60-foot-tall mountain decorated with waterfalls and a cave.

Opryland Railroad: tour the park on a train with a vintage locomotive.

Rock 'n' Roller Coaster: spiral roller coaster races through the treetops.

Screamin' Delta Demon: six-passenger wheeled sleds careen through a serpentine 1,700-foot-long, 12-foot-wide chute.

Sky Ride: ride in a cable car for an exceptional view of the park.

Tennessee Waltz: feel a wavelike sensation as you swing from this ornate German carousel.

Tin Lizzies: four-passenger cars resembling Model Ts.

Wabash Cannonball: corkscrew roller coaster races through two giant loops while traveling at 50 miles per hour.

KIDDIE RIDES

Dune Buggies: fun driving for little ones.

Mini Ferris Wheel: a down-scaled version of the big wheel.

Mini Rock 'n' Roller Coaster: a pint-sized version of the adult ride.

Red Baron Airplanes: kids can pilot their own colorful planes.

Surrey With the Fringe on Top: a little surrey ride.

ATTRACTIONS AND GAMES

General Jackson Showboat: the 300-foot-long, four-deck paddle wheel showboat offers year-round cruises with live entertainment and sightseeing on the Cumberland River. Daytime cruises last two hours, and evening cruises last three hours. Day-long cruises are offered in the spring and fall, and festive holiday cruises are scheduled in November and December.

Big "G" Kid Stuff: activity area designed for younger children, with a miniature space needle, boat ride, ball crawl, big playhouse, and more.

Arcades: two arcades house over 130 video games.

Games of Skill: located throughout the park, including baseball toss and ring toss.

SHOWS

Country Music U.S.A.: anthology of country music that honors the stars and sounds of Nashville with traditional and contemporary country music, as well as hoedown and clogging.

Way Out West: a rip-roaring, lighthearted show full of your favorite Western characters and featuring songs, dances, and comedy from the Old West.

And the Winner Is: a fast-paced production celebrating tunes that have been honored with Oscar, Tony, Grammy, Dove, and CMA awards. The show boasts 18 singers and dancers and a 12-piece orchestra.

Shake, Rattle, and Rock: a group of 14 performers and musicians takes you back to the rocking '50s and '60s with hits from legends such as Elvis Presley, Roy Orbison, the Beatles, and the Motown sound.

The Mike Snider Show: Grand Ole Opry star Mike Snider delights audiences with his brand of country humor and expert banjo picking. Appearing with Snider is his three-piece band.

Sing the Glory Down: the Cumberland Boys quartet combines great gospel sounds of the past with the best of today.

The Country Cajun Show: a high-energy, fast-paced group that plays everything from Cajun to country, including trick fiddling and vocals.

The Country and Bluegrass Show: a blend of bluegrass, mountain folk, and country songs combine for a rousing performance.

The Country Club: today's country hits with precise harmony and energy add up to a show-stopping performance.

The Laughing Place: magic shows for children of all ages.

SPECIAL ANNUAL EVENTS

Easter at Opryland: a celebration for kids in April, complete with bunnies and an Easter egg hunt.

American Music Festival: annual junior and high school band and choral performances from around the country in May.

Country Music Concerts: some of the biggest names in country music perform special concerts throughout the season in week-long engagements.

Gospel Jubilee: two days of gospel music concerts in May.

Independence Festival: fireworks, flags, and patriotic face painting highlight this week-long celebration around the Fourth of July.

Kids' Fest: kids will have a great time with special shows and activities just for them in early August.

Bluegrass Festival: two days in August of the best performers in bluegrass music.

Country America Lifestyles: September weekends feature exhibits and activities focusing on crafts, cooking, the outdoors, and traditional country living.

Grand Ole Opry Birthday: join the October birthday celebration of the world's longest-running radio show, featuring autograph and photograph sessions and concerts.

Howl-O-Ween at Opryland: trick-or-treating and storytellers add to the spirit of this spooky end-of-October holiday.

RESTAURANTS

Seafood Wharf

Cafe Mardi Gras: New Orleans–style food, including Monte Cristo sandwiches and salads.

Country Kettle: barbecue, beans, cornbread.

Rudy's Country Kitchen: sausage, biscuits, eggs, grits.

Longhorn Barbecue: barbecue plates, sandwiches, beans.

Riverside Plantation: catfish, vegetables.

Plaza Inn: entrees, salads, hot vegetables, fresh baked bread and desserts.

SNACK BARS

Kahn's: hot dogs.

Christie Cookies: cookies, ice cream.

Chubby's: burgers, fries, shakes.

Julio's Pizza

Zack's: frozen yogurt.

Chaos Concessions: ice cream, soft drinks.

Cofelts: fudge, taffy.

El Grande Taco

Mark Twain Ice Cream

Funnel Cakes: funnel cakes, ice cream.

CATERING

Contact Melanie Fly at (615) 889-6600.

SOUVENIR SHOPS

The Ragin' Cajun Shirt Shop

The Toy Chest

Opry Collection: records, Opry memorabilia.

Grizzly Mercantile: country hats and mountain crafts.

Other shops located throughout the park sell gifts, shirts, hats, music boxes, country arts and crafts, puppets, and Opryland memorabilia.

HINTS FOR TRAVELING WITH CHILDREN, ELDERLY, HANDICAPPED

Handicapped guests have access to most of the park's rides. Some restrictions apply, so check with hosts and hostesses. All restrooms have wheelchair facilities.

TEXAS

AQUARENA SPRINGS

Aquarena Springs is a 75-acre water and nature fun park located just 45 minutes north of San Antonio on the banks of Spring Lake in beautiful San Marcos, Texas. Host to approximately 250,000 guests per year, this picturesque spot includes such favorite attractions as excursions in glass bottom boats, Submarine Underwater Theatre starring "Ralph" the swimming pig, Alpine Sky Ride, the beautiful Hillside Gardens, and Texana Village, a re-created frontier Texas town of 100 years ago. Excellent eateries, comfortable picnic areas, and entertaining shows make this a delightful destination for a family outing.

ADDRESS AND TELEPHONE

Aquarena Springs
P. O. Box 2330
San Marcos, TX 78666

1-800-999-9767

LOCATION

Aquarena Springs is two minutes west of I-35 in San Marcos, Texas. From I-35 take the Aquarena Springs Drive exit and follow the signs to Aquarena Springs.

OPERATING SEASONS AND HOURS

Open daily year-round. Hours: 9 A.M. to 9 P.M. in summer; 9 A.M. to 5:30 P.M. in fall and winter.

ADMISSION FEES

Adults: $14.95. Children ages 4 to 15: $11.95. Seniors: $12.95.

TRANSPORTATION AND ACCOMMODATIONS WITHIN THE PARK

The Aquarena Springs Inn: is a historic bed-and-breakfast inn with a golf course and Olympic-sized swimming pool. For information or reservations call 1-800-999-9767.

GUEST SERVICES

Restrooms, strollers, first aid. Visa, MasterCard, American Express, and Diners Club cards accepted.

RIDES

Alpine Sky Ride: view the park as you travel high above the crystal blue waters of Spring Lake on your way to the Hillside Gardens.

Sky Spiral: takes you 300 feet above the park for a panoramic view of the area.

ATTRACTIONS AND GAMES

Glass Bottom Boats: view a whole new world of underwater splendor including water plants, bubbling springs, and fish.

Hillside Gardens: a nature lover's paradise of lush flowering shrubs and giant oak trees, as well as a 100-year-old grist mill, a restored 1848 log cabin, the reconstructed remains of an old Spanish mission, and live alligators.

Texana Village: authentic buildings of 100 years ago including a complete frontier saloon, a candle-making factory, a barbershop, an old jail, the oldest home in San Marcos (circa 1846), and a blacksmith's shop.

Rare Aquatic Life: home of more than 100 varieties of aquatic life including several endangered species not found anywhere else on earth.

9-Hole Golf Course

SHOWS

Submarine Underwater Theatre: an entertaining underwater show with aquamaids performing a graceful ballet, an aquamaid picnic, entertaining aquamen who will make you laugh, and "Ralph" the swimming pig performing his swine dive.

Birds of Paradise: four beautiful, trained macaw parrots demonstrate their talents including bicycling, playing basketball, and playing horseshoes.

River Theatre: a video production of the award-winning *River of Innocence* film that reveals the secrets of the San Marcos River.

RESTAURANTS

The Restaurant on the Lake:
Pepper's at the Falls: burgers, salads.

CATERING

Contact Jo Anne McCully at 1-800-999-9767.

SOUVENIR SHOPS

T-shirts, caps, Texas souvenirs, fudge, ice cream, candy, jellies.

ASTROWORLD

AstroWorld, a member of the Six Flags family, is located on 75 acres in Houston and is host to about 2 million guests per year. There are more than 100 rides, shows, and attractions, divided into 12 themed worlds that represent classic cultures and eras of America's past, including Americana Square, turn-of-the-century America; Alpine Valley, a visit to the Swiss Alps; Bugs Bunny in Enchanted Kingdom, a little people's paradise; Coney Island, back to the heyday of amusement parks; European Village, a scenic European atmosphere; International Plaza, modern and contemporary U.S.A.; Nottingham Village, a touch of Olde England; Oriental Corner, a touch of the Far East; Plaza de Fiesta, a corner of Old Mexico; Thunder River, a world of white water and nature; Western Junction, the Old West revisited; and XLR-8 Plaza, a state-of-the-art futuristic adventure. Together with restaurants, shops, and live shows, the park offers a variety of fantasy and fun for every member of the family.

ADDRESS AND TELEPHONE

AstroWorld
9001 Kirby
Houston, Texas 77054

(713) 799-1234

LOCATION

AstroWorld is located off the 610 loop at the Fannin Street exit in Houston. Guests enter the park via a privately owned bridge that spans Interstate 610.

OPERATING SEASONS AND HOURS

Open weekends from mid-March through Memorial Day and from Labor Day through mid-October. Open daily from Memorial Day through Labor Day. Opens at 10 A.M. on weekends and 11 A.M. on weekdays. Closing times vary, so check with the park upon arrival.

ADMISSION FEES

Adults: $19.95. Children under 48 inches: $10.95.

TRANSPORTATION AND ACCOMMODATIONS WITHIN THE PARK

A tram service transports guests from the parking lot to the front gate.

GUEST SERVICES

Restrooms, telephones, storage cages, wheelchairs, strollers, check cashing, ATM services, information booths, baby changing and feeding area, lockers, lost parents area, lost and found, first aid, camera rental. Visa, MasterCard, American Express, and Discover cards accepted.

RIDES

Alpine Carousel: an original 1895 Dentzel carousel.
Antique Taxis: old-fashioned autos on a ¼-mile track.
AstroNeedle: circular elevator ride rising 270 feet in the air.

AstroWay: cable car ride that rises 100 feet over the park.
Bamboo Shoot: a water flume ride.
Condor: climb into a bird-shaped car and be lifted more than 110 feet in the air, spinning parallel to the ground.
Excalibur: a tubular roller coaster with a 60-foot dip.
Greezed Lightnin': a chilling 360-degree shuttle loop coaster.
Gunslinger: modeled after the famed flying Dutchman rides of carnival midways.
Joustabout: a scrambler ride.
Looping Starship: a 360-degree looping orbit.
SkyScreamer: the ultimate thrill ride with the sensation of jumping off a 10-story building.
Texas Cyclone: a giant wooden roller coaster that has a 92-foot lift and free-falls onto a 53-degree-angle drop.
Thunder River: river rapids ride.
Tidal Wave: ride over a waterfall and plunge through a 20-foot wall of water.
Ultra Twister: dive 92 feet straight down before making a 360-degree rotating turn forward, then backward.
Viper: a steel loop coaster.
Wagon Wheel: a spinning ride shaped like a wheel from a Conestoga wagon.
Warp 2000: an elevated scrambler ride.
XLR-8: a high-tech suspended roller coaster.

KIDDIE RIDES

Designed specifically for young children, the Enchanted Kingdom offers a magical land where they can discover, conquer, explore, and have fun. The following rides are featured:
Bugs Bunny Carrot Patch
Foghorn Flyers
The Fudd Mobile
Henry Hawk Hideaway
Porky Pig Pen
Speedy Boats
Sylvester Roadsters
Tasmanian Express
Tweety Twirlers
Wile E. Coyote Cliffs
Yosemite Sam Dry Gulch Pass

ATTRACTIONS AND GAMES

Discovery Mountain: children will find creative activities that call upon their senses of sight and hearing; they will discover their shadow in a colorful aura, create musical notes, and see themselves in funny shapes in convex mirrors. At the Enchanted Kingdom.

Video and Arcade Games: located throughout the park.

SHOWS

Bugs Bunny Wonder Circus: kids can be circus stars with Bugs Bunny and his Looney Tunes friends. At the Bugs Bunny Theatre.

Dolphins of the Deep: trained dolphin duo performs incredible feats. At the Aquarena Theatre.

Bugs Bunny Cartoon Theatre: kids can join Bugs Bunny at his very own theater where every day is a Bugs Bunny cartoon festival. At Discover Mountain.

Horizons: 70-millimeter Sens-O-Sphere on a 180-degree screen. At the Horizons Theatre.

Fireworks Spectacular: patriotic fireworks light up the sky. At the Showboat Lagoon Theatre.

Blast Puppet Show: featuring some of America's most adored stars, this elaborate celebrity puppet show will knock the family's socks off. At the Showcase Theatre.

The Great Texas Longhorn Revue: features true Western entertainment performed by a unique group of animated "cowboys." At the Texas Cow Palace.

Country Hoedown: a toe-tapping, hand-clapping good time with a two-man singing and picking group. At the Texas Cow Palace.

The Wild West Show: an old-fashioned gunfight in the streets of Western Junction.

Cornelius D. Crow: see this humorous and cynical crow of Alpine Valley.

SPECIAL ANNUAL EVENTS

July Fourth Celebration

Fright Nights: Halloween celebration in late October.

Holiday in the Park: celebrations in November and December.

RESTAURANTS

The Festhalle: gourmet hot dogs and hamburgers, pizza, nachos, fries.

Los Tios: tacos, enchiladas, burritos, nachos.

Gabby's Bar-B-Que: beef brisket dinners, sandwiches.

Chat-n-Chew: hamburgers, cheeseburgers, chili dogs, desserts.

Shanghai Grill: char-grilled chicken, hot dogs, hamburgers.

La Cantina: hamburgers, hot dogs, chicken nuggets.

Spanky's Pizza Parlour

Plaza Pizza

Popeye's: chicken.

SNACK BARS

Coney Island Hot Dog Stand

Ralph's Refreshment Center

Corny Dog Corner

Alpine Food Court: baked potatoes, gyros/pita sandwiches, Belgian waffles, candy, shakes, nachos, tacos, pizza.

Columbo Yogurt

Ice Cream Parlour

Malt Shoppe

Other food stands are located throughout the park.

CATERING

Contact Group Sales at (713) 794-3291

SOUVENIR SHOPS

There are 31 shops throughout the park that offer souvenirs as well as a variety of merchandise from Mexican to European.

HINTS FOR TRAVELING WITH CHILDREN, ELDERLY, HANDICAPPED

Disabled guests needing special assistance to the front gate of the park should alert a host at the toll plaza for an escort. Inquire at Guest Relations for a guide to help during the visit.

SCHLITTERBAHN RESORTS & WATERPARK

Schlitterbahn, which means "slippery road," is a family water theme park situated on 65 acres on the Comal River in south Texas. The park uses an ingenious method of pumping spring-water out of the Comal and circulating it through the rides to keep the water cool, even on the hottest Texas days. Schlitterbahn's attractions offer a choice of nine inner tube chutes that send riders through a maze of twists, turns, and dips; 17 water slides that end in a splash-down pool; a wave pool; swimming pools; hot tubs; restaurants; and a miniature golf course. For the park's youngest visitors there's Pollywog Pond featuring colorful mushroom slides. The newest addition to the park is the Surfenburg area with the Squirt 'n' Sliden children's park and the Boogie Bahn surfing ride.

ADDRESS AND TELEPHONE

Schlitterbahn Resorts & Waterpark
305 West Austin
New Braunfels, TX 78130

(512) 625-2351

LOCATION

Schlitterbahn is located 30 minutes north of San Antonio and 45 minutes south of Austin on I-35.

OPERATING SEASONS AND HOURS

Open weekends from late April through May and from the end of August to mid-September. Open daily from late May through August. Hours: 10 A.M. to 8 P.M.

ADMISSION FEES

All-day pass: Adults: $16.97. Children ages 3 to 11: $13.74. Midday (3:30 P.M.) pass: Adults: $11.58. Children: $9.43. Spectator admission: $8.35. Children age 3: free. Two-day pass: Adults: $27.48. Children: $22.09.

TRANSPORTATION AND ACCOMMODATIONS WITHIN THE PARK

Schlitterbahn Resort "at the Bahn": 140 units including motel rooms, apartments, and cottages, adjacent to the water park. For reservations call (512) 625-5510.

Schlitterbahn Resort "at the Rapids": 89 units on the Comal River, adjacent to the new Surfenburg addition to the park. For reservations call (512) 620-9010.

GUEST SERVICES

Restrooms, telephones, showers, changing area, lost and found, first aid, locker rental, life jackets, and children's tubes. Visa, MasterCard, American Express, and Diners Club cards accepted.

RIDES

Banzai Tube Slide: get ready to scream on this superfast tube slide.

Boogie Bahn: surf's up for boogie boards.

Castle Body Slides: get swept down a flume by a flood of water.

Cliffhanger Tube Chute: leisurely floating with a sheer-drop finish.

Comal Express: float to the Comal River.

Congo River Ride: relax on a lazy river ride.

Curley Shuffle Tube Chute: enjoy a lazy tube float ride.

Der Bahn: a foam-padded speed slide.

Double Loop Slides: twist along a fast body slide.

Hillside Tube Chute: a twisting, turning tube float.

Paddleboats: paddle down the waterway.

Raging River Tube Chute: toss and turn on the river rapids.

Raindrop: splash through a water curtain.

River Tube Chute: a natural tube float.

Schlittercoaster: ride a sled over the edge of a cliff to a splashy ending.

Soda Straws: speed through curving straws.

Tunnel Tube Chute: it takes a full 45 minutes to float through this one.

Whitewater Tube Chute: shoot the chute.

KIDDIE RIDES

Pollywog Pond: a playground full of giant water-spraying mushrooms and padded water slides.

Tadpool: shallow kiddie pool and small slide.

Squirt n' Sliden: giant submarine with octopus slides on top, and a life-sized fire truck with 34 hands-on children's activities.

ATTRACTIONS AND GAMES

The Beach: ride the waves in this wave pool

Lagoon Swimming Pool: swim and float in a million-gallon pool.

Gator Bowl: activity pool for the little ones with foam creatures to play on.

Hot Tubs: two for everyone; another for adults only.

Water Volleyball

Tennis Courts

Miniature Golf: an 18-hole course with a Bavarian theme.

Arcade: 100 video games.

SPECIAL ANNUAL EVENT

Fourth of July: party with fireworks and live music.

RESTAURANTS

BBQ Restaurant: barbecue platters and sandwiches.

Pizza Restaurant: pizza, sandwiches.

Riverwalk Cafe: breakfast (eggs, pancakes, cereal, breads, juice), lunch (sandwiches, burgers, fries).

Schlitter Grill: turkey legs, shish kebab, fajitas, sausage-on-a-stick.

Hot Stuff: finger foods, entrees.

SNACK BARS

Concession stands located throughout the park serve cotton candy, ice cream, sodas.

CATERING

Contact Group Sales at (512) 625-2351.

SOUVENIR SHOPS

Gift Shop T-shirts, swimsuits, hats, visors, park souvenirs.

Surf's Up Gift Shop

SEA WORLD OF TEXAS

Situated on 250 acres in lovely San Antonio, Sea World of Texas ranks among the world's largest marine parks. It boasts more than 25 shows, educational exhibits, and attractions, including performances by killer whale Shamu and other whales and dolphins. Visitors can also enjoy the antics of sea lions, walrus, and penguins, as well as the daring feats of professional water skiers.

ADDRESS AND TELEPHONE

Sea World of Texas
10500 Sea World Drive
San Antonio, TX 78251

1-800-422-7989

LOCATION

Sea World of Texas is located in northwest San Antonio, 16 miles from downtown, at the intersection of Ellison Drive and Westover Hills Boulevard, just off State Highway 151, between Loop 410 and Loop 1604. There is city bus service from downtown San Antonio.

OPERATING SEASONS AND HOURS

Open weekends in fall and spring. Hours: 10 A.M. to 6 P.M. Open daily June through September. Hours: 10 A.M. to 11 P.M.

ADMISSION FEES

Adults: $20.95. Children ages 3 to 11: $14.95. Children under 3: free. Two-day passes also available.

TRANSPORTATION AND ACCOMMODATIONS WITHIN THE PARK

None.

GUEST SERVICES

Restrooms, telephones, stroller and wheelchair rental, coin lockers, first aid, lost parents, pet shelters, camera rentals, lost and found, reentry battery jumps, wheelchair facilities, diaper-changing facilities, nursing mother facilities, foreign currency exchange.

RIDES

Rio Loco: river rapids water ride.
Texas Splashdown: log flume ride.

ATTRACTIONS AND GAMES

Cap'n Kid's World: a four-acre, nautically themed playground featuring 16 elements that combine play and learning for youngsters up to age 14.
Garden of Flags: crowning one of the highest elevations in San Antonio.
Le Grande Marche: a grand staircase leading to a panoramic view of the San Antonio skyline.
Koi Pond: admire the gilded beauty of the Asian carp.
Cypress Gardens West: a 16-acre botanical wonderland showcases more than 200,000 blooming annuals in season.
Texas Walk: an inspiring journey through Texas history.
United States Map: a one-acre scale map of the country. Trace the routes of Lewis and Clark and other explorers.
Sharks and the Coral Reef: come head-to-teeth with many predators swimming in a 450,000-gallon shark tank. Another circular aquarium displays smaller sharks and rays, and a 300,000-gallon reef exhibit presents a kaleidoscope of tropical fish.
Marine Mammal Pool: shake flippers with the friendly dolphins.
Avian Exhibits: see one of the world's largest waterfowl and exotic bird collections.
Seal and Sea Lion Community: feed seals, otters, and sea lions.
Penguins: step onto a moving walkway and see more than 200 penguins frolic with alcids and other birds in a re-created subantarctic polar environment. Includes Learning Hall.
Midway Games: games of skill and video challenges at the Games Center.

SHOWS

Shamu Celebration: watch killer whales perform aquatic feats.
Cetacean Sensation: a dolphin and whale show that educates as well as entertains.
Spooky, Kooky Castle: rib-tickling sea lion, walrus, and otter show.
Gold Rush: exciting Wild West water-ski show performed at the Water Ski Stadium on the shores of a picturesque 12-acre lake.
Summer Nights: a nighttime extravaganza that includes fireworks, live music, and parades, every night during the summer.

RESTAURANTS

Blue Bonnet Grill: Mexican food, southwestern cuisine.

Chicken 'n' Biscuit: fried and barbecued chicken.

Oaks Cafe and Grill: burgers, barbecued beef, fish sandwiches.

De Lido Ristorante: pizza, pasta.

SNACK BARS

Snack carts located throughout the park sell hot dogs, popcorn, ice cream, beer, margaritas, soft drinks.

CATERING

Contact Group Sales at (512) 523-3600.

SOUVENIR SHOPS

Shamu Photo: your picture taken with costumed Shamu.

Joplin Square: T-shirts, souvenirs.

Oceans Treasures: tropical and shark-related gifts and souvenirs.

Main Mast: Sea World and Texas gifts and souvenirs.

Kid's Treasures: Sea World memorabilia.

Pirate's Cove: fine nautical gifts and Sea World mementos.

Ship to Shore Fashions: sportswear.

Shamu's Emporium: whale, dolphin, and Sea World souvenirs.

Nature's Kingdom: books and learning aids about animals.

HINTS FOR TRAVELING WITH CHILDREN, ELDERLY, HANDICAPPED

Sea World of Texas offers many shady rest areas. The park is also completely accessible to the handicapped.

SIX FLAGS OVER TEXAS

Six Flags Over Texas is one of the Lone Star State's top single tourist attractions, playing host to some 3 million visitors each year. The theme park spreads over 205 acres of what was once ranchland in Arlington, midway between Dallas and Fort Worth. The park draws its name and theme from the flags of the six sovereign governments that have flown over Texas during its rich history. Six Flags Over Texas features more than 100 rides, shows, and other attractions, ranging from a special revue featuring Six Flags' celebrity host Bugs Bunny to a full-scale musical. Among the park's most popular attractions is the Texas Giant, a huge wooden roller coaster towering more than 14 stories into the sky. For small children there is Looney Tunes land with special rides just for kids.

ADDRESS AND TELEPHONE

Six Flags Over Texas
P. O. Box 191
Arlington, TX 76010

(817) 640-8900

LOCATION

Six Flags Over Texas is located at I-30 and State Highway 360 in Arlington.

OPERATING SEASONS AND HOURS

Open weekends in the spring and fall. Open daily in the summer. Hours vary greatly, so check with the park before arriving.

ADMISSION FEES

Adults: $21.95. Children under 48 inches and seniors 55 and over: $15.95.

TRANSPORTATION AND ACCOMMODATIONS WITHIN THE PARK

None.

GUEST SERVICES

Restrooms, telephones, stroller rental, wheelchairs, diapering and nursing center, picnic area, lost parents area, kennels. Visa, MasterCard, and American Express cards accepted.

RIDES

Antique Cars: take a turn at the wheel of a miniature antique car.
Avalanche Bobsled: speed and turn on this thrilling adventure.
Casa Magnetica: a place where everything appears to defy gravity.
Conquistador: the flying ship of Spain swings in a dizzying arc.
El Sombrero: twist and shake on this thrill ride.
Flashback: towering coaster that turns you upside down six times, three times forward and three times backward, at high speed and heights up to 125 feet.
Great Six Flags Air Racer: takes you nearly 100 feet in the air aboard a biplane that flies in a circle at 36 miles per hour.
Judge Roy Scream: plunge and soar along the park's entryway lake on this traditional wooden coaster.
Log Flumes: splash down from each of two flumes.
Roaring Rapids: experience the excitement of a raft trip down the raging Colorado River.
Runaway Mine Train: a roller coaster that lives up to its name.
Shock Wave: long, tall, and fast double-loop roller coaster.
Silver Star Carousel: an antique, handcarved classic.
Splash Water Falls: 20-passenger boats climb five stories in the air before plunging off a waterfall at a 35-degree angle into a 250-million-gallon lake. Prepare to get soaked!

Texas Chute Out: take a breathtaking ride 200 feet into the sky, then drop at free-fall speed until the parachute plunges to a safe landing.
Texas Cliffhanger: four-passenger gondolas drop from the top of a 128-foot tower, providing the sensation of having stepped off a 10-story building.
Texas Giant: this tall wooden roller coaster is a park favorite.

KIDDIE RIDES

Daffy Duck Lake: little boats go sailing.
Elmer Fudd Fewwis Wheel: a down-scaled Ferris wheel.
Flying Aces: kids fly high in their own little planes.
Porky Pig Play Pen: huge air pillows for bouncing barefoot.
Road Runner Runaround: a mini car drive.
Tweetie Bubbles: a ball crawl.

ATTRACTIONS AND GAMES

Oil Derrick Tower: see the skylines of Dallas and Fort Worth from the observation platform atop this 300-foot-tall tower.
Cartoon Greeters: the park's official greeters are Bugs Bunny, Daffy Duck, Sylvester, Foghorn Leghorn, and Yosemite Sam.
Video Games: latest video electronic games.
Shooting Gallery: everyone's favorite shooting games.
Games of Skill: located throughout the park.

SHOWS

Dolphin & Sea Lion Show: sea creatures cavort.
Crazy Horse Saloon: fast-paced country music show.
Bugs Bunny Show: catch Bugs Bunny and other costumed characters at the Good Time Theatre.
Texas Magic: multimedia laser show.
Gunfire Comedy Show: a tongue-in-cheek shoot-out.
Major Musical Revue: enjoy a tuneful revue at the Southern Palace.

Amphitheater Music Show: top-name entertainment at this 10,000-seat amphitheater.

SPECIAL ANNUAL EVENTS

Holiday in the Park: Christmas ice show, music shows, carolers, and special shops during the Christmas season.
Fright Nights: Halloween scares during that season.

RESTAURANTS

Casa de los Banderos: enchiladas, tacos, Tex-Mex specialties.
Chicken Plantation: fried chicken, corn on the cob.
Dixie Belle's: barbecued beef.
The Colonel's Cafe: pizza.
Chubbie's: burgers, fries, club sandwiches.

SNACK BARS

Newman's Corn Dogs
Smokehouse: smoked turkey legs.
Gourmet Burger
  Snack stands located throughout the park sell fried chicken, barbecue, Mexican specialties, burgers, ice cream, soft drinks.

CATERING

Contact Group Sales at (817) 640-8900.

SOUVENIR SHOPS

Spectrum: T-shirts, posters, caps, jewelry.
Looney Tunes Shop: stuffed animals from Warner Bros.
Mercado: mini carousel horses, glassware.
Indian Village Trading Post: jewelry, American Indian novelties, leather goods.
Shirt Market: sportswear, T-shirts.
Candy Kitchen

Glass Blower Shop
  Other souvenir stands throughout the park sell T-shirts, sportswear, Six Flags mementos.

HINTS FOR TRAVELING WITH CHILDREN, ELDERLY, HANDICAPPED

Wheelchairs are provided on a first-come, first-served basis. A special diapering and nursing facility is provided at the Baby Care Center in Looney Tunes Land. Rocking chairs and privacy are provided for nursing moms.

TIPS ON MAKING YOUR VISIT MORE ENJOYABLE

Families should plan to spend a minimum of eight hours in the park.

WET'N WILD

Wet'n Wild is a 24-acre water theme park situated in a suburb of Dallas, Texas. The park features 10 different body flumes, a wave pool, an activity pool, a children's play pool, and the newest ride, Bub-a-Tub.

ADDRESS AND TELEPHONE

Wet'n Wild
12715 LBJ Freeway
Garland, TX 75041

(214) 271-5637

LOCATION

Wet'n Wild is located at the intersection of Northwest Highway and LBJ Freeway, northeast of Dallas.

OPERATING SEASONS AND HOURS

Open daily from Memorial Day to Labor Day. Hours: 10 A.M. to 6 P.M. from Memorial Day to mid-June; 10 A.M. to 9 P.M. from mid-June to Labor Day. Open selected weekends prior to Memorial Day; check with the park before arriving.

ADMISSION FEES

Adults: $13.95. Children ages 3 to 12: $11.95. Seniors 55 and over: $7.52.

TRANSPORTATION AND ACCOMMODATIONS WITHIN THE PARK

None.

GUEST SERVICES

Restrooms, telephones, information booth, first aid, lockers, lost and found, flotation device rental. Visa, MasterCard, and American Express cards accepted.

RIDES

Body Flumes: soar and twist down 10 different flumes.
Bonsai Bogan: ride a water coaster down a slide and across a pool.
Bub-a-Tub: a four-person inner tube drops from a six-story tower down a triple-dip slide to a splash landing pool below.

Dragon's Tail
Flash Flood
Geronimo: experience this free-fall drop.
Rapids Ride: in a tube.

ATTRACTIONS AND GAMES

Activity Pool: float, dunk, splash, and swim.
Wave Pool: ride the surf in this large wave pool.
Children's Play Pool: gentle sprays and water activities for kids.

RESTAURANTS

None.

SNACK BARS

Burger Barn: burgers, nachos, hot dogs, pizza.
Ice Cream Parlor
Surfer's Cove: shaved ice, cookies, fruit drinks.

CATERING

Not available.

SOUVENIR SHOP

Swimwear and other water-related paraphernalia.

ROCKY MOUNTAIN AND SOUTHWEST

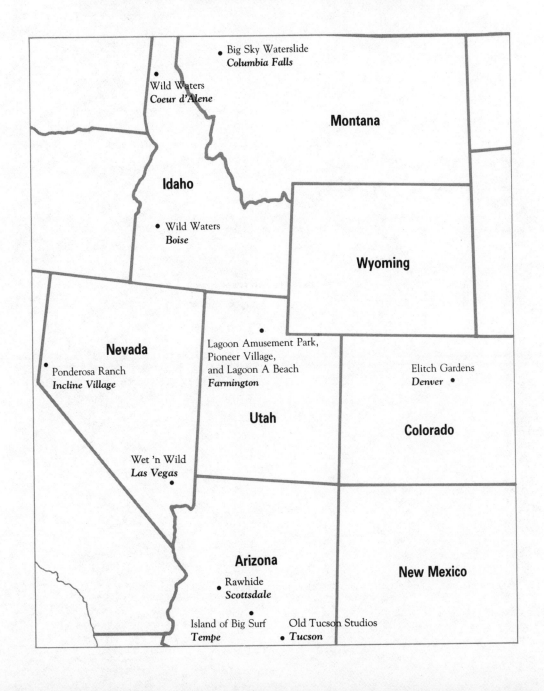

Big Sky Waterslide
Columbia Falls

Wild Waters
Coeur d'Alene

Montana

Idaho

Wild Waters
Boise

Wyoming

Nevada

Ponderosa Ranch
Incline Village

Lagoon Amusement Park,
Pioneer Village,
and Lagoon A Beach
Farmington

Elitch Gardens
Denver •

Utah

Colorado

Wet 'n Wild
Las Vegas

Arizona

Rawhide
Scottsdale

New Mexico

Island of Big Surf   Old Tucson Studios
Tempe   • *Tucson*

ARIZONA

ISLAND OF BIG SURF

Island of Big Surf is a 20-acre watery wonderland in the midst of the Arizona desert. With an exotic adventure for every member of the family, this theme park features one of the world's largest oceanlike wave pools and water slides such as the Waikiki Wipeout and Maui Wowie. Kids can explore Mennehune Cove, a water activity area, and look for lost treasure at Lava Bay. Other highlights are refreshing river walks, an adults-only lounge, and lots of misted shade.

ADDRESS AND TELEPHONE

Island of Big Surf
1500 North McClintock Road
Tempe, AZ 85281

(602) 947-SURF (7873)

LOCATION

Big Surf is located on McClintock Road between McDowell and University, just south of McKellips.

OPERATING SEASONS AND HOURS

Open daily from Memorial Day to Labor Day. Opens at 10:30 A.M. Closing times vary, so check with the park upon arrival.

ADMISSION FEES

Adults: $10.95. Children ages 4 to 11: $8.95. Children 3 and under: free.

TRANSPORTATION AND ACCOMMODATIONS WITHIN THE PARK

None.

GUEST SERVICES

Restrooms, telephones, bathhouses with showers, first aid (a trained medical staff is present at all times), lost and found, locker rental, raft rental, and free life jackets for everyone 48 inches and under. Visa, MasterCard, and American Express cards accepted.

RIDES

Maui Wowie: a water slide complex featuring a corkscrew slide.

Raging River Rides: choose from three different rides and careen down the river in an inner tube. Snake through a hillside and take a quick plunge into a pool, or build up speed as you head in a straight line into the pool, or glide gently along the river.

Waikiki Wipe Out: this water slide complex contains two pretzel slides and a 4½-story dropout slide.

KIDDIE RIDES

Volcano Bay Play Area: lava tubes (underground tube slides), cargo nets, wet and wild water slides, water cannons, exploding geysers, and more.

ATTRACTIONS AND GAMES

North Shore Wave Pool: ocean-sized waves are created in this giant wave pool; you can even bodysurf up to 200 feet.

Mennehune Cove: an activity area for little people who can play in tubes, boats, and climbing structures.

Video Arcade

Volleyball: four sand courts.

RESTAURANTS

Hang Ten Lounge: adults can enjoy special drinks such as mai tais and piña coladas, as well as beer and wine.

The Outrigger: hamburgers, hot dogs, fries, burritos, subs, drinks.

SNACK BARS

Snack Shack: burgers, fries, pizza, chili, pretzels, shakes, candy, drinks.

Polly's Ice Cream Parlor: hand-dipped ice cream, yogurt.

CATERING

Contact the Marketing Department at (602) 947-2477.

SOUVENIR SHOP

Surf and Bikini Shop: T-shirts, tank tops, tanning products, sunglasses, thongs, shorts.

HINTS FOR TRAVELING WITH CHILDREN, ELDERLY, HANDICAPPED

Bring sunblock, beach tents, and beach chairs. Note that there is a large expanse of sandy beach with no wheelchair or stroller access. Only plastic baby bottles are allowed in the park.

HELPFUL TIP ON MAKING YOUR VISIT MORE ENJOYABLE

Leave food, glass containers, and aerosol cans at home.

OLD TUCSON STUDIOS

Host to over 500,000 guests a year, Old Tucson Studios is a world famous 320-acre Western theme park and motion picture studio located in beautiful Tucson Mountain Park. Just 15 minutes west of central Tucson, the 52-year-old movie set of frontier and adobe buildings has been featured in more than 300 Western films and television shows including the recent television series "The Young Riders." The sets provide a unique atmosphere for Old Tucson's scheduled live gunfights, stunt demonstrations, saloon revues, special effects shows, stagecoach rides, Kids Korral play area, petting corral, games, rides, and more.

ADDRESS AND TELEPHONE

Old Tucson Studios
201 South Kinney Road
Tucson, AZ 85746

(602) 883-6457

LOCATION

Old Tucson Studios is located 15 minutes west of I-10 in Tucson, Arizona. Take Speedway Boulevard west from I-10 and follow the signs over Gates Pass Road. RVs and buses take Ajo Way west from I-10 and follow the signs to Old Tucson.

OPERATING SEASONS AND HOURS

Open daily year-round except Thanksgiving and Christmas days. Hours: 9 A.M. to 9 P.M.

ADMISSION FEES

Adults: $9.95. Children ages 4 to 11: $5.95. Children 3 and under: free. After 5 P.M.: Adults: $5.95. Children: $5.20.

TRANSPORTATION AND ACCOMMODATIONS WITHIN THE PARK

None.

GUEST SERVICES

Restrooms, telephones, information center, camera and video recorder rentals, lost and found, stroller and wheelchair rentals, first aid and full-time emergency medical technician. Visa, MasterCard, American Express, and Discover cards accepted.

RIDES

Antique Cars: take a drive in the desert riding in a replica 1910 American Mercer.

Carousel: everyone's favorite.
C. P. Huntington Train: this narrow-gauge train circles Old Tucson.
Mine Ride: ride through this newly discovered mine and look for gold, silver, and Spanish treasures.
Old Tucson Stage Lines: take a ride on an authentic 1880s stagecoach (additional charge of $1).

ATTRACTIONS AND GAMES

Kids Korral: this play area designed for small children includes a miniature Old Tucson Western town set, ball crawl, air bounce, rope climb, maze. Also includes the Petting Corral.
Grandpa Donald's Petting Corral: feed the many farm animals.
Old West Sets: visit sets used in movies and television shows, throughout the park.
Iron Door Shooting Gallery: test your skills against Old West cowboys.
Silverlake Park Games Area: enjoy America's favorite arcade and games of skill in this unique setting.
Remote Control Boats: skipper your own boat around the Silverlake Park pond.
Simmons Gun Museum: more than 1,000 weapons collected from around the world.

SHOWS

Hollywood in the Desert: a film reliving the history of Old Tucson.
Royal Oak Soundstage Tour: a 17-minute behind-the-scenes look at movie-making.
Raid on Phillips Ranch: a 15-minute reenactment of the life of a courageous storekeeper as he maintains law and order in the 1800s.
Wizard of the West: a 25-minute presentation of magic and illusion.
Red Dog Palace Saloon: enjoy Ruby's Red Garter Revue or a country/Western show.
Stunt Show: learn the secrets of your favorite movie and television stunts.
Bank Robbery: share the excitement as a sheriff and gang attempt to steal a payroll.

J. P. Shysler & Co.: Jonah P. Shysler's great-grandson attempts to demonstrate the inventions passed down to him.

SPECIAL ANNUAL EVENTS

University of Arizona Rodeo: March and November.
Nightfall Halloween: in October.
Western Music Festival: in November.

RESTAURANTS

Big Jakes Ramada: barbecue ribs, sandwiches, chicken baskets, burgers.
Golden Nugget: ice cream, hot dogs, snacks.
Iron Door Cafe: pizza, Mexican dishes.
Coyote Cafe: hamburgers, hot dogs, fries, onion rings, drinks.
Ma Shelton's Bakery: homemade cookies, muffins, yogurt, coffee, tea.
Red Dog Palace: cocktails, beer, musical revues.

SNACK BARS

Last Outpost: homemade fudge, peanuts, candy.
Photo Sipper: hot pretzels, churros, drinks.

CATERING

Contact the Sales Department at (602) 883-0100, Ext. 269.

SOUVENIR SHOPS

Emporium: movie memorabilia, take an Old West photo of yourself.
Manyins Provisions: sundries, novelty gifts, film, postcards.
General Store: toys, souvenirs, jellies, jams, gifts, clothing.
Latigo Leather Shop: handcrafted leather goods
Southwest Collectibles: handcrafted stained glass and gifts.

Western Wear Co.: complete Western outfitting.
Sagebrush Gallery: limited edition prints, paintings, ceramics, unique gifts.
T-shirt Factory: T-shirts, hats, jackets, sweatshirts.
Indian Trading Post: native jewelry, baskets, pottery, rugs.
Last Outpost: southwestern gifts, souvenirs, toys, cards.

RAWHIDE

Rawhide is a Western theme park with an authentic replica of an entire 1880s Old West town set in the middle of 160 acres of natural desert. Visitors can experience this exciting period in history through various attractions and amusements, gunfights and live reenactments by colorful entertainers, and displays of Western antiques and memorabilia. The park offers visitors an authentic glimpse of life in the Old West with stagecoach and burro rides, a working blacksmith shop, general store, old-fashioned ice cream parlor, tin-type photo studio, and artisans and crafts people at work. Rawhide also offers various dining options, shops, and galleries. Close to 850,000 guests visit the park every year, making it the state's largest Western-themed attraction.

ADDRESS AND TELEPHONE

Rawhide
23023 N. Scottsdale Road
Scottsdale, AZ 85255

(602) 563-5111

LOCATION

Rawhide is located in Scottsdale, outside of Phoenix, near several interstate highways.

OPERATING SEASONS AND HOURS

Open daily year-round. Hours: October through May weekends: 11 A.M. to 10 P.M.; weekdays: 5 P.M. to 10 P.M. June through September: 5 P.M. to 10 P.M.

ADMISSION FEES

Free admission to the park except during special events. Certain attractions and amusements require a fee.

TRANSPORTATION AND ACCOMMODATIONS WITHIN THE PARK

None.

GUEST SERVICES

Restrooms, telephones, first aid, lost and found, message centers, wheelchairs. Visa, MasterCard, and American Express cards accepted.

RIDES

Stagecoach Ride: an antique stagecoach takes you on a ride through the desert.
Train Ride: authentic miniature replica of a steam locomotive takes you on a scenic ride through the beautiful Arizona desert.

KIDDIE RIDES

Burro Ride: burros take the children for a ride on Main Street.

ATTRACTIONS AND GAMES

Petting Ranch: featuring buffalo, goats, sheep, and many other Western ranch animals.
Kid's Territory: children's play area including Ghost Town, Fort Apache, and Miniature Train.

Shooting Gallery
Gold Panning: the park's miner will show you how.
Old West Museum: more than 5,000 antiques.
Authentic 1880s Town: see a newspaper office, sheriff's office, blacksmith shop, and cemetery.
Carriage Exhibit: display of horse-drawn vehicles from the 1880s.
Covered Wagon Circle: display of antique Conestoga wagons.
Arcade: coin-operated antique machines throughout the park.
Fortune Teller: take a peek into your future.
Mine Exhibit: explore the underground tunnel and mining equipment.

SHOWS

Street Shows: shoot-outs, stunt shows, and cowboy comedy on Main Street.
Six Gun Theatre: live-action Western drama.
Live Country-Western Bands: performances on Main Street on the weekends, and daily in the Steakhouse and the Saloon.

SPECIAL ANNUAL EVENTS

Parada del Sol Rodeo: late January.
Triple Salute Weekend: President's Day Weekend celebration featuring parades, fireworks, and special entertainment.
Fourth of July: fireworks display, live music, family barbecue.
Wrangler Jeans Rodeo: early October.
Halloween Haunted House: last two weeks of October. Safe trick-or-treating and a costume parade takes place on October 31.
Holiday Season Celebration: a variety of special family activities, from Thanksgiving weekend through New Year's Day.

RESTAURANTS

Rawhide Steakhouse: mesquite-broiled steaks, barbecue ribs and chicken, prime rib, trout, deep-fried rattlesnake, hot apple pie with cinnamon swirl ice cream.

Cafe: hamburgers, hot dogs, chicken sandwiches, nachos, salads, ice cream, cookies.

SNACK BARS

Ice Cream Parlour: old-fashioned soda fountain.
Candy Shop: prickly pear lemonade, gourmet popcorn, soft pretzels.
The Pits: barbecue beef, sandwiches.
Margarita Bar: margaritas, beer.

CATERING

Contact Ernie McDonald at (602) 563-5600.

SOUVENIR SHOPS

Old-Fashioned Photo Studio: dress up in 1880s-style clothing for a photo.
Western Wear Shop: traditional hats, boots, clothing, accessories.
Indian Jewelry Shop: turquoise and silver jewelry.

Spirit West Gallery: southwestern originals and prints.
General Store: old-fashioned figurines, curios, toys, candy.
Import Shop: Mexican imports including rugs, ponchos, hats.
Pottery Shop: handcrafted decorative pots, night-lights, wall hangings.
The Gold Prospector: gold jewelry.
Blacksmith Shop: authentic hand-forged gifts.
T-Shirt Company: hundreds of styles.
Print Shop: unique cards, Western books, custom-printed items such as "Wanted" posters.
Senor Chile's: southwestern condiments and salsas, chili pepper items.
Needles and Blooms: live cactus and cactus-related arts and crafts.
Old Adobe Shop: decorated southwestern women's wear and accessories.
Rock Shop: rocks, minerals, pewter, pottery, crystal.
Gift Shop: souvenirs, toys.
Arizona Sun Care Shop: skin products formulated especially for the Arizona climate.

COLORADO

ELITCH GARDENS

Elitch Gardens is a traditional amusement park made special by the spectacular gardens throughout its 28 acres. Visitors can view colorful marigolds, lilies, geraniums, petunias, snapdragons, periwinkles, and more as they stroll the grounds. In addition, the park features a variety of classic amusement rides, including a turn-of-the-century carousel, sky ride, and wooden roller coaster. Between 850,000 and 1 million guests visit the park each year.

ADDRESS AND TELEPHONE

Elitch Gardens
4620 W. 38th Avenue
Denver, CO 80212

(303) 455-4771

LOCATION

Take the Lowell Boulevard exit south off I-70, then turn right (west) on 38th Avenue. The park is located between Tennyson and Wolff streets in the northwest section of Denver.

OPERATING SEASONS AND HOURS

Open weekends from mid-April to May. Open daily from June to Labor Day. Opens at 10 A.M. Closing times vary from 10 P.M. to 12 A.M., so check with the park upon arrival.

ADMISSION FEES

Weekdays: Adults: $12.50 or $7.50 for gate admission only. Children under 52 inches: $10. Children under 3: free (if they want to ride: $5). Seniors over 55: $5 for gate admission only.
   Weekends: Adults: $14.50 or $8 for gate admission only. Children under 52 inches: $12. Children under 3: free (if they want to ride: $5). Seniors over 55: $5 for Saturday gate admission only, Sunday free.

TRANSPORTATION AND ACCOMMODATIONS WITHIN THE PARK

None.

GUEST SERVICES

Restrooms, telephones, information booth, first aid, lost and found, lockers, strollers. Visa and MasterCard accepted.

RIDES

Carousel: an ornate turn-of-the-century beauty.
Casino: spin on the roulette wheel.
Ferris Wheel: ride up and down again on this park favorite.
Holland Express: go forward, then backward, as fast as you can.
Paradise: speed and spin on this thrill ride.
Rainbow: ride in a full 360-degree circle.
Round Up: stand up as you spin in circles.
Scooters: bumper cars in the round.
The Sidewinder: a brand-new steel-launch loop roller coaster.
Sky Ride: catch a great view of the park, gardens, and the Rockies from your skytop gondola.
Spider: experience stomach-wrenching chills as you ride in cars on the legs of the spider.
Splinter: a water log ride through scenes of the Old West.
Thing-a-ma-jig: glide like a paratrooper coming in for a landing.
Tilt-a-Whirl: sit, spin, tilt, and whirl.
Troika: enjoy a smooth ride in the sky.
Twister: speed through two 360-degree curves and the pitch-black "tunnel on the turn."
Wave Swinger: swing through the air in chairs suspended by cables.
Wild Cat: try this camelback coaster. It's older than the Twister but also hair-raising.

KIDDIE RIDES

Bumper Boats: just like the big kids' cars, only on water.
Ding Dong Dock: boat ride in the round.
Mini-Flume: ride down Adventure River.
Mini Scooters: pint-sized bumper cars.
Mini Wave Swinger: the kids' version of the adult ride.
Red Baron: airplanes that kids can control themselves.
Swinger: enclosed cars swing back and forth, round and round.

ATTRACTIONS AND GAMES

Gardens: stroll through magnificent flowering gardens located throughout the park. Don't miss the Elitch Gardens' working flower clock.
Soft Play Area: play activities for the little ones including a ball crawl, punching bag forest, rope maze, cable swing, slides, bridges, and walkways.
Games of Skill: located throughout the park.

SHOWS

Beach Babes: a '60s and '70s rock and roll music revue performed every two hours (alternates with Way Out West).
Way Out West: an old-fashioned medicine show set to music. Performed every two hours (alternates with Beach Babes).
Pirates of the Caribbean High-Dive Team: expert divers plunge from as high as 80 feet into a tiny pool of water. Performed every two hours.
Other musical and comedy shows are also performed throughout the season.

RESTAURANTS

Palace Restaurant: barbecue, salads, drinks.
Wheels Restaurant: hamburgers, hot dogs. Live musical revues.

SNACK BARS

Stands located throughout the park serve pizza, calzones, burgers, hot dogs, tacos, ice cream, cotton candy, funnel cakes, candy, frozen yogurt, soft drinks.

CATERING

Contact Paula Barkman at (303) 455-4771.

SOUVENIR SHOP

The Corner Store: T-shirts, specialty gifts, carousel horses, candles, sunscreen, candy.

IDAHO

WILD WATERS

Wild Waters is a water slide theme park located in picturesque Boise, Idaho. Visitors to the park can race and splash on any of the many water slides that twist and turn down the 60-foot-high mountain. For the not so daring there are the relaxing River Run and the Spa. The park also offers minislides for little folks, an arcade full of the latest gaming challenges, as well as a cafeteria and gift shop.

ADDRESS AND TELEPHONE

Wild Waters
1850 Century Way
Boise, ID 83709

(208) 322-1844

LOCATION

Wild Waters is located in Boise. Take S. Sale Road to Century Way. Wild Waters is just off Overland Road.

OPERATING SEASONS AND HOURS

Open daily from mid-May to Labor Day. Hours: 11 A.M. to 7 P.M.

ADMISSION FEES

Adults: $9.95. Children ages 4 to 11: $8.50. Children 3 and under: free.

TRANSPORTATION AND ACCOMMODATIONS WITHIN THE PARK

None.

GUEST SERVICES

Restrooms, telephones, lost and found, showers, lockers. Visa and MasterCard accepted.

RIDES

Big Spur: several slides for your enjoyment.
Bonzai: soar down two speed slides.
Cliffhanger: hold on to a T-bar, then drop into refreshing water.
Corkscrew Slide: speed around curves.
Drop Off Slides: two slides that send you splashing into a deep pool.
Intermediate Slides: two for middle-level sliders.
River Run: float in an inner tube.
Roundhouse: splash through curves on this slide.

Sidewinder: twist through this water slide.

ATTRACTIONS AND GAMES

Water World: a castle with a water fountain, tire swings, and rope ladder for the little ones.
Arcade Room
Outdoor Games: water balloon tosses and sponge races are held throughout the week.
Volleyball Court

RESTAURANT

Sunshine Cafe: burgers, corn dogs, hot dogs, pizza, burritos, churros, nachos, fries, onion rings, pretzels, ice cream, popcorn, soft drinks.

SNACK BAR

Candy Store

CATERING

Not available.

SOUVENIR SHOP

Swimwear, shorts, tops, suntan lotion, sunglasses, hats, goggles, cards.

WILD WATERS

Sister to Wild Waters in Boise, this Coeur d'Alene theme park also features water slides and activities. Visitors can splash their way down and around five large slides and several smaller ones, or they can enjoy the peaceful River Ride and the Spa. The park also offers minislides for little folks, an arcade full of the latest gaming challenges, and a snack bar and gift shop.

ADDRESS AND TELEPHONE

Wild Waters
2119 North Government Way
Coeur d'Alene, ID 83814

(208) 667-6491

LOCATION

Wild Waters is about 30 miles east of Spokane, Washington. Take Interstate 90 and exit at Lincoln Way (Highway 95) in Coeur d'Alene. Go north one block to Appleway and east one block to Government Way. A right turn will take you to the entrance.

OPERATING SEASONS AND HOURS

Open daily from mid-May to Labor Day. Hours: 11 A.M. to 7 P.M.

ADMISSION FEES

Adults: $9.95. Children ages 4 to 11: $8.50. Children 3 and under: free.

TRANSPORTATION AND ACCOMMODATIONS WITHIN THE PARK

None.

GUEST SERVICES

Restrooms, telephones, lost and found, showers, lockers. Visa and MasterCard accepted.

RIDES

Cruiser: plunge down a speed slide.
Double Trouble: twister with two tunnels.
Drop Off: curl and drop your way down to a deep pool.
Skidder: twister with a tunnel.
Twister: spin down this splash-filled curlicue.

Drop Off Slides: three slides send you splashing down into a deep pool.

Gyro: twist and rotate in this human-powered gyrating hoop.

River Ride: float through three pools in an inner tube.

KIDDIE RIDE

Jersey Cream: two minislides for tots.

GAMES

Arcade Room

Outdoor Games: water balloon tosses, sponge races, and coloring contests held throughout the week; floating basketball hoop in the pool.

RESTAURANTS

None.

SNACK BARS

Doughnut Stand

Paradise Candy

Wild Waters Snack Bar: hot dogs, hamburgers, fries, burritos, drinks, slushy ice drinks.

CATERING

Not available.

SOUVENIR SHOP

Swimwear, shorts, tops, suntan lotion, sunglasses, hats, goggles, cards, novelty gifts.

MONTANA

BIG SKY WATERSLIDE

Big Sky Waterslide is among Montana's first water parks. Nestled in the heart of the northern Rockies, just north of Kalispell and east of Whitefish, it's a convenient and refreshing stop on your way to or from Glacier National Park. This 15-acre water park features nine slides geared to the beginner or expert, in addition to a hot tub, activity pool, large picnic area, space-age video arcade, and gift shop.

ADDRESS AND TELEPHONE

Big Sky Waterslide
Box 2311
Junction of Highways 2 and 206
Columbia Falls, MT 59912

(406) 892-2139 or (406) 892-5025

LOCATION

Big Sky Waterslide is located 15 miles south of Glacier National Park, on Highway 2 at the junction of Highway 206. Take the Amtrak train to Whitefish, Montana, then drive seven miles to the park. Or fly into Glacier International Airport in Kalispell and drive 15 miles to the park.

OPERATING SEASONS AND HOURS

Open weekends from May to mid-June. Hours: 11 A.M. to 6 P.M. Open daily from mid-June to Labor Day. Hours: 10 A.M. to 8 P.M.

ADMISSION FEES

Adults: $9.50. Children ages 4 to 11: $7. Non-riders: $4. At twilight: Adults: $6.50. Children ages 4 to 11 and seniors: $5. Non-riders: $3. (Additional fee for miniature golf.)

TRANSPORTATION AND ACCOMMODATIONS WITHIN THE PARK

None.

GUEST SERVICES

Restrooms, telephones, lost and found, first aid, changing rooms, locker rentals.

RIDES

Big Splash River Ride: experience the sensation of white water rafting. Cascade down a river of churning water in an inner tube.

Bonzai Speed Slide: shoot down a double drop-off speed slide.

Geronimo: a 70-foot free-fall speed slide drops you seven stories in less than five seconds.

Twister Slides: drop, bend, twist, and turn on four rides, each 350 to 400 feet long.

KIDDIE RIDES

Intermediate Slides: children 9 and under can slip and slide before splashing down in a three-foot pool.

ATTRACTIONS AND GAMES

Activity Pool: wading pool with water games and toys geared to young children.

Picnic Grounds

Barbecue Area

Hot Tub

Golf Course: miniature greens. Open in summer. Hours: 10 A.M. to 10 P.M. Additional fee: Adults: $4.50. Children: $3.50.

Arcade

RESTAURANTS

None.

SNACK BARS

Concession stands located throughout the park serve chips, candy, ice cream bars, nachos, pretzels, hot dogs, burritos, corn dogs, raw hamburgers to barbecue, soft drinks.

CATERING

Contact Roger Elliott at (406) 892-5025.

SOUVENIR SHOP

Towels, flotation device rentals, Big Sky mementos.

NEVADA

PONDEROSA RANCH

Ben Cartwright's Ponderosa Ranch is the theme park used by the "Bonanza" television show's tour guides. Fans of the now-classic TV series can experience firsthand the hospitality of the Cartwright clan's ranch house. Visitors explore an entire Western town with its carriages, buggies, vintage cars, and other Western memorabilia, while enjoying the breathtaking view of Lake Tahoe, one of America's most scenic recreation areas.

ADDRESS AND TELEPHONE

Ponderosa Ranch
P. O. Box A.P.
Incline Village, NV 89450

(702) 831-0691

LOCATION

Ponderosa Ranch is located off Highway 28 in Incline Village, Nevada.

OPERATING SEASONS AND HOURS

Open from May to October. Hours: 9:30 A.M. to 5 P.M. Hayride breakfast from Memorial Day to Labor Day. Hours: 8 A.M. to 9:30 A.M.

ADMISSION FEES

Adults: $7.50. Children ages 5 to 11: $5.50. Children under 5: free. Hayride breakfast: Adults: $9.50. Children ages 5 to 11: $7.50. Children ages 3 and 4: $2. Children under 3: free.

TRANSPORTATION AND ACCOMMODATIONS WITHIN THE PARK

Transportation is available for people who have difficulty walking the park's distances.

GUEST SERVICES

Restrooms, telephones, information booth, first aid, lost and found, baby strollers, wheelchairs. Visa, MasterCard, American Express, and Discover cards accepted.

RIDE

Hayride Breakfast: ride through the Ponderosa's tall timbers to a hearty all-you-can-eat breakfast. Savor Ben's scrambled eggs and Hop Sing's sausages, flapjacks, juice, and coffee while enjoying the view of Lake Tahoe.

ATTRACTIONS AND GAMES

Cartwright Ranch House: see the home of Ben, Adam, Hoss, and Little Joe.
Western Memorabilia: Western town, antique carriages, vintage cars, "Bonanza" props.
Petting Farm: pet the cuddly barnyard animals.
Pony Rides: for kids.
Shooting Gallery and Arcade: family fun.

RESTAURANTS

Gunnysack Cafe: Hoss burgers, hot dogs, corn dogs, pizza, barbecued beef sandwiches, fries, onion rings, corn on the cob, baked beans.
Silver Dollar Saloon: popcorn, nachos, candy, sarsaparilla, lemonade, spirits, iced tea, coffee, cocoa.

SNACK BARS

Fudge Confections
Ice Cream Store

CATERING

Not available.

SOUVENIR SHOPS

General Store: Cartwright memorabilia.
Western Store: cowboy hats, belts, buckles, boleros, spurs, guns.

Indian Store: jewelry, pottery, moccasins, headdresses, bows and arrows, leather vests.

HELPFUL TIP ON MAKING YOUR VISIT MORE ENJOYABLE

The breakfast hayride is the best way to see the entire Ponderosa Ranch.

WET 'N WILD

Wet 'n Wild is a 16-acre water park located right on the glittering Las Vegas strip. It features more than a dozen ways to beat the heat of the desert, from thrilling slides to relaxing rides for all ages. Featured at the park are the Surf Lagoon wave pool, the Banzai Boggan water roller coaster, the Willy Willy whirlwind ride, and other fast, splashing water rides. More than 500,000 visitors a year cool off in the park's 1½ million gallons of fresh temperature-controlled water.

ADDRESS AND TELEPHONE

Wet 'n Wild
1050 E. Flamingo #320
Las Vegas, NV 89119

(702) 734-0088

LOCATION

Wet 'n Wild is located on the Las Vegas strip.

OPERATING SEASONS AND HOURS

Open daily from mid-April through September. Opens at 10 A.M. Closing times vary, so check with the park upon arrival.

ADMISSION FEES

Adults: $15.95. Children ages 3 to 12: $12.95. Children under 3: free.

TRANSPORTATION AND ACCOMMODATIONS WITHIN THE PARK

None.

GUEST SERVICES

Restrooms, telephones, information booth, check cashing, first aid, lockers, towels, lost and found. Visa, MasterCard, and American Express cards accepted.

RIDES

Banzai Boggan: a water roller coaster that takes riders down a 45-degree chute and across the water's surface.
Blue Niagra: two intertwined looping blue tubes.
Der Stuka: free-fall 76 feet to a straight 100-foot runway that slows riders down before they reach a splashpool.
Flash Flood/Hydra-Maniac: riders are sent down flumes in a burst of water for a high-speed splash landing.
Lazy River: leisurely float along at two miles per hour for about 10 minutes.
Raging Rapids: riders in inner tubes are carried over a slippery fall before plunging into the pool below.
Whitewater Slideways: three water slides for the twisting and turning ride of a lifetime.
Willy Willy: named for an Australian whirlwind, it carries riders on inner tubes around a clockwise course in a pool at a rate of 10 miles per hour.

ATTRACTIONS AND GAMES

Surf Lagoon: from experienced swimmers to small children, all enjoy the mighty four-foot waves in this 500,000-gallon pool.

Children's Water Playground: a giant water playground for kids with a 1930s-style zeppelin, water games, and sea squirts.
Suntan Lagoon: relax under the cascading waterfall while you take in the sun.
Bubble Up: a giant colorful bubble with cascading water fountain for climbing, slipping, and sliding.
Arcade
Bankshot Basketball

RESTAURANTS

None.

SNACK BARS

Snack Bar: hot and cold sandwiches, hot dogs, hamburgers.
Snack bars located throughout the park serve pizza, ice cream, and more.

CATERING

Contact Group Sales at (702) 737-7873.

SOUVENIR SHOP

Souvenirs, swimwear, suntan lotion, sportswear, accessories.

HELPFUL TIPS ON MAKING YOUR VISIT MORE ENJOYABLE

Glass containers and alcoholic beverages are not allowed in the park. You may bring your own picnic lunch.

UTAH

LAGOON AMUSEMENT PARK, PIONEER VILLAGE, AND LAGOON A BEACH

One million guests a year visit Lagoon, outside of Salt Lake City, Utah. The park is really three parks in one: Lagoon Amusement Park, with its many rides, shows, attractions, restaurants, and snack bars; Pioneer Village, a 15-acre reconstructed frontier community typical of the 1880s; and Lagoon A Beach, the new action water park. The park also offers a full-service RV park adjacent to the Lagoon.

ADDRESS AND TELEPHONE

Lagoon Amusement Park
P. O. Box N
Farmington, UT 84025

(801) 451-0101

LOCATION

The park is located 15 minutes on the freeway from Salt Lake City or Ogden. The park can be reached by car: take I-15 to the Lagoon Drive exit. Bus transportation is available from Salt Lake City or Ogden with the Utah Transit Authority. Check with the UTA at (801) 263-3737 for schedules.

OPERATING SEASONS AND HOURS

Open weekends from mid-April to mid-May and from September to mid-October. Open daily from Memorial Day to Labor Day. Opens at 11 A.M. Closing times vary between 7 P.M. and 11 P.M., so check with the park upon arrival.

ADMISSION FEES

All-day passport: $16.95.

TRANSPORTATION AND ACCOMMODATIONS WITHIN THE PARK

Pioneer Village Campgrounds: full-service campground with 250 spaces. For reservations call (801) 451-2812.

GUEST SERVICES

Restrooms, telephones, information booth, check cashing, first aid, lockers, lost and found, stroller and wheelchair rental. Visa, MasterCard, American Express, and Discover cards accepted.

RIDES

Boomerang: bumper cars.

Centennial Screamer: start flat, then move to a vertical position and spin around.

Colossal Fire Dragon: this coaster is nearly 85 feet high at the highest point.

Dracula's Castle: enter the dark world of the prince of the night.

Flying Aces: guide yourself in a circle as you fly through the air.

Flying Carpet: go 80 feet in the air, circle, then move backward.

Freefall Slide: experience the sensation of dropping from 65 feet above the ground at this Lagoon A Beach water slide.

Hump Slide: Lagoon A Beach's "liquid lightning."

Jet Star II: zoom along a steel coaster.

Lagoon Merry-Go-Round: choose from a menagerie of handcarved animals to ride round and round.

Lagoon Roller Coaster: climb to over 70 feet above the ground and reach speeds of 45 miles per hour on this wooden coaster.

Log Flume: soar down this flume into a splash pool.

Mooch's Mainstream: an island cruise that will float you past tropical waterfalls, fountains, and waves.

Musik Express: hit top speeds while enjoying whirling lights and hot music.

Paratrooper: fly up and down.

Rock-o-Plane: cars at both ends of this ride take you up and over.

Roll-o-Plane: individual cars take you up in the air, then topsy-turvy.

Serpentine Slides: three winding slides at Lagoon A Beach drop you from a 56-foot tower and send you twisting and splashing to the bottom.

Skeeter Boats: paddle around a lake.

Sky Ride: an aerial view from a tram of the park and midway.

Skyscraper: a 150-foot-high Ferris wheel.

Space Scrambler: move and shake in several directions simultaneously.

Speedway: drive your own motorcar on a track.

Stagecoach: a real stagecoach is pulled by Clydesdale horses.

Terror Ride: take this dark journey if you dare.

Tidal Wave: a giant boat swings back and forth.

Tilt-a-Whirl: a park tradition.

Tube Slides: four speedy slides that are "totally tubular."

Turn of the Century: swing around in a circle.

Wild Kingdom Train: while riding a steam engine around the lake, see the park's collection of animals, including lions, tigers, bears, bobcats, buffaloes, elk, llamas.

KIDDIE RIDES

Baby Boats: boats along a water channel.

Bulgy the Whale: a little whale.

Helicopter: kids fly in a circle in copters that go up and down.

Moonraker: minispaceships fly in a circle.

Puff the Little Fire Dragon: a pint-sized coaster.

Red Baron: little biplanes.

Scallawagger: friendly bugs that go in a circle.

Scamper: bumper cars for little ones.

Sky Fighter: tiny planes with play guns.

Speedway Jr.: kids "drive" their own little cars around a track.

ATTRACTIONS

Pioneer Village: a 15-acre restoration of pioneer Utah, complete with log schoolhouse, smokehouse, old mill, pioneer bakery, post office, dental office, barbershop, print shop, general store, horse-drawn carriage collection, gun collection, exhibits of Indian and pioneer artifacts, and a music hall exhibit with live demonstrations.

Lake Park Terrace: built in 1886, this structure is reminiscent of a bygone era and is just one of 25 picnic areas at Lagoon.

Zoo: see lions, tigers, bears, mountain lions, buffaloes, elk, llamas, and more in the second largest zoo in Utah.

Lagoon A Beach: this action water park has a South Seas theme and features water rides, an adult wave pool, a children's activity area, sand volleyball courts, a surf shop, and more.

SHOWS

Music USA: a musical revue with a new theme each season.

Lagoon All-Star Band: a 30-piece marching band that performs on the midway twice daily.

Summer Rhythm: a live rhythm and blues band that performs three times a day.

Wild West Shoot-Out: good guy versus bad guy brawl in Pioneer Village, four times daily.

L. A. Goon Band: this brass clown band performs in the early afternoon.

Costumed characters parade around the park throughout the day.

RESTAURANT

Gaslight Sandwich Shop: deli sandwiches, ice cream.

SNACK BARS

Stands located throughout the park sell hot dogs, burgers, tacos, soft drinks.

CATERING

Contact Peter O'Bagy at (801) 451-0101.

SOUVENIR SHOPS

Rad Brad's Surf Rags: swimwear, T-shirts, towels, hats, magazines, souvenirs.

General Store: T-shirts, hats, toys, novelties.

Carts: park mementos.

HELPFUL TIPS ON MAKING YOUR VISIT MORE ENJOYABLE

To beat the crowds visit the park on Sunday or Monday. It's also a good idea to arrange a definite time and place for your family to meet later in the day, but avoid the crowded entrance area as a meeting place. Pets can be taken into the park provided they are leashed at all times.

PACIFIC WEST

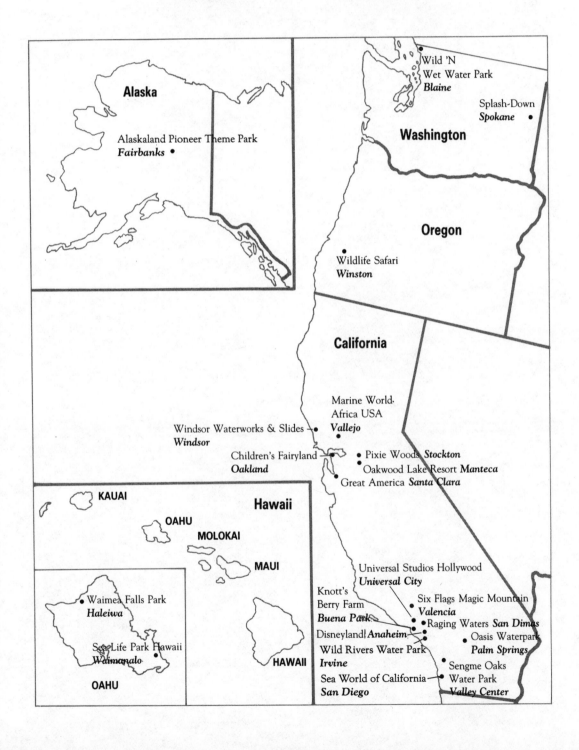

Alaska

Alaskaland Pioneer Theme Park
Fairbanks •

Wild 'N
Wet Water Park
Blaine

Splash-Down
Spokane •

Washington

Oregon

• Wildlife Safari
Winston

California

Marine World
Africa USA
Windsor Waterworks & Slides — • *Vallejo*
Windsor

Children's Fairyland — • Pixie Woods *Stockton*
Oakland • Oakwood Lake Resort *Manteca*
• Great America *Santa Clara*

KAUAI

Hawaii

OAHU

MOLOKAI

MAUI

• Waimea Falls Park
Haleiwa

Sea Life Park Hawaii
Waimanalo •

HAWAII

Universal Studios Hollywood
Universal City

Knott's
Berry Farm
Buena Park

Six Flags Magic Mountain
• *Valencia*
• Raging Waters *San Dimas*

Disneyland| *Anaheim* —
Wild Rivers Water Park
Irvine
Sea World of California —
San Diego

• Oasis Waterpark
Palm Springs

• Sengme Oaks
• Water Park
Valley Center

OAHU

ALASKA

ALASKALAND
PIONEER THEME PARK

Alaskaland Pioneer Theme Park, situated on 44 acres on the Chena River in Fairbanks, Alaska, receives close to 150,000 visitors a year. This historical theme park was created to celebrate the hundredth anniversary of Alaska's becoming part of the United States. The attractions include three National Historic Landmarks; Gold Rush Town, with actual cabins belonging to the first frontier settlers in Alaska gathered from around the state; Mining Valley, with artifacts from the mining days of Alaska's history; and Native Village, museums and homes from Alaska's first settlers, the Indians. There are also recreation and play areas.

ADDRESS AND TELEPHONE

Alaskaland Pioneer Theme Park
P. O. Box 71267
Fairbanks, AK 99707-1267

(907) 459-1087

LOCATION

Alaskaland is near the heart of Fairbanks where the Alaska Railroad and Borough bus stations are located. It is on Airport Road, one of Fair-banks's main roads, leading directly to the Fairbanks International Airport and the Fairbanks City Center area.

OPERATING SEASONS AND HOURS

Open daily from Memorial Day to Labor Day. Hours: 11 A.M. to 9 P.M.

ADMISSION FEES

None. (Some of the attractions have individual fees.)

TRANSPORTATION AND ACCOMMODATIONS WITHIN THE PARK

None.

GUEST SERVICES

Restrooms, telephones, information booth, check cashing, lost and found, message center, first-aid station.

RIDES

Crooked Creek and Whiskey Island Railroad: take a train ride that circles the park twice and gives passengers a guided tour of the many attractions of the park.
Lydie Lou Carousel: a 77-year-old carousel.

ATTRACTIONS AND GAMES

The Sternwheeler Nenana: the second largest wooden vessel still in existence and recently granted the status of National Historic Landmark.
The Harding Car: the railroad car that President Warren G. Harding rode to drive the golden spike into the completed Alaska Railroad. Also a National Historic Landmark.
Judge James Wickersham House: the third National Historic Landmark in the park, this is the house of the first territorial judge in Alaska.
The Pioneer Aviation Museum: vintage aircraft from the early pioneer days in Alaska.
Gold Rush Town: actual cabins from around the state belonging to the first frontier settlers in Alaska.
Mining Valley: artifacts from the mining days of Alaska's history.
Native Village: museums and homes from Alaska's first settlers, the Indians.
The Farthest North Miniature Golf Courses: two 18-hole courses.
Volleyball: play on a sand court.
Boating Dock
Horseshoe Pits
Bicycle Path: parallels the Chena River and passes through Alaskaland.
Large Playground Areas

SHOWS

Vaudeville Show: at the Palace Saloon.
Big Stampede Show: view six 10-feet-by-20-feet paintings as you listen to a narrative explanation of the chronological history of the Gold Rush coming to Alaska.

Northern Inua Show: a miniversion of the World Eskimo Indian Olympics.
Potlatch Show: a celebration through dance of the Athabascan Indians.

SPECIAL ANNUAL EVENTS

Golden Days: a re-creation of Alaska's Gold Rush boom and bust days, in July.
The Art Festival: a weekend-long folk festival with entertainment, in July.
Fourth of July: food and games.
Labor Day Sidewalk Sale: the stores in Gold Rush Town have sale tables set up outside.
Christmas Bazaar: crafts and other goods are sold, starting on the Saturday after Thanksgiving.

RESTAURANTS

The Alaska Salmon Bake: all-you-can-eat salmon, halibut, ribs, steak.

SNACK BARS

Souvlaki: Greek food, submarine sandwiches.
Country Kitchen: burgers, soups, salads, sandwiches.
Pretzel Cache: hot dogs, pretzels, candy.
Frosty Paws: frozen yogurt, soft-serve ice cream.
Goldrush Ice Cream Parlor: ice cream, sandwiches, nachos, candy, hot dogs.

CATERING

Not available.

SOUVENIR SHOPS

Gold Rush Town: 27 gift shops sell original crafts, original clothing, jewelry, fresh fish, souvenirs, old-time photos of guests, and sundries.

HINTS FOR TRAVELING WITH CHILDREN, ELDERLY, HANDICAPPED

The park is wheelchair accessible. It is advisable that parents with young children bring their own strollers.

HELPFUL TIP ON MAKING YOUR VISIT MORE ENJOYABLE

Alaskan weather is very changeable so visitors are encouraged to bring rain gear, sweaters, light jackets, and umbrellas.

CALIFORNIA

CHILDREN'S FAIRYLAND

Children's Fairyland theme park contains more than 60 colorful sets re-creating such nursery rhymes, fairy tales, and popular legends as Pinocchio, Billy Goats Gruff, and Alice in Wonderland. Geared to young children and their families, the park also features costumed fairy tale characters such as Mother Goose, Thumbelina, and a seven-foot-tall Lost Dragon, as well as live goats, lambs, ducks, and chickens. A variety of kiddie rides and daily puppet shows are other features of this 10-acre park.

ADDRESS AND TELEPHONE

Children's Fairyland
1520 Lakeside Drive
Oakland, CA 94612

(415) 452-2259

LOCATION

Children's Fairyland is located in Lakeside Park on the corner of Grand and Bellevue. Take Highway 880 to Oak Street. Continue on Oak/Lakeside to Grand Avenue. Make a right on Grand and go one block to Lakeside Park. By train, take BART to 19th and Broadway. By bus, take AC Transit bus number 12, 18, or 34.

OPERATING SEASONS AND HOURS

Open Wednesday to Sunday in April, May, and September. Hours: 10 A.M. to 4:30 P.M. Open daily from June to August. Hours: Monday to Friday, 10 A.M. to 4:30 P.M.; Saturday and Sunday, 10 A.M. to 5:30 P.M. Open weekends from October to March. Closed for one week in late October.

ADMISSION FEES

Adults: $2. Children ages 12 and under: $1.50. (Kiddie rides have separate fees.)

TRANSPORTATION AND ACCOMMODATIONS WITHIN THE PARK

None.

GUEST SERVICES

Restrooms, telephones, first aid, lost and found.

RIDES

None.

KIDDIE RIDES

Chinese Tree House: a terrace for kids and adults too.
Dragon Slide: a slide for tots, located in the Chinese Tree House.
Jolly Trolley Train: a journey in a colorful car.
Magic Web: a pint-sized Ferris wheel.
Toyland Boat Ride: mini bumper boats.
Wonder-Go-Round: a small merry-go-round.

ATTRACTIONS

Fairy Tale Re-Creations: colorful re-creations of fairy tales, nursery rhymes, and legends. See the Old Woman's Shoe, Jolly Roger Pirate Ship, Alice in Wonderland Rabbit Hole, the Yellow Brick Road, and more.
Costumed Characters: visitors can bump into a fairy tale character in full regalia, including Mother Goose, Peter Pan, Pinocchio, and others.

SHOW

Puppet Show: a colorful puppet show that kids will love. Performed daily at 11 A.M., 2 P.M., and 4 P.M.

SPECIAL ANNUAL EVENTS

Easter Egg Roll
Fairyland Birthday: enjoy a slice of a 15-foot cake as the park celebrates its birthday in August.
Jack-o-Lantern Jamboree: visitors and Fairyland inhabitants dress up in costume for this Halloween extravaganza in October.

RESTAURANTS

None.

SNACK BAR

Mrs. Pucker's Pumpkin: hot dogs, nachos, sandwiches, fruit drinks.

CATERING

Contact Birthday Party Catering at (415) 452-2259.

SOUVENIR SHOP

The Duchess House: T-shirts, small toys, books, postcards, park mementos.

DISNEYLAND

World-renowned Disneyland, nicknamed "the happiest place on earth," occupies 80 acres of land in Anaheim, California. The Magic Kingdom creates its own times and journeys in seven lands with different themes: Adventureland, with its exotic regions of Asia, Africa, and the South Pacific; Critter Country, a down-home backwoods setting for "Splash Mountain" and the Country Bear Playhouse; Fantasyland, a happy kingdom of storybook enchantment; Frontierland, the exciting realm of pioneers and a return to the heritage of the Old West; Main Street, U.S.A., a composite of small-town America, circa 1900; New Orleans Square, home of ghosts, pirates, and quaint shops; and Tomorrowland, the world of the future. Rides, shows, shops, eateries, and, of course, Mickey Mouse and friends annually delight millions of guests from all over the world.

ADDRESS AND TELEPHONE

Disneyland
P. O. Box 3232
Anaheim, CA 92803

(714) 999-4565

LOCATION

Disneyland is located approximately 27 miles southeast of the Los Angeles Civic Center, adjacent to the I-5 exit at Buena Vista. Buses from Los Angeles International Airport and Orange County Airport (John Wayne Airport) stop at the Disneyland Hotel, located across the street from the park.

OPERATING SEASONS AND HOURS

Open daily year-round. Hours in the summer months: 8 A.M. to 1 A.M. Hours in the winter months: 10 A.M. to 6 P.M., and 9 A.M. to 12 A.M. on weekends. Seasonal schedules vary, so write or call the park for a schedule before arriving.

ADMISSION FEES

Adults: $27.50. Children ages 3 to 11: $22.50.

TRANSPORTATION AND ACCOMMODATIONS WITHIN THE PARK

Disneyland Monorail: travels round-trip between Disneyland and the Disneyland Hotel.
Disneyland Hotel: located opposite the park at 1150 West Cerritos Avenue, Anaheim, CA 92802. For information and reservations call (714) 778-6600.

GUEST SERVICES

Restrooms, telephones, information (City Hall), first aid, kennel, lockers, lost and found, message center, lost children's area, stroller and wheelchair rental, tape recorders for blind guests. Bank of America inside the Magic Kingdom is open every day. All major credit cards including Visa, MasterCard, and American Express accepted.

RIDES

Big Thunder Mountain Railroad: a thrilling ride on a runaway mine train.
Davy Crockett's Explorer Canoes: cruise the rivers of America with a wilderness guide and your own paddle.
Disneyland Railroad: all aboard an old-fashioned steam train for a grand circle tour of Disneyland.
Fantasyland Autopia: a scenic freeway minus the traffic jams.
Haunted Mansion: the 999 "happy haunts" in this old house are just dying to see you.
Jungle Cruise: cruise on tropical rivers for a mystery-filled adventure.
Mad Tea Party: spinning cups and saucers whirl about.
Mark Twain Steamboat: a stately steam-powered sternwheeler.
Matterhorn Bobsleds: hold on to your hats on this thrilling ride and icy encounter with the Abominable Snowman.
Mike Fink Keelboats: a rustic cruise through backwoods waterways.
Motor Boat Cruise: tricky currents and challenging rapids test your skills as a captain.
Mr. Toad's Wild Ride: a reckless joyride on the road to "nowhere in particular."
Omnibus: take in all the sights on Main Street from atop a double-decker bus.
Pirates of the Caribbean: glimpse a pirate's life on this wild adventure ride.
Rafts to Tom Sawyer Island: journey to Tom Sawyer Island where you'll find balancing rocks, secret caves, and a barrel bridge.
Rocket Jets: enjoy a soaring aerial adventure high above Tomorrowland.
Sailing Ship Columbia: sail the rivers of America on a sailing ship.
Skyway to Tomorrowland: journey high above the Magic Kingdom.
Space Mountain: touch the outer reaches of the universe on this high-speed roller coaster.

Splash Mountain: log flume ride on which you experience a five-story drop at a 47-degree angle of descent, leading to a musical finale. This is Disneyland's newest ride.

Star Tours: an intergalactic adventure featuring R2-D2 and C3PO of *Star Wars* fame.

Submarine Voyage: an underwater cruise to the North Pole and back.

KIDDIE RIDES

Mostly in Fantasyland, including:

Alice in Wonderland: a date with Alice and the White Rabbit.

Casey Jr. Circus Train: the little train that knew he could takes a trip around Storybook Land.

Dumbo the Flying Elephant: kids fly atop this endearing storybook character.

It's a Small World: the happiest cruise that ever sailed around the world.

King Arthur Carousel: 72 prancing horses.

Peter Pan's Flight: pirate galleons soar past the second star on the right, then straight on till morning.

Pinocchio's Daring Journey: Pinocchio finds Pleasure Island isn't so pleasurable.

Snow White's Scary Adventure: a trip to the witch's castle.

ATTRACTIONS AND GAMES

Horse-Drawn Street Cars: ride a horse-drawn trolley down the turn-of-the-century Main Street thoroughfare.

The Walt Disney Story, featuring Great Moments with Mr. Lincoln: exhibits honoring the man behind the mouse, plus a salute to the country's sixteenth president.

Main Street Cinema: the Disney gang stars in cartoon classics.

Swiss Family Treehouse: the treetop home of the Robinson family.

Big Thunder Ranch: an Old West homestead.

Sleeping Beauty Castle: dioramas re-create the story of Sleeping Beauty.

Disney Characters: Mickey Mouse, Minnie Mouse, Goofy, and the gang can be spotted throughout the park. (Mickey usually hangs out in Town Square.)

Penny Arcade: games, fortunes, and old movies for a penny, nickel, dime, or quarter.

Teddi Barra's Swinging Arcade: frontier fun and games for a dime or quarter.

Starcade: two floors of the most popular video games.

Frontierland Shootin' Arcade

SHOWS

Country Bear Playhouse: a foot-stompin', knee-slappin' hoedown featuring lovable bear-itones.

Golden Horseshoe Jamboree: song and dance revue.

Captain EO: 3-D musical motion picture space adventure starring Michael Jackson.

Imagination: spectacular high-tech multimedia after-dark presentation on the Rivers of America in Frontierland.

RESTAURANTS

Town Square Cafe: eggs, omelets, burgers, salads, desserts.

Plaza Pavilion: chicken, spaghetti, salads.

Plaza Inn: hot entrees, salads, sandwiches, desserts.

Tahitian Terrace: teriyaki steak, shrimp, chicken, fish.

Cafe Orleans: sandwiches, salads, desserts.

Blue Bayou Restaurant: seafood, chicken, beef, Monte Cristo sandwiches.

French Market Restaurant: fried chicken, salads, desserts.

Hungry Bear Restaurant: burgers, hot dogs, chicken, sandwiches, salads, desserts.

Casa Mexicana: tacos, burritos, enchiladas.

Golden Horseshoe: cold sandwiches, chips, beverages.

River Belle Terrace: pancakes, waffles, eggs, sandwiches, salads.

Big Thunder Barbecue: barbecue chicken, ribs, beans, corn on the cob.

Village Haus Restaurant: burgers, hot dogs, beverages.

Carnation Ice Cream Parlor: ice cream, sandwiches, soups, salads.

SNACK BARS

Main Street Cone Shop: ice cream, frozen yogurt.

Tiki Juice Bar: pineapple spears, Dole pineapple whip, pineapple juice, coffee.

Royal Street Veranda: fritters, Mardi Gras juleps.

Harbor Galley: hot and cold seafood, drinks.

Mile Long Bar: Mickey Mouse pretzels, apple cider, drinks.

Stage Door Cafe: burgers, hot dogs, brownies.

Wheelhouse: hot dogs, ice cream, cookies, drinks.

Yumz: hot dogs, pizza bread, nachos, drinks.

Ice Cream Train: frozen juice and ice cream bars, canned soda.

The Space Place: burgers, hot dogs, salads, ice cream, shakes.

Lunching Pad: hot dogs, popcorn, lemonade.

Other snack bars and stands located throughout the park serve hot dogs, burgers, ice cream, frozen treats, popcorn, cookies, doughnuts, churros, pastries, burritos, fruit, juice.

CATERING

Not available.

SOUVENIR SHOPS

Emporium: buttons, pens, pennants, toys, clothing, calculators, and other Disneyland memorabilia.

Crystal Arcade: Disney character T-shirts, sweatshirts, souvenirs.

Main Street Menagerie: cuddly versions of Disney characters.

New Century Timepieces: Mickey Mouse watches and clocks, and other Disney timepieces.

Mad Hatter Shop: hats, from mouse ears to chapeaus.

Disneyana: rare and unusual Disney collector merchandise.

The Disney Showcase: a brand-new shop containing up-to-the-minute Disney films and TV merchandise.

Disney Clothiers, Ltd.: Disney character clothing.

Carefree Corner: toys, greeting cards, stationery, gift wrap, party supplies.

Disney Gallery Collector's Room: posters, books, limited edition lithographs.

Crocodile Mercantile: Black Hills gold and gold nugget jewelry, Splash Mountain souvenirs, toys.

Tinkerbell Toy Shop: dolls, toys, Disney character clothing.

Small World Gifts: Disney character toys, souvenirs, T-shirts.

Other souvenir and gift shops located throughout the park sell a variety of items from clothing, watches, handicrafts, glassware, collectibles, and jewelry to stuffed animals, fragrances, candy, items with a Western and Indian theme, wood carvings, and Christmas decorations.

HINTS FOR TRAVELING WITH CHILDREN, ELDERLY, HANDICAPPED

Strollers are a good idea since Disneyland encompasses 80 acres and children get tired easily. Baby care is offered in the Baby Center; it has child-sized flush toilets for tots. Changing tables are available, and a limited selection of juices and strained baby foods are for sale at a nominal fee. A special room for nursing mothers is available as well.

Elderly guests should read Disneyland literature carefully before arrival so that the park layout is as familiar as possible; that way they can avoid extra steps. It's a good idea to save the less strenuous Main Street attractions, such as "Great Moments with Mr. Lincoln," for the end of the day.

Handicapped visitors can write for or pick up "The Disneyland Handicapped Guest Guide" at Disneyland City Hall. It offers helpful information and lists the attractions that are accessible to handicapped guests. For blind guests a tape recorder with a cassette describing the park is available at City Hall. Guide dogs are allowed in almost all areas of the park.

HELPFUL TIPS ON MAKING YOUR VISIT MORE ENJOYABLE

Get your reservation for the Golden Horseshoe Show immediately after arriving in the park. Ride the most popular attractions—Splash Mountain, Star Tours, Space Mountain, and Big Thunder Mountain Railroad—early in the day or during parades.

GREAT AMERICA

This 100-acre theme park is regarded by many as the most elaborate in northern California. Great America is composed of several areas with different themes: Hometown Square, a quaint American town of the 1920s; County Fair, a turn-of-the-century fairground and midway; Yukon Territory, an 1898 Gold Rush mining town; Smurf Woods, a play area for kids; Yankee Harbor, a late-eighteenth-century New England seaport; Hanna-Barbera's Fort Fun, a play-action area for kids; and Orleans Place, a re-creation of the New Orleans French Quarter, circa 1850. Highlights at Great America are its five roller coasters, live stage shows, ice skating show, costumed characters, and a state-of-the-art, giant-screen 3-D movie.

ADDRESS AND TELEPHONE

Great America
P. O. Box 1776
Santa Clara, CA 95052

(408) 988-1800

LOCATION

Great America is located five minutes north of downtown San Jose along Great America Parkway between highways 101 and 237. Take Santa Clara County Transit Light Rail Line from downtown San Jose. County transit buses connect Great America to BART (Bay Area Rapid Transit) at its Fremont Terminus.

OPERATING SEASONS AND HOURS

Open selected weekends beginning late March and from Labor Day to mid-October. Open daily from June 1 to Labor Day and the week before Easter. Opens at 10 A.M. Closing times vary, so check with the park upon arrival.

ADMISSION FEES

Adults: $20.95. Children ages 3 to 6: $10.45. Children 2 and under: free. Seniors 55 and over: $13.95.

TRANSPORTATION AND ACCOMMODATIONS WITHIN THE PARK

None. (Nearby hotels offer shuttle service to the park.)

GUEST SERVICES

Restrooms, telephones, information booth, check cashing, stroller and wheelchair rental, lockers, infant care center, lost parents area, first aid, lost and found. Visa, MasterCard, American Express, and Optima cards accepted.

RIDES

Ameri-Go-Round: antique carousel.
Barney Oldfield Motor Speedway: take the wheel of an antique auto—kids can be drivers too.
Berzerker: race along banking curves in this low-riding train.
The Carousel Columbia: experience the fun of a double-decker carousel.
The Demon: zoom along a steel coaster with two 360-degree loops and a double helix.
Eagles Flight/Delta Flyer: touch the treetops on this aerial tram ride.
The Edge: a free-fall plunge.
Fiddler's Fling: swirl and spin.
Great America Scenic Railway: journey around the park.
The Grizzly: speed up and down the largest wooden coaster in northern California.

The Lobster: dip, turn, and swirl on this amusement park classic.

Logger's Run: swoosh down a water flume.

Orleans Orbit: feel centrifugal force as you spin.

The Revolution: board a ship that swings 360 degrees in the air.

Rip Roaring Rapids: splash down this white water raft ride.

Rue Le Dodge: bumper cars.

Skyhawk: strap yourself into the cockpit, close the hatch, grab the joystick, and you're in control, streaking through the sky at 60 feet in the air.

Sky Tower: climb to a platform 200 feet in the air for a panoramic park view.

Tidal Wave: brave a shuttle loop steel coaster.

Triple Wheel: a triple-armed Ferris wheel.

Vortex: enjoy Great America's exciting new stand-up coaster.

Whitewater Falls: splash through a spillwater ride.

Yankee Clipper: get ready to get wet on this water flume ride.

KIDDIE RIDES

The Blue Streak: a scaled-down coaster for kids.

Brainy's Buggies: self-drive buggies.

Buzzin' Bees

Handy's Biplanes: biplanes for little pilots.

Hanna-Barbera Carousel: a park favorite.

Huck's Hang Gliders: tyke-sized gliders.

Lazy's Snail Trains

Li'l Dodge'em: pint-sized bumper cars.

Yakki Doodle's Lady Bugs: a circle of colorful ladybugs.

ATTRACTIONS AND GAMES

Remote Control Boats

Games of Skill: located around the park.

Games Gallery: favorite amusement park games.

Northwest Shooting Gallery

Cirque Electrique Games and Arcade: games of skill and video games.

SHOWS

It's Magic: a lively combination of music, dance, and illusion.

The Flintstones Broadway on Ice: a skating spectacular with Fred Flintstone, Barney Rubble, and Dino.

The Last Buffalo: an all new 3-D experience.

Bird Land Theater: amazing exotic birds to entertain and delight children of all ages.

Rockin' Scooby: Puppet Tree Theater presents performances by Scooby Doo, Yogi Bear, and George Jetson.

SPECIAL ANNUAL EVENT

Carousel to Coaster 10k and 5k Run: in September.

RESTAURANTS

Sprouts, the Salad Bar: self-serve salad bar with fresh vegetables and fixings.

Klondike Cafe: barbecued ribs, chicken, burgers.

Maggie Brown's: fried chicken dinners.

Harbor Inn: seafood, Oriental dinners.

Mexican Cantina: burritos, taco salads.

Hometown Grill: burgers, hot dogs, fries, soft drinks.

All-American Hot Dog Shop: hot dogs, beer, soft drinks.

Pizza Luigi: pizza, beer, soft drinks.

Pizza Orleans: pizza, beer, soft drinks.

Great Northwest Roast Beef Shop: roast beef sandwiches, hot dogs, beer, soft drinks.

Yeoman's Grill: burgers, hot dogs, fries, soft drinks.

A La Burger: burgers, hot dogs, fries, soft drinks.

Snowshoe Saloon

Yogi's Picnic Basket: burgers, hot dogs, fries, soft drinks for kids.

Greedy's Goodies: snacks and beverages for kids.

SNACK BARS

The Yogurt Station: frozen yogurt with assorted toppings.
Country Coolers and California Shakes
The Cache: hot dogs, corn dogs, soft drinks.
Yukon Soft Serve
Farmer's Market: 11 international food stands serve tacos, ice cream, nachos, burgers, croissant sandwiches, hot dogs, Oriental food, corn dogs, fries.
Always on Sundae: ice cream.
Allie's Cookie Kitchen: cookies, baked goods, hot chocolate, coffee.
Hometown Ice Cream
R. B. Floats: root beer floats.
Sticky Fingers: cotton candy, frozen slushes.
Sweet Tooth: funnel cakes, cotton candy, soft drinks.

CATERING

Contact Group Sales at (408) 988-1776.

SOUVENIR SHOPS

Gateway Gifts: a complete selection of souvenirs and gifts.
Happy Hatter: hats for the entire family.
Carousel Plaza Shirts: fun and fashionable T-shirts.
Triple Wheel Souvenirs: candy, stuffed toys, T-shirts.
Hanna-Barbera Collection: stuffed toys and souvenirs.
Moosejaw Trading Post: Western gifts, hats, toys.
Sport Stop: gifts for the sports enthusiast, specializing in baseball and football items.
Fun Shop: colorful gifts and toys for kids.
Mardi Gras Emporium: Great America's biggest selection of gifts, souvenirs, clothing.
Radical! Surf and Skate Shop: posters, T-shirts, and other radical gifts.
Kid's Clothing and Keepsakes: infant and youth clothing, gifts.
Rip Roaring Rapids Souvenirs: T-shirts, ride mementos.

Coaster Station: souvenirs of your favorite rides.
The Painted Shirt: personalized shirts while you wait.
Cartoon Clubhouse: clothing, gifts and plush toys of your favorite cartoon characters.
California Beach Club: fashion for the young and young at heart.
Bayside Boutique: clothing and gifts.
Captain's Quarters: clothing and gifts.
Amazing Pictures: computer-generated pictures on clothing and gifts.
Plaza Camera and Film Shop: featuring free loan of cameras.

HINTS FOR TRAVELING WITH CHILDREN, ELDERLY, HANDICAPPED

Strollers and wheelchairs are available for rent, but guests are usually more comfortable in equipment brought from home. An Infant Care Center in Fort Fun dispenses a complimentary diaper when a child runs short; the center is also a good spot to feed or nurse babies. The lost parents area is also located here, should adults become separated from their children. It's a good idea to carry recent photos of your children, mentally note what each is wearing, and advise kids to ask only costumed park employees for help should they get lost.

HELPFUL TIP ON MAKING YOUR VISIT MORE ENJOYABLE

If you want to exit and reenter, make sure you get your hand stamped.

KNOTT'S BERRY FARM

One of the nation's most popular independently owned family theme parks, Knott's Berry Farm features five areas with different themes: Camp Snoopy, a children's wonderland; Ghost Town, an action-packed authentic Old West mining town; Fiesta Village, a festive salute to California's early Spanish heritage; Roaring '20s, a look back at the colorful amusement parks of the

1920s; and Wild Water Wilderness, a turn-of-the-century California river wilderness park. The 150-acre Knott's Berry Farm, located just 10 minutes from Disneyland, also features a wide assortment of shows and attractions as well as high-energy thrill rides, restaurants, and unique shops.

ADDRESS AND TELEPHONE

Knott's Berry Farm
8039 Beach Boulevard
Buena Park, CA 90620

(714) 220-5200

LOCATION

Knott's Berry Farm is located just 10 minutes north of Disneyland and 40 minutes south of Los Angeles, adjacent to I-5; exit at Buena Park.

OPERATING SEASONS AND HOURS

Open daily year-round. Summer hours: 9 A.M. to 11 P.M., Sunday through Thursday; 9 A.M. to midnight, Friday and Saturday. Winter hours: 10 A.M. to 6 P.M., Monday through Friday; 10 A.M. to 10 P.M., Saturday; 10 A.M. to 7 P.M., Sunday. Closed Christmas Day. Check the park for special holiday hours.

ADMISSION FEES

Adults: $21.95. Children ages 3 to 11: $19.95. Seniors 60 and over: $14.95.

TRANSPORTATION AND ACCOMMODATIONS WITHIN THE PARK

None.

GUEST SERVICES

Restrooms, information center, stroller and wheelchair rental, message center, first aid, lockers, diaper-changing stations, check cashing. Visa, MasterCard, American Express, and Discover cards accepted.

RIDES

Bigfoot Rapids: an exhilarating rafting trip down a raging white water river.
Boomerang: a European-designed roller coaster.
Carousel: an authentic Dentzel carousel.
Kingdom of the Dinosaurs: ride back in time to see the gigantic beasts that ruled the world.
Montezooma's Revenge: soar from 0 to 55 miles per hour in less than five seconds.
Parachute Sky Jump: fall 20 stories in a parachute.
Timber Mountain Log Ride: this log flume ride takes you on a journey through a logging camp and a picturesque forest.
XK-1: you control the flight of your craft seven stories above the ground.

KIDDIE RIDES

High Sierra Ferris Wheel: a scaled-down wheel for kids.
Red Baron: little airplanes.
Timberline Twister: a mini roller coaster.
Walter K. Steamboat: a seaworthy vehicle for a gentle journey.

ATTRACTIONS AND GAMES

Camp Snoopy: a children's wonderland with a California High Sierra theme and featuring Snoopy and his Peanuts friends.
Ghost Town: an action-packed, authentic 1880s Old West mining town complete with cowboys, cancan girls, and gold panning.
Fiesta Village: a festive salute to California's early Spanish heritage, featuring thrill rides.
Roaring '20s: a look back at a colorful amusement park of the 1920s, featuring the Kingdom of the Dinosaurs ride.
Wild Water Wilderness: a turn-of-the-century California river wilderness park

featuring Bigfoot Rapids, an outdoor white water river ride.

Artisans/Craftspeople: stroll through Ghost Town and see their handiwork.

Midway Games: games of skill are located throughout the park.

Buffalo Nickel Arcade: one of the largest west of the Mississippi.

SHOWS

Wild West Stunt Show: watch the high-flying antics of the Wild West.

Old Time Melodramas: soap operas of yesteryear can be viewed in the Bird Cage Theatre.

3-D Movie: watch an old-fashioned 3-D flick in the Cloud 9 Ballroom.

Chevrolet/Geo Good Time Theatre: enjoy musical extravaganzas and celebrity concerts.

SPECIAL ANNUAL EVENT

Halloween Haunt: the park is transformed from "berry" farm to "scary" farm. Rides and attractions are re-themed, and employees dress in Halloween costumes during 10 special nights in October.

RESTAURANTS

Mrs. Knott's Chicken Dinner Restaurant: chicken dinners, salads, vegetables, desserts, drinks. (Located just outside the park.)

The Knott's Family Steakhouse: steaks, seafood, desserts, drinks. (Located just outside the park.)

The Garden Terrace: menus with international flair and themes. Sunday champagne brunches.

SNACK BARS

More than 60 snack stands located throughout the park sell hot dogs, barbecued ribs, Mexican foods, burgers, pizza.

CATERING

Contact the Catering Department at (714) 220-5074.

SOUVENIR SHOPS

Virginia's Gift Shop: souvenirs, decorator items, jewelry, paintings.

Bigfoot Rapids Gift Shop: swimsuits, towels, beachwear, park mementos.

Fiesta Village Gift Shop: Mexican gifts, hats, T-shirts, and other mementos.

Ghost Town Shops: shops located in Ghost Town include a silversmith, glassblower, woodcarver, weaver, candy maker, and more.

The Toy Box: located in Camp Snoopy, sells toys and Peanuts character merchandise.

Gift stands located throughout the park sell T-shirts, Knott's Berry Farm jellies and jams, Snoopy and Peanuts merchandise, and more.

MARINE WORLD AFRICA USA

Marine World Africa USA is the only combination wildlife park and oceanarium in the United States, with 160 acres to showcase animals of land, sea, and air. Visitors experience the animals performing in shows, roaming in innovative habitats, and strolling with their trainers throughout the park. Marine World's unique approach is to provide education through entertainment for approximately 1.5 million visitors each year. In addition to the fast-paced shows and entertainment, some of the most memorable attractions are Butterfly World, a walk-through butterfly habitat; Elephant Encounter, six activity areas to highlight the intelligence and personality of 11 truly magnificent animals; Seal Cove, a sea lion and harbor seal breeding colony; and Tiger Island, home of the park's hand-raised Bengal tigers. Marine World also features "Whale-of-a-Time World" children's playground, a variety of eateries and gift shops, and beautifully landscaped grounds for photographs and picnicking.

ADDRESS AND TELEPHONE

Marine World Africa USA
Marine World Parkway
Vallejo, CA 94589

(707) 643-ORCA

LOCATION

Take I-80 to Marine World Parkway (State Highway 37) exit in Vallejo. High-speed catamaran ferry service is offered daily from San Francisco.

OPERATING SEASONS AND HOURS

Open daily from Memorial Day to Labor Day, and Wednesday through Sunday all year long. Opens at 9:30 A.M. Closing times vary, so check with the park upon arrival.

ADMISSION FEES

Adults: $19.95. Children ages 4 to 12: $14.95. Children 3 and under: free. Seniors 60 and over: $16.95.

TRANSPORTATION AND ACCOMMODATIONS WITHIN THE PARK

None.

GUEST SERVICES

Restrooms, telephones, ATM, information center, lost and found, lost children's area, first aid, diaper-changing areas, storage lockers, wheelchair and stroller rental. Visa, MasterCard, American Express, and Discover cards accepted.

RIDE

Elephant Rides: separate fee.

ATTRACTIONS

Aquarium: galleries display a wide variety of sea life in habitats that range from temperate to tropical.

Butterfly World: the only walk-through, free-flight butterfly habitat west of the Mississippi, featuring more than 500 species.

Elephant Encounter: six activity areas, including log-pull demonstrations, tug-of-war challenges, animal rides, elephant pool, and showers. Designed to be both stimulating for the animals and entertaining for the audience.

Reptile Discovery: get closer and learn more about some of the world's most misunderstood creatures.

Lorikeet Aviary: a free-flight aviary filled with brightly colored, hand-raised lorikeets. Guests can feed the birds.

Gentle Jungle: animal encounter areas with petting corral featuring sheep, goats, llamas, and more; also, small animal exhibits and interactive exhibits geared to children.

Seal Cove: a breeding colony of California sea lions and harbor seals; guests can feed these aquatic creatures.

Tiger Island: habitat for the park's hand-raised Bengal tigers; trainers play, swim, and relax with the cats.

Animal Nursery: where many of the animals born at the park are hand-raised.

Giraffe Feeding Dock: feed the long-necked favorites.

Whale-of-a-Time World Playground: creative play area just for kids featuring punching bag forest, ball crawl, slab slide, tube slide, air bounce, net climb, and more.

Bill's Big Backyard: larger-than-life-sized romping ground for very young tots.

SHOWS

Killer Whale & Dolphin Show: orcas and bottlenose dolphins perform.

Sea Lion Show: a comical and educational show performed by trained sea lions and seals.

Water Ski & Boat Show: the 25-member Marine World International Ski Team demonstrates high-speed feats in a fast-paced show.

Tiger Show: 12 Bengal tigers and two lions perform in a 20-minute show.

Chimpanzee Show: fast-paced and funny, this show highlights the incredible learning abilities and talents of the park's chimpanzees.

Bird Show: exotic birds and birds of prey perform in a clever, informative show.

Wildlife Theatre: an informative show featuring servals, snakes, ferrets, a cheetah, snow leopard, owl, and squirrel monkeys.

Showcase Theatre: a 3,000-seat covered amphitheater offering spectacular new entertainment acts each year for the whole family.

SPECIAL ANNUAL EVENTS

Fourth of July: fireworks display.

Budweiser International Water Ski Championships: first weekend in June, with world-class competition in slalom skiing, freestyle, and distance jumping.

RESTAURANTS

Lakeside Market: farmer's market–style collection of restaurants featuring fried chicken, deli sandwiches, corn dogs, nachos, fries, beer.

The Broiler: burgers, hot dogs, fries, soft drinks.

Captain Mobe's Sea Food: salads, fresh seafood.

Pizza Safari: pizza, beer, wine, margaritas, soft drinks.

SNACK BARS

Kiosks and specialty carts located throughout the park serve corn dogs, nachos, fish and chicken platters, chili, ice cream, and soft drinks.

CATERING

Contact Steve Ramirez at (707) 644-4000, ext. 336.

SOUVENIR SHOPS

Main Gift Shop: gifts, clothing, film, park souvenirs.

Safari and Whale Photos: have your picture taken with an animal or "riding" a life-sized "orca."

Additional shops located throughout the park sell gifts, park mementos, and books.

HELPFUL TIPS ON MAKING YOUR VISIT MORE ENJOYABLE

Be sure to arrive early; it takes a full day to take in all of the park's attractions.

OAKWOOD LAKE RESORT

Oakwood Lake Resort is a 300-acre water theme park and a four-star RV campground. One of the regional summertime attractions of northern California, the park was established 19 years ago and attracts a yearly attendance of 220,000. Oakwood features nine waterslides as well as several other water attractions including The Rampage, a speed slide with a three-story drop. Visitors can also relax by the 75-acre lake's sandy beach or take advantage of the volleyball courts, horseshoe pits, softball fields, and race cars. There is an amphitheater that attracts major concerts. The newest attraction is Castaway Bay, a kiddie cove.

ADDRESS AND TELEPHONE

Oakwood Lake Resort
874 East Woodward
Manteca, CA 95336

(209) 239-2500

LOCATION

Oakwood Lake Resort is located between Stockton and Modesto, between Interstate 5 and Highway 99. Take Highway 120 to Airport Way. Exit south, then go west off Woodward Avenue.

OPERATING SEASONS AND HOURS

Open weekends in May and September. Hours: 10 A.M. to 5 P.M. Open daily from Memorial Day to Labor Day. Hours: from Memorial Day to June 12, 10 A.M. to 5 P.M.; from June 13 to Labor Day, 10 A.M. to 7 P.M.

ADMISSION FEES

General admission and all-day pass: $15.95. General admission and half-day pass: $10.95. Admission only (does not include unlimited use of all rides): $8.95. Children under 48 inches: free.

TRANSPORTATION AND ACCOMMODATIONS WITHIN THE PARK

An RV campground with full hookups is available. (Separate fee.) For information and reservations call (209) 239-9566.

GUEST SERVICES

Restrooms, telephones, information booth, first aid, lockers, lost and found. Visa and MasterCard accepted.

RIDES

The Rampage: after a three-story drop, skim out over the water.
Rapids Ride: swoosh down simulated river rapids in your own inner tube.
The Turbo Tube: launch yourself onto the water in an inflatable boat.

Waterslides: nine different water slides, including the famous Manteca Water Slide, offer lots of slipping, sliding, and sledding fun.

KIDDIE RIDES

Kiddie Slide: a gently sloping slide for the youngest guests.

ATTRACTIONS AND GAMES

Castaway Bay: a kiddie cove for tiny tots.
Oakwood Lake: a 75-acre lake with white sandy beaches.
Volleyball
Softball
Horseshoes
Picnic Grounds
Games

SHOWS

The Oakwood Amphitheatre features concerts throughout the season. Check the park for its schedule.

SPECIAL ANNUAL EVENT

Fourth of July: airshow and fireworks display.

RESTAURANTS

None.

SNACK BARS

Pazzelli's: pizza.
Sweet Shop & Deli: sandwiches, cones, sundaes, banana splits, floats, milk shakes.
Jeremiah's: burgers, fries, hot dogs, nachos.

CATERING

Contact Canteen Corp. at (209) 239-3005.

SOUVENIR SHOPS

Gazebo Gift Shop: towels, sunglasses, shirts, sweatshirts, hats, beach bags.
Print Shop: personalized champagne glasses, buckets, buttons.
Also visit the country store and shopping arcade.

OASIS WATERPARK

Oasis Waterpark is a resort-style water park located in the world-class resort town of Palm Springs, 100 miles east of Los Angeles. Approximately 250,000 patrons visit the surf and slide playground each year. Among the park's attractions are its nine water slides, including the seven-story-tall Scorpions and 45-mile-per-hour Rattlers. Oasis Waterpark, which calls itself "Western America's Deluxe Waterpark," also features California's largest wave pool, private cabana rentals, and sand volleyball courts.

ADDRESS AND TELEPHONE

Oasis Waterpark
1500 Gene Autry Trail
Palm Springs, CA 92264

(619) 325-7873

LOCATION

To get to Oasis Waterpark, take Interstate 10 east from Los Angeles to Gene Autry Trail, then go south 4½ miles. The park is five minutes from downtown Palm Springs.

OPERATING SEASONS AND HOURS

Open weekends in September and October. Hours: 11 A.M. to 6 P.M. Open daily from March 15 to Labor Day. Hours: 11 A.M. to 7 P.M.

ADMISSION FEES

Adults: $15.95. Children 40 inches to 60 inches and seniors: $10.95.

TRANSPORTATION AND ACCOMMODATIONS WITHIN THE PARK

None.

GUEST SERVICES

Restrooms, telephones, private cabanas, lockers and changing rooms, life vests, swim trunks, body-and surfboard rental, private inner tube rentals, first aid. Visa and MasterCard accepted.

RIDES

Inner Tube Slide: swoosh down a wet and wild open inner tube slide.
Rattlers: twist and turn at top speeds on these two thrill slides.
Scorpions: experience a unique thrill on twin 70-foot free-fall slides.
Tube Slides: speed down two enclosed tube slides.
Whitewater River: ride an inner tube on a leisurely 600-foot tour around Island Palms Cafe.

KIDDIE RIDES

Squirt City: children's play area featuring kiddie slide, fountain, low-pressure water cannons, and sea monster.
Tortoise and Hare: minislides for kids 2½ to 6 years old.

ATTRACTIONS AND GAMES

Wave Action Pool: one acre of surface and 850,000 gallons of water form the largest wave action pool in California.

European-Style Health Club: features weight machines, rowing machines, and other health equipment as well as steam room, therapy spa, sauna, and showers. (Separate admission.)

Volleyball: two beach-sand courts.

SHOWS

Occasional concerts in a 5,000-capacity amphitheater. Check the park for its performance schedule and show times.

SPECIAL ANNUAL EVENTS

Spring Break Weeks: water activities with a college theme during March and April.

SNACK BARS

Beach Club Cafe: ham, turkey, and other sandwiches, salads.

Beach Club Walk-Up Window: hot dogs, sub sandwiches, chef salads, nachos, pretzels, wine coolers, beer, soft drinks.

Island Palms: hot dogs, corn dogs, burgers, pizza, fries, candy, chips.

Beach Front: hot dogs, burgers, steak sandwiches, chef salads, candy, chips.

CATERING

Contact Elayne Tunnell at (619) 327-0499.

SOUVENIR SHOP

Balboa Beach Company: beach items and park souvenirs.

PIXIE WOODS

Visitors who pass through the Rainbow Gates of Pixie Woods enter a park filled with lush trees and clear lagoons. But the main feature of the eight-acre theme park is its re-creations of nursery rhyme and fairy tale settings, including Old MacDonald's Farm, Three Little Pigs, Mary Had a Little Lamb, and Alice in Wonderland. Youngsters can also travel forward through time at the Space Center or go back in time at the Frontier Village. Geared to families with young children, the park also offers its 65,000 annual guests rides on the Pixie Queen, a replica of a paddle wheel steamer, and rides on the family carousel.

ADDRESS AND TELEPHONE

Pixie Woods
Louis Park (Monte Diablo and Occidental)
Stockton, CA 95202

(209) 466-9890

LOCATION

Pixie Woods is located in Louis Park in Stockton. Take the Monte Diablo Avenue exit west from Interstate 5 and proceed to the park, at Monte Diablo and Occidental.

OPERATING SEASONS AND HOURS

Open weekends and holidays from the last Sunday in February to the second Sunday in June, and September and October. Hours: noon to 5 P.M. Open Wednesday to Sunday from June to Labor Day. Hours: 11 A.M. to 5 P.M. (except 6 P.M. on Saturday and Sunday).

ADMISSION FEES

Adults: $1.25. Children 12 and under: $1. (Separate fees for rides.)

TRANSPORTATION AND ACCOMMODATIONS WITHIN THE PARK

None.

GUEST SERVICES

Restrooms, telephones, first aid.

RIDES

Merry-Go-Round: whirl around on this full-sized carousel.
Pixie Queen: a 10-minute boat ride on a replica of an old paddle wheel steamer. You pass the lagoon, the erupting Magical Volcano, Pirate Island, Japanese Garden, and more.

KIDDIE RIDE

Merry-Go-Round: a tyke-sized ride. (Free.)

ATTRACTIONS AND GAMES

Tree House: a play area for tots. Inner tubes, slides, and climbing are all situated around a tree.
Fairy Tale and Nursey Rhyme Settings: see re-creations of Mary Had a Little Lamb, Old MacDonald's Farm, Three Little Pigs, and more. Some feature live animals.
Frontier Village: a miniature replica of a Western town where kids can play, climb, and slide on the mini jail, saloon, bank, and barbershop.
Magical Volcano: erupts on the hour with a wonderful spray. Visitors can view it from the paddleboat ride.
Space Center: play area for kids with modernistic play equipment.

SHOWS

Toadstool Theatre: special shows and entertainment for kids.

SPECIAL ANNUAL EVENTS

Easter Special Fun Day: candy for kids, prizes, and drawings on Easter Sunday.
Pixie Woods Special Anniversary: Ronald McDonald visits and entertains on the second Sunday in June.
Christmas in July: Santa visits Pixie Woods and kids get gifts on the second Sunday in July.
Halloween Party: kids dress up in costumes and participate in a costume parade on the last Sunday in October.

RESTAURANTS

None.

SNACK BAR

Hot dogs, burritos, tacos, corn dogs, cotton candy, candy, popcorn, ice cream, drinks, and more.

CATERING

Not available.

SOUVENIR SHOP

T-shirts, bumper stickers, park mementos.

HINT FOR TRAVELING WITH CHILDREN, ELDERLY, HANDICAPPED

Restrooms and walkways are stroller and wheelchair accessible.

RAGING WATERS

Raging Waters, on 44 lush acres, features 5 million gallons of water attractions, sandy beaches, slides, rides, chutes, lagoons, and a children's activity pool. Favorites among its many water rides are the Amazon Adventure, a seemingly endless river ride; the Dark Hole, a two-person raft ride through total darkness; the Drop Out, with a seven-story drop; and, for the park's littlest visitors, Typhoon Lagoon, a children's activity area with floating bridges, slides, and fountains. The park also features nine restaurants and snack shops and an authentic Southern California Beach Shop. Approximately 650,000 guests visit the park annually.

ADDRESS AND TELEPHONE

Raging Waters
111 Raging Waters Drive
San Dimas, CA 91773

(714) 592-6453

LOCATION

Raging Waters is centrally located where the San Bernardino Freeway (10) and Foothill Freeway (210) meet in San Dimas. Exit at Raging Water Drive and drive east to the park entrance.

OPERATING SEASONS AND HOURS

Open weekends in May, early June, September, and to mid-October. Hours: 10 A.M. to 6 P.M. Open daily from early June to Labor Day. Hours: on weekdays, 10 A.M. to 9 P.M.; on weekends, 9 A.M. to 10 P.M.

ADMISSION FEES

Adults: $16.95. Children 42 inches to 48 inches: $8.95. Children under 42 inches: free. Seniors 55 and over: $8.95. Nonparticipants: $8.95.

TRANSPORTATION AND ACCOMMODATIONS WITHIN THE PARK

None.

GUEST SERVICES

Restrooms, telephones, information booth, first aid, lost and found, lockers, free life vests for children, picnic facilities.

RIDES

Amazon Adventure: a seemingly endless river of tropical lagoons, waterfalls, and cool relaxing fun.
Bermuda Triangle: spiral down three 100-foot-long tunnels at speeds up to 25 miles per hour.
Canyon Chute: try this one bareback or with an inner tube.
The Dark Hole: ride in a covered tunnel in total darkness in these two-person inner tubes.
Drop Out: two slides with a seven-story drop reached in less than four seconds, while hitting speeds up to 40 miles per hour.
Raging Rivers: ride an inner tube down a quarter of a mile of churning waterways, complete with whirlpools, white water rapids, dams, and spillways.
Raging Rocket and Screamer: descend from a drop of eight stories at 25 miles per hour.
Rampage: speed 150 feet down this hydro-sled ride to a refreshing splashdown.
Slide Mountain: swoosh down a furious speed slide.
Thunder Run: a speeding chute ride.
Treetop Twister: twist and soar down another chute ride.

ATTRACTIONS AND GAMES

Wave Cove: splash about in a pool featuring three-foot ocean waves.
Typhoon Lagoon: a children's activity island featuring floating bridges, slides, fountains, waterfalls, and water cannons.

Raging Water Pavilion: houses a video and game arcade with 30 of kids' favorite challenges.

RESTAURANTS

None.

SNACK BARS

Food concessions located throughout the park serve hot dogs, burgers, ribs, chicken, pizza, hot fudge sundaes.

CATERING

Contact Group Sales at (714) 592-8181, ext. 205.

SOUVENIR SHOP

Beach Shop: swimwear, T-shirts, sportswear, suntan lotion, film, gifts, park souvenirs.

SEA WORLD OF CALIFORNIA

Sea World of California, a 150-acre marine life park on San Diego's Mission Bay, features more than 20 major exhibits and attractions. Guests have the opportunity to see and interact with marine life at three aquariums: World of the Sea, Marine Aquarium, and the Freshwater Aquarium. At the Dolphin Pool and Forbidden Reef they can touch and feed bottlenose dolphins and bat rays and at the Penguin Encounter are more than 300 of the flightless birds in a simulated Antarctic environment. Sea World features more than six live shows, including Baby Shamu Celebration, Pirates of Pinniped, a tale starring sea lions and otters, and New Friends, a show spotlighting dolphins and small whales. The newest exhibit, a specialized shark habitat, offers a tropical reef environment fea-

turing 300-pound sand tiger sharks, one of the largest displays of these sharks.

ADDRESS AND TELEPHONE

Sea World of California
1720 South Shores Road
Mission Bay
San Diego, CA 92109-7995

(619) 222-6363 or (619) 222-3901

LOCATION

From north or south, exit west from Interstate 5 onto Sea World Drive. From the east, exit from Interstate 8 onto West Mission Bay Drive to Sea World Drive east. Sea World is also accessible by San Diego Transit buses. Call (619) 233-3004 for schedules and routes. The park is also included in a number of sightseeing bus packages.

OPERATING SEASONS AND HOURS

Open daily year-round. Hours: 9 A.M. to dusk. Summer hours from June 12 to Labor Day: 9 A.M. to 11 P.M.

ADMISSION FEES

Adults: $22.95. Children ages 3 to 11: $16.95. Children under 3: free. Seniors 55 and over: $18.35.

TRANSPORTATION AND ACCOMMODATIONS WITHIN THE PARK

None.

GUEST SERVICES

Restrooms, telephones, stroller and wheelchair rental, guided tours, Home Federal Star automated teller machine, camera rental, information center, lost children area, lost and found.

Visa, MasterCard, Carte Blanche, and Diners Club cards accepted.

RIDES

Bayside Skyride: round-trip six-minute skyride along the shore of Mission Bay.

Skytower Ride: see all of Sea World and San Diego on this 265-foot spiral into the sky. Both rides require separate admission.

ATTRACTIONS AND GAMES

Shark Exhibit: a 600,000-gallon encounter with tropical sharks and coral fishes. An acrylic viewing tube that transects the exhibit allows park guests panoramic viewing of some of the largest sharks at any marine life park.

Marine Aquarium: fishes and colorful invertebrates from around the world as well as the Under Water Ski Lagoon stadium.

Freshwater Aquarium: piranhas, four-eyed fish, upside-down catfish, and other amazing freshwater species.

World of the Sea Aquarium: undersea communities of coral reefs, kelp beds, schooling fishes, and game fishes.

Dolphin Pool: meet and feed bottlenose dolphins.

California Tide Pool: touch sea stars, sea urchins, and other amazing inhabitants of California's shallow coastal waters.

Walrus Exhibit: feed the walruses their favorite fishy treats.

Penguin Encounter: more than 300 Antarctic penguins and Arctic alcids in an icy polar environment with entertaining and educational video presentations and continuous viewing.

Avian Exhibits: birds from all over the world.

Forbidden Reef—Bat Ray Shallows & Moray Eel Caverns: feed bat rays as they glide past in a shallow lagoon. Venture below water level and come face-to-face with mysterious moray eels.

Killer Whale Skywalks: rising 10 feet over the Shamu Stadium backstage, the Skywalks are a great place to view and learn about killer whales between shows.

Sea Turtles: fascinating endangered marine turtles.

Seal & Sea Lion Exhibit: feed California sea lions and harbor seals.

Beached Animal Exhibit: feed seals and sea lions rescued from local beaches and nursed back to health at Sea World.

Alaska Sea Otters: these Alaska sea otters were rescued from the Prince William Sound oil spill and remain at Sea World for long-term care and study.

Cap'n Kid's World: more than a dozen creative playground adventures for children.

Cap'n Kid's Boardwalk Games & Remote-Controlled Boats: challenging games of skill for all ages.

SHOWS

Baby Shamu Celebration: Baby Shamu joins Shamu in a spectacular presentation (guests in the first 12 rows may get very wet). At Shamu Stadium.

New Friends Dolphin & Whale Show: several species of whales and dolphins from oceans all over the world perform together in a heartwarming show. At Dolphin Stadium.

Sea Lion and Otter Show—Pirates of Pinniped: join sea lions Clyde and Seamore on yet another saga of high seas comedy.

Spotlight on Commerson's Dolphins: the only Commerson's dolphins on exhibit in the Western Hemisphere in an educational and entertaining presentation. (Doors close promptly at scheduled show times.) At the Underwater Theatre.

Window to the Sea: become an explorer on a fantastic video voyage that opens a window to rarely seen wonders of the sea.

Beach Blanket Ski Party: world-class water-skiers put the sizzle in a '60s-style beach party. At the Water Ski Lagoon.

RESTAURANTS

Harborside Cafe: breakfast and lunch indoors and outdoors; seafood, grilled fajitas, salads, sandwiches, fresh-baked desserts.

Cascades Grill & Cafe: carved roast beef sandwiches, charburgers, deli sandwiches, salads, fresh-baked desserts.

Luigi's Italian Kitchen: pizza, chicken, cannelloni, spaghetti, salads, fresh-baked desserts.

Bakery: cinnamon rolls, sticky buns, muffins, cookies, turnovers, cheesecakes, continental breakfast.

Margaritas: nachos, wine, margaritas, beer.

Chicken 'n' Biscuit: fried chicken, biscuits, fresh-baked desserts.

SNACK BARS

Frosty Cones & Frozen Yogurt: frosty and nonfat frozen yogurt cones and sundaes.

Candy Shop: premium candies, homemade fudge, hand-dipped apples.

A selection of snacks is available in all show areas including popcorn, churros, Mexican-style donuts, ice cream novelties, and soft drinks.

CATERING

Contact Bess Eberhardt at (619) 222-6363, ext. 2090.

SOUVENIR SHOPS

Gifts from Shamu: Shamu gifts, film, sunglasses, inflatables, cameras, sundries, Sea World T-shirts, sweatshirts, hats and caps.

California Clothes & Gifts: beachwear, resort wear, jewelry, sweatshirts, T-shirts, shorts, film.

San Diego/California Gift Shop: San Diego and California souvenirs, T-shirts, sweatshirts, film, baby needs, suncare products.

Shamu Photo Spot: take your picture with costumed Shamu.

Neptune's Locker: unusual gifts, greeting cards, souvenirs, inflatable and plush toys.

Sea World Photo Express: one-hour photo processing with convenient drop-off locations.

Kodak Image Center: film, cameras, and camera rentals including video recorders.

The Whale Shop: whale-themed gifts, apparel, jewelry, posters, and books.

Square Rigger: nautical gifts, selection of brass, souvenirs, shells, film, jewelry, collectibles.

Forbidden Treasures: sterling and gold sea life jewelry, fine collectible figurines, crystal, watches, collector's steins, music boxes, pearl jewelry.

Bat Ray Shallows Souvenirs & Gifts: large selection of apparel, jewelry, sunglasses, plush toys, souvenirs, sundries.

Gems of the Sea: select an oyster and have your pearl mounted in a fine settings.

Amazing Pictures: computerized video photograph on T-shirts, mugs, or posters.

Glassblower: a third-generation artisan creates works of art before your eyes.

California Surf: beachwear, swimwear, sandals, suncare products, straw hats and purses.

Kids' Treasures: toys, novelties, souvenirs.

Cap'n Kid's Photo Key Chain: souvenir photos taken in the Entrance Plaza available for viewing here without obligation.

Penguin Gift Shop: penguin gifts, toys, and apparel.

The Parent's Store: educational toys, globes, science kits, books, games, school supplies. More than 10,000 book titles.

HINTS FOR TRAVELING WITH CHILDREN, ELDERLY, HANDICAPPED

Diaper-changing facilities are located adjacent to several restrooms; check the park maps for locations. For the disabled, Sea World provides special parking, restrooms, telephones, and access to shows and exhibits. Check at the information center if you have special needs.

SENGME OAKS WATER PARK

Sengme Oaks is a small water theme park located near the La Jolla Indian Campground.

The family park features a mushroom waterfall and gentle water slides for young children as well as several speed slides for older visitors. Meadows and woods surround the park and enhance its relaxing setting.

ADDRESS AND TELEPHONE

Sengme Oaks Water Park
Box 158
Valley Center, CA 92082

(619) 742-1921 or (619) 742-1922

LOCATION

Sengme Oaks Water Park is located in the La Jolla Indian Reservation northeast of San Diego and seven miles west of Lake Henshaw along Highway 76. From San Diego take I-15 north to Valley Center Parkway in Escondido. Continue north to Highway 76 and go east 8½ miles to the entrance. From Orange, Riverside, and Los Angeles counties, take I-15 south to Highway 76, then go east. Follow the signs to the park.

OPERATING SEASONS AND HOURS

Open Wednesday to Sunday from May to September. Hours: 10 A.M. to 5:30 P.M. on weekdays; 10 A.M. to 6 P.M. on weekends.

ADMISSION FEES

Adults: $9.95. Children ages 4 to 11: $8.95. Children 3 and under: free. Seniors 65 and over: $5.

TRANSPORTATION AND ACCOMMODATIONS WITHIN THE PARK

None.

GUEST SERVICES

Restrooms, telephones, showers, lockers, tube vests for small children, barbecue pit, and picnic area. Visa and MasterCard accepted.

RIDES

Giant Slides: two giant 350-foot slides end in a large pool.
Rampage: sled down this speed slide.
Speed Slides: plunge 500 feet on these two speed slides.

KIDDIE RIDES

Kiddie Slides: two gentle slides in the activity pool.

ATTRACTIONS AND GAMES

Activity Pool: splash about under the mushroom fountain, then try the ramp slide.
Children's Playground
Volleyball
Horseshoe Pitch

RESTAURANTS

None.

SNACK BAR

Hot dogs, tacos, nachos, burgers, fries, corn dogs, candy, chips, soft drinks.

CATERING

Not available.

SOUVENIR SHOPS

None.

SIX FLAGS MAGIC MOUNTAIN

Six Flags Magic Mountain is a 260-acre family theme park offering more than 100 rides, shows, and attractions for enthusiasts of all ages. The newest ride is Psyclone, a relentless classic wooden roller coaster replica of New York's legendary Coney Island Cyclone. Roller coaster fans will also enjoy Colossus, Revolution, Ninja, and Viper, the world's tallest looping roller coaster. Roaring Rapids, Freefall, Tidal Wave, and many more exciting rides are also featured. The family will enjoy musical reviews, magic shows, high-dive exhibitions, and browsing through Cyclone Bay, a new beachfront boardwalk themed area. There are also patriotic fireworks and laser shows and, just for kids, Bugs Bunny World featuring pint-sized rides and the Wile E. Coyote Critter Canyon Animal Farm and Petting Zoo.

ADDRESS AND TELEPHONE

Six Flags Magic Mountain
P. O. Box 5500
Valencia, CA 91385

(805) 255-4111

LOCATION

Magic Mountain is located 25 minutes north of Hollywood and one hour south of Bakersfield. Take I-5 north and exit at Magic Mountain Parkway.

OPERATING SEASONS AND HOURS

Open weekends and school holidays from Labor Day to Memorial Day. Open daily from Memorial Day to Labor Day. Opens at 10 A.M. Closing hours vary, so check with the park upon arrival.

ADMISSION FEES

Adults: $24. Children below 48 inches: $14. Children 2 and under: free. Seniors over 55: $16.

TRANSPORTATION AND ACCOMMODATIONS WITHIN THE PARK

None.

GUEST SERVICES

Restrooms, telephones, information booths, check cashing, first aid, kennels, lockers, lost children, lockers, pet kennels, ATM terminals, lost and found, stroller and wheelchair rentals, camera rentals, baby care center, picnic facilities. Citibank Classic MasterCard, Visa, American Express, and Discover cards accepted.

RIDES

Buccaneer: climb aboard a pirate ship that runs amok.
Colossus: one of the world's tallest, longest, and fastest dual-track coasters with a 115-foot hill.
Eagle's Flight: soar high in an aerial gondola.
Freefall: discover the sensation of weightlessness during an unrestricted 10-story drop.
Gold Rusher: experience a runaway mine train adventure.
Grand Carousel: a nostalgic ride on a restored 1912 carousel.
Jet Stream: sleek boats zoom you around a scenic hillside.
Log Jammer: a smooth and splashy journey in a hollowed-out log.
Metro: a monorail takes you to the top of Samurai Summit.
Ninja: experience high-speed spirals and daring vertical drops at speeds up to 55 miles per hour.
Orient Express: a tram ride to the top of Samurai Summit.
Psyclone: an all new replica of the famous Coney Island Cyclone, this relentless wooden coaster begins with a 95-foot drop and continues with five fan-banked turns, 10 more drops, and a 183-foot tunnel.
Reactor: an updated fast, thrill ride.
Revolution: a daring ride at 55 miles per hour through steep drops and a 360-degree vertical loop.

Roaring Rapids: a rafting excursion through rapids, crosscurrents, and waterfalls.

Sandblasters: classic bumper cars.

Sky Tower: take an elevator up 380 feet for a spectacular view of the park.

Subway: gravity plays havoc in the darkness.

Tidal Wave: hop aboard 20-passenger boats that plunge over a 50-foot waterfall, then splash down and create a 20-foot-tall wave of water.

Turbo: stand and spin.

Viper: the world's tallest looping roller coaster.

Z-Force: step inside the cockpit of a Navy fighter for a furious flight, complete with two 360-degree vertical loops.

KIDDIE RIDES

At Bugs Bunny World:

Baron Von Fudd: kids control mini prop planes.

Bunny Hole: tunnels and tunnels of fun.

The Carousel: beautiful ponies on a minicarousel.

Daffy Duck Duners: little ones speed away on dune buggies.

Elmer Fudd Orchard: round and round a big red apple in a wacky worm.

Honey Bunny Bugs: colorful ladybugs circle a giant mushroom.

Merlin the Magic Mouse Cars: mini mice cars circle a giant Swiss cheese.

Road Runner Racers: Grand Prix–style race cars.

Schmatterhorn: a colorful ocean of plastic balls.

Tasmanian Devil Cycles: excitement on three-wheel cycles.

Tweety Bird Cage: kids spin around in Tweety's bird cage.

Wile E. Coyote Coaster: minihills and minithrills.

Yosemite Sam Pirate Ship: kids stow away on a pirate ship.

At Critter Canyon:

Granny Gran Prix: miniature antique car ride through Wile E. Coyote Critter Canyon.

ATTRACTIONS AND GAMES

Wile E. Coyote Critter Canyon: a "please touch" petting zoo with dozens of cuddly goats and sheep and more than 55 species of rare and exotic animals.

Bugs Bunny Snapshot Photo Spot: take your picture with the Looney Tunes characters during scheduled appearances. (Check with the park for a schedule.)

After Hours Dance Club: state-of-the-art open-air dance club, open nightly from dusk to closing.

Cyclone Bay: home of the Psyclone, the all new beachfront area reminiscent of the boardwalk scene of yesteryear.

Center Ring Games: challenging games of skill with fun and prizes.

Mining Town Games & Arcade: games of skill and video challenges.

The Palace Arcade: Skee ball and other arcade games.

Boomball and Arcade: challenging games of skill including air-powered cannons and the largest game room arcade in the park.

Sharkey's Shooting Gallery: lets you test your skills in an electronic shooting gallery, located in the Cyclone Bay.

SHOWS

The Bugs Bunny Magic World of Kids: Bugs leads a cast of Looney Tunes characters through feats of magic, song, and dance.

U. S. High-Dive Stage and Stunt Show: world-class high divers perform amazing and often humorous feats.

Foghorn Leghorn Wild Animal Show: educational show featuring exotic animals.

Strictly U.S.A.: red, white, and blue fireworks extravaganza nightly from June to September.

Over the Hill Ninja Show: puppet show atop Samurai Summit.

Six Flags also features a variety of concerts and special events throughout the summer. Check with the park for its schedule.

SPECIAL ANNUAL EVENT

Toys for Tots: admission is free to anyone bringing a new toy, valued at $5 or more, on the first two weekends in December.

RESTAURANTS

Four Winds Restaurant: seafood, salad bar, sandwiches.

Timbermill Restaurant: roast beef, chicken strips, burgers, desserts.

Food Etc.: barbecue, tacos, pasta, deli subs, salads, frozen yogurt, baked goods.

Suzette's Bakery: cinnamon rolls, muffins, funnel cakes.

Wascal's: burgers, chicken strips, fries, salads, shakes, drinks.

Guido's: pizza.

Ninja Dog: grilled hot dogs, chili dogs, fries, drinks.

The Waterfront: burgers, pizza, ice cream.

Katy's Kettle: burgers, chicken strips, fries, salads, drinks.

Colossus Cookery: burgers, chicken strips, fries, salads.

Dock Side Deli: sandwiches, pizza.

Valencia Terrace Chicken Plantation: fried chicken, fish and chips, drinks.

Carnation Corner: ice cream, drinks.

Time Out: hot dogs, corn dogs, fries, drinks.

Baja Cantina: nachos, burritos, tacos.

SNACK BARS

Stands located throughout the park serve ice cream, pretzels, popcorn, ices, soft frozen lemonade, soft drinks.

CATERING

Contact Group Sales at (805) 255-4500.

SOUVENIR SHOPS

Holiday Bazaar: Magic Mountain merchandise, clothing, glassware, sunglasses, stuffed toys, film, cameras.

Remember When: Looney tunes merchandise and handcrafts, Coca-Cola collector items, nostalgic gifts.

Totally Tunes: Looney Tunes and Tiny Tunes giftware.

Tidal Wave Shop: T-shirts, hats, clothing, beachwear.

Head Gear: hats with free name embroidery on certain styles.

Ninja Ride Shop: coaster merchandise.

Amazing Pictures: photograph your face on a new body.

Pair-A-Scopes: photo souvenirs.

At Cyclone Bay:

Bay Glass and Jewelry: hand-twisted wire name jewelry, hand-blown glass figures.

T.A.G.S.: active-wear clothing.

California Precious Cargo: shell and rock collectibles, figurines.

Psyclone Souvenirs: Psyclone ride souvenirs, shark paraphernalia.

Muscle Beach Airbrush and Arcade: hand-painted T-shirts, video arcade.

Pacific Coast Candles

Santa Cruz Accessories

Bay Shore Candy

Big Daddy's Photographic Emporium

UNIVERSAL STUDIOS HOLLYWOOD

Universal Studios Hollywood offers a unique, behind-the-scenes look at the world's biggest motion picture and television studio. A seven-hour excursion through Universal's famed 420-acre front and back lots is highlighted by an encounter with a 6½-ton, 30-foot-tall King Kong; "Earthquake . . . the Big One," a stunning re-creation of an upheaval measuring 8.3 temblor on the Richter scale; as well as the great white shark Jaws, a collapsing bridge, and Flash Flood. Walk along Streets of the World, accessible-to-the-public motion picture sets from your favorite movies. And experience "The E.T. Adventure," where you soar to the stars on a bicycle. Visitors also can participate in special effects on a sound stage and view such live special-effects shows as *Star Trek Adventure*,

Miami Vice Action Spectacular, Animal Actors Stage, Conan, and *The Riot Act.*

ADDRESS AND TELEPHONE

Universal Studios Hollywood
100 Universal City Plaza
Universal City, CA 91608

(818) 508-9600

LOCATION

Universal Studios Hollywood is located just off the Hollywood Freeway (101) at either Universal Center or the Lankershim Boulevard exit.

OPERATING SEASONS AND HOURS

Open daily year-round except Christmas and Thanksgiving. Hours: 9 A.M. to 5 P.M.

ADMISSION FEES

Adults: $24.50. Children ages 3 to 11 and seniors 60 and over: $19.00. Children under 3: free.

TRANSPORTATION AND ACCOMMODATIONS WITHIN THE PARK

Tram tour.

GUEST SERVICES

Restrooms, telephones, information booths, message centers, first aid, kennels, lockers, lost and found, strollers, wheelchairs. Visa, MasterCard, American Express, Diners Club, and Carte Blanche cards accepted.

RIDES

The E.T. Adventure: riders climb aboard star-bound bicycles and, with the help of a dazzling array of never-before-seen special effects, venture with E.T. across the endless universe in an effort to save his home.

ATTRACTIONS

Guided Tram Excursions: this guided open-air super tram tour offers a rare look at Universal Studios' famed back lot. Before you're even around the first turn you're intercepted by alien creatures piloting a Cylon tank. They blast the tram into a giant spaceship. Visitors view the Battle of Galactica, the world's largest permanent laser display, ride past the Burning House, then see such creatures as 30-foot-tall King Kong and experience the collapsing bridge, the parting of the Red Sea, the Doomed Glacier Expedition, and Earthquake . . . the Big One.

Streets of the World: walk among famous Hollywood movie sets including Baker Street in London, Sherlock Holmes's famous haunt; Mel's Diner from *American Graffiti*; and Faber College of *Animal House.*

K.I.T.T.: the sleek, black, talking car from TV's "Knight Rider" answers visitors' questions.

Costumed Characters: filmdom's most famous characters, including Charlie Chaplin, the Phantom of the Opera, Woody Woodpecker, Frankenstein, W. C. Fields, and Beetlejuice, can be found throughout the park.

Lucy: A Tribute: in this one-of-a-kind tribute full of rare memorabilia, film footage, and family photographs, fans can literally "walk through" the public and private life of that famous redhead, Lucille Ball.

The World of Cinemagic: reveals rare behind-the-scenes glimpses and interactive participation in the thrilling world of Hollywood motion picture technology.

SHOWS

The Star Trek Adventure: audience members, using costumes, sets, film footage, and special effects, seemingly appear in a feature alongside costars William Shatner as Admiral Kirk and Leonard Nimoy as Captain Spock.

Miami Vice Action Spectacular: live-action extravaganza featuring more than 50 live stunts and special effects within a 15-minute show. Held in a 3,000-seat outdoor arena with a West Indies theme.

The Adventures of Conan: inspired by the films *Conan the Barbarian* and *Conan the Destroyer*, the show features 20 minutes of death-defying stunts, special effects, and lasers.

The Riot Act: a 15-minute show where stunt experts use their skills dodging shotgun blasts, having bottles broken over their heads, riding wild horses, and falling 30 feet to the ground.

Animal Actors Stage: Mickey the Chimp, Hoby the Cat, and other animal stars re-create their television and movie tricks.

An American Tail: this children's attraction brings to life one of the most popular American films with a full musical stage production and the world's most unusual playground featuring 15-foot banana peel slides and giant lobster traps.

RESTAURANTS

Moulin Rouge: herb chicken, spinach soufflé, seafood croissants, wine, beer, drinks.

Mel's Diner: burgers, hot dogs, apple pie, sundaes, fare of the 1950s.

Winston's Grill: English foods, bangers, barbecued chicken, ribs, desserts.

Hollywood Cantina: tacos, tostadas.

Il Ristorante: pasta, pizza.

Alfa Inn: an English pub and full-service bar.

Studio Commissary: pizza, salads, chili, chicken filets.

SNACK BAR

River Boat: hot dogs, pretzels, popcorn, soft drinks.

CATERING

Contact Rayanne Myers at (818) 777-3950.

SOUVENIR SHOPS

Silver Screen Store: posters, celebrity porcelain dolls, movie-abilia, including personally autographed artifacts from stars such as Gary Cooper, Jayne Mansfield, and Humphrey Bogart.

Emporium: Universal mementos and traditional souvenirs.

Woody's Cartoon Corner: Woody the Woodpecker drawings, Woody plush toys.

Cote de California: California casual clothing and gear.

Lucy Shop: Lucille Ball merchandise.

Studio Store: movie memorabilia.

HELPFUL TIP ON MAKING YOUR VISIT MORE ENJOYABLE

Bring plenty of film because photo opportunities abound (such as snapping a picture of your child in the grasp of King Kong).

WILD RIVERS WATER PARK

Wild Rivers Water Park, Orange County's newest water theme park, is located on 20 tropical acres. The park offers a plethora of water rides and activities, including WIPEOUT! in which 200 gallons of water "flush" you down a super flume ride; Serengeti Surf Hill, made up of seven lanes of ultrafast downhill sliding; and Monsoon Lagoon, a gentle wave pool. For the park's youngest visitors there's Typhoon Lagoon with its scaled-down version of many of the adult water rides.

ADDRESS AND TELEPHONE

Wild Rivers Water Park
8770 Irvine Center Drive
Irvine, CA 92718

(714) 768-WILD

LOCATION

South of Los Angeles, Wild Rivers is located just off the 405 San Diego Freeway at Irvine Center Drive, adjacent to Irvine Meadows Amphitheatre. From the 405 San Diego Freeway, take the Irvine Center Drive exit south ½ mile. From the I-5 Santa Ana Freeway, take the Lake Forest Drive exit west to Irvine Center Drive and go north one mile.

OPERATING SEASONS AND HOURS

Open weekends from mid-May to mid-June and in September. Hours: 11 A.M. to 5 P.M. Open daily from mid-June to early September. Hours: 10 A.M. to 8 P.M.

ADMISSION FEES

Adults: $15.95. Children ages 3 to 9: $11.95. Seniors 55 and over, spectators, and guest admitted after 4 P.M.: $7.95.

TRANSPORTATION AND ACCOMMODATIONS WITHIN THE PARK

None.

GUEST SERVICES

Restrooms, telephones, first aid, lost and found, locker rentals. Visa and MasterCard accepted.

RIDES

Bombay Blasters: feel as if you're being shot from a cannon barrel before plunging into water.

The Cobra: enjoy breathtaking twists and turns from top to bottom.
Congo River Rapids: white water inner tubing down the side of a mountain.
Hurricane Harbor: bodyboard on one perfect wave after another.
Lake Victoria: adult pool with a speed slide.
Nairobi Express: a high-speed ride through a dark mountain tunnel.
Safari River Expedition: grab an inner tube, then float and relax for a quarter of a mile.
Serengeti Surf Hill: seven lanes across of superfast downhill sliding for the entire length of a football field.
Sweitzer Falls: take a speedy slide down the falls, then shoot out three feet above water.
Wahtubee: a high-speed double-drop slide.
WIPEOUT!: 200 gallons of water "flush" you down a spectacular flume ride.

KIDDIE RIDES

Dinosaur Slide: a slide and a swing on a lovable two-headed dinosaur.
Pygmy Pond: less than one foot deep, this features a gorilla swing and an elephant slide.
Typhoon Lagoon: miniversions of Congo River Rapids, The Cobra, and other adult water rides.

ATTRACTIONS AND GAMES

Monsoon Lagoon: bodysurf, ride an inner tube, or surf on these gentle waves.
Water Walk: stroll through a trail surrounded by geysers.
Mombasa Hot Springs: giant-sized Jacuzzi pools.
Sun 'n' Sand Volleyball: a real sand volleyball court.
Tim-buk-tu Arcade

RESTAURANT

Colonel Hawkins Outpost: sandwiches, fries, snacks, drinks.

SNACK BARS

Pizza Junction
Carnation Ice Cream Hut

CATERING

Contact Quality Food Service at (714) 581-6840.

SOUVENIR SHOP

Trader Robbie's Safari Outfitters: swimsuits, towels, suntan lotion, film, souvenirs.

WINDSOR WATERWORKS & SLIDES

Windsor Waterworks & Slides is a complete family recreation park located in Sonoma County, California. Main attractions are its four 400-foot water slides where visitors can speed and spiral through tunnels and slopes, finally landing in a splashdown pool. The park also offers a swimming pool, children's wading pool, and landscaped picnic grounds with barbecues. Visitors can entertain themselves at the horseshoe pits, Ping-Pong tables, video arcade, snack bar, and souvenir shop.

ADDRESS AND TELEPHONE

Windsor Waterworks & Slides
8225 Conde Lane
Windsor, CA 95492

(707) 838-7360

LOCATION

Located six miles north of Santa Rosa, Windsor Waterworks is next to Highway 101; take the Windsor exit.

OPERATING SEASONS AND HOURS

Open daily from mid-June to Labor Day. Hours: weekdays from 11 A.M. to 7 P.M.; weekends from 10 A.M. to dusk. Also open weekends in May and September. Hours may vary, so check with the park before arriving.

ADMISSION FEES

Weekends: Adults: $10. Children ages 2 to 12: $9. Children under 2: free.
  Weekdays: Adults: $9. Children ages 2 to 12: $8. Children under 2: free.

TRANSPORTATION AND ACCOMMODATIONS WITHIN THE PARK

None.

GUEST SERVICES

Restrooms, showers, locker rentals. Visa and MasterCard accepted.

RIDES

Body Flumes: four 400-foot flumes. You lie on a foam rubber mat, take a 42-foot drop, then speed through tunnels, around spirals, and up and over slopes, finally landing in a splashdown pool.

ATTRACTIONS AND GAMES

Swimming Pool
Wading Pool: for small children.
Video Arcade
Ping-Pong Tables
Horseshoe Pits

RESTAURANTS

None.

SNACK BAR

Pizza pockets, hot dogs, candy, popcorn, drinks.

CATERING

Not available.

SOUVENIR SHOP

Park mementos, T-shirts, shorts, tank tops.

HAWAII

SEA LIFE PARK HAWAII

Located an easy 30-minute drive from Waikiki, Sea Life Park Hawaii is home to thousands of marine creatures. At Whaler's Cove, performing whales and dolphins help tell tales of old Hawaii in an entertaining water show. An all new ⅝-scale replica of the whaling ship *Essex* lets you go below deck to get a special underwater view of the whales, dolphins, and the world's only known living "wholphin," a unique hybrid of a whale and a dolphin. Other attractions include the Hawaii Ocean Theatre, Kolohe Kai sea lion show, Hawaii Reef Tank, Pacific Whaling Museum, sea lion feeding pool, and Turtle Lagoon.

ADDRESS AND TELEPHONE

Sea Life Park Hawaii
Makapuu Point
Waimanalo, HI 96795

(808) 259-7933 or (808) 923-1531

LOCATION

Sea Life Park is on the easternmost tip of Oahu. Take Kalanianaole Highway east to Makapuu Point; the park entrance is on your left. Many tour companies offer sightseeing packages that include a visit to the park. The park can also be reached by city bus. (Check the park for schedules.)

OPERATING SEASONS AND HOURS

Open daily year-round. Hours 9:30 A.M. to 5 P.M., except until 10 P.M. on Friday.

ADMISSION FEES

Adults: $14.25. Children ages 7 to 12: $9.50. Children ages 4 to 6: $4.95.

TRANSPORTATION AND ACCOMMODATIONS WITHIN THE PARK

None.

GUEST SERVICES

Restrooms, telephones, information area, first aid, stroller rental, wheelchairs. Visa, MasterCard, American Express, and JCB cards accepted.

RIDES

None.

ATTRACTIONS

Pacific Whale Museum: collection of authentic scrimshaw and historical whaling artifacts.

Shark Gallery: everything you wanted to know about sharks.

Sea Lion Feeding Pool: purchase fish to feed to a colony of sea lions.

Seal Pool

Hawaiian Monk Seal Care Center: endangered species of seals are cared for here until they can be returned to their native home.

Touch Tank Environment: touch marine creatures.

Turtle Lagoon: several species of turtles flap their flippers in this special exhibit.

Hawaiian Reef Tank: view thousands of colorful creatures living in a 300,000-gallon aquarium.

Rocky Shores: an exhibit that reproduces the conditions of the intertidal zone with its pounding surf, wave-swept rocks, and quiet pools.

Bird Sanctuary: red-footed and brown boobies, gooney birds, and iwa birds.

Penguin Habitat: this exhibit houses the world's only endangered penguin species—the Humboldt penguin.

SHOWS

Whaler's Cove: the whaling days of old Hawaii are recalled by a team of dolphins and island maidens.

Hawaiian Ocean Theatre: dolphins display their talent in this open-air amphitheater.

Kolohe Kai Sea Lion Show: these rascals of the sea strut their stuff.

In addition, each Friday night at 8:30 P.M. Hawaii's best entertainers perform on the Sea Lion Cafe Stage.

SPECIAL ANNUAL EVENTS

Humpback Whale Awareness Month: conservation program, including lectures, and marine artist youth competition in February.

Zoo and Aquarium Month: features free behind-the-scenes tours and special educational activities in June.

RESTAURANTS

Rabbit Island Bar & Grill: burgers, hot dogs, salads, sandwiches, and such local Hawaiian dishes as Kahlua pig and Lomi Lomi salmon.

Sea Lion Cafe: a variety of hot entrees, hamburgers, salads, and island food.

SNACK BARS

Snack stands located throughout the park serve hot dogs, nachos, ice cream, soft drinks.

CATERING

Contact the Sales Office at (808) 923-1531.

SOUVENIR SHOPS

Sea Life General Store: island gift items and Sea Life Park memorabilia, items with a nautical theme.

Makapuu Marketplace: unusual mementos of Hawaii.

HINTS FOR TRAVELING WITH CHILDREN, ELDERLY, HANDICAPPED

Sea Life Park Hawaii is ramped to accommodate wheelchairs and handicapped persons. Baby strollers are available to rent.

WAIMEA FALLS PARK

Situated within a historic and beautiful 1,800-acre Hawaiian valley, Waimea Falls Park showcases more than 30 tropical and subtropical gardens. The park offers spectacular cliff-diving exhibitions, hula demonstrations, and guided tours of the grounds and historic sites. Visitors can also see native wildlife and try their hand at such ancient games as o'o'ihe (spear throwing) and 'ulu maika (lawn bowling).

ADDRESS AND TELEPHONE

Waimea Falls Park
59-864 Kamehameha Highway
Haleiwa, HI 96712

(808) 638-8511 or (808) 923-8448

LOCATION

From Honolulu, drive west on the H-1 freeway to H-2 freeway and then to Kamehameha Highway. The park's entrance will be on the right, across from Waimea Bay.

OPERATING SEASONS AND HOURS

Open daily year-round. Hours: 10 A.M. to 5:30 P.M.

ADMISSION FEES

Adults: $13.95. Children ages 7 to 12: $7.50. Children ages 4 to 6: $2.75

TRANSPORTATION AND ACCOMMODATIONS WITHIN THE PARK

An open-air minibus offers a narrated scenic tour of the trip to the park's 45-foot waterfall and back. (The tram leaves every 15 minutes.)

GUEST SERVICES

Restrooms, telephones, information booth, first aid, lost and found, wheelchairs. Visa, MasterCard, and American Express cards accepted.

RIDES

None.

ATTRACTIONS AND GAMES

Botanical Gardens: in the park's major attraction there are more than 30 gardens containing tropical and subtropical flora from Hawaii and around the world. Regional gardens contain flora from Guam, Sri Lanka, and Madagascar, and there is also a lei garden. Native Hawaiian plants and flowers are featured, and the gardens contain many rare and exotic species.

Wildlife Area: see lemurs from Madagascar, nene geese (a rare and protected species, and the Hawaiian state bird), and the Hawaiian stilt.

Educational Center: learn about plant life.

Ancient Hawaiian Historical Sites: visit actual archaeological sites and get a taste of Hawaiian history.

Guided Park Tours: trained park guides lead walking tours throughout the day that highlight different sections of the park. Tours include the Burial Temple Tour and the Upper Valley Garden Tour. Check with the park for a schedule.

Moonwalk: stroll to the waterfall and back under a full moon two evenings per month in a relaxing guided tour. Check with the park for dates and times. (A donation to the Waimea Arboretum Foundation is suggested: $1 for individuals, $5 for families.)

Hawaiian Games Site: guests can participate in such ancient Hawaiian games as o'o'ihe (spear throwing), 'ulu maika (lawn bowling), and moa pahe'e (dart sliding).

SHOWS

Cliff-diving: world-class divers plunge into a pool five times daily.

Hula: the kahiko (ancient) Hawaiian hula is presented by the park's resident hula troupe four times daily.

SPECIAL ANNUAL EVENTS

Makahiki Festival: a two-day celebration of Hawaiian history and culture, including hula competition, hula performances, arts and crafts, Hawaiian games and foods—on the first weekend in October.

Keiki (Children's) Fishing Festival: fun and prizes for children 3 to 10 years old in September.

RESTAURANTS

Pikake Pavilion: this open-air dining facility overlooking a meadow serves lunch and dinner. Dishes include barbecued ribs, mahimahi, Hawaiian-style pork, and chicken.

Proud Peacock Restaurant: island fish, burgers, salads, beef, pork, chicken, sandwiches, desserts, drinks. (Dinner only.)

SNACK BARS

Snack stands located throughout the park serve sandwiches, burgers, ice cream, shaved ice, drinks.

CATERING

Contact Sales Office at (808) 923-8448.

SOUVENIR SHOPS

Charlie's Country Store: Hawaiian arts and crafts, books, videos, T-shirts, hats, park memorabilia.

Logo Shop: Waimea Falls T-shirts, hats, glasses, towels.

HELPFUL TIPS ON MAKING YOUR VISIT MORE ENJOYABLE

Plan to spend an entire day exploring the park. A good agenda is first to ride the tram to the waterfall, then take a leisurely walk back down, enjoying the numerous gardens and trails along the way either on your own or with a guided tour.

OREGON

WILDLIFE SAFARI

Wildlife Safari is Oregon's natural wildlife experience. The 600-acre drive-through animal park is home to more than 600 creatures of distinction from Africa, Asia, and North America. The variety of species includes African lions, Bengal tigers, African elephants, Damara zebras, cheetahs, bears, and various feathered friends. These animals can be studied up close while they are interacting in their natural habitats. Additional attractions include elephant and train rides, the Safari Village with its sparkling new White Rhino Restaurant, live animal shows, and a petting zoo. The park draws an annual attendance of more than 170,000 guests.

ADDRESS AND TELEPHONE

Wildlife Safari
P. O. Box 1600
Winston, OR 97496-0231

(503) 679-6761

LOCATION

Wildlife Safari is located in southern Oregon. Take Oregon Interstate 5 to Winston exit 119 (Highway 42 west) by Roseburg. Follow the well-marked signs to the park.

OPERATING SEASONS AND HOURS

Open daily year-round. Opens at 9 A.M. in the fall and spring and 8:30 A.M. in the summer. Closing times vary from 4 P.M. to 8 P.M., so check with the park upon arrival.

ADMISSION FEES

Adults: $8.95. Children ages 4 to 12: $5.75. Children under 4: free. Seniors 65 and over: $7.50. Vehicle charge: $1.

TRANSPORTATION AND ACCOMMODATIONS WITHIN THE PARK

Rental vehicles are available by reservation. Self-contained RV facilities are available.

GUEST SERVICES

Restrooms, telephones, information booth, kennels, lost and found. Visa, MasterCard, American Express, Discover, Carte Blanche, and Diners Club cards accepted.

RIDES

Elephant Rides: straddle the back of a 6,000-pound African elephant.

Train Rides: journey through the Safari Village which has an extraordinary view of the beautiful valley and exotic animals.

ATTRACTIONS

Petting Zoo: pet barnyard animals.

Wildlife Photo Booths: take your picture with one of the Safari Village's show animals.

SHOWS

Live Animal Shows: programs include elephants, birds of prey, and reptiles, with keeper talks and more; daily in the summer and on weekends in the fall and spring.

Wildlife Films: these 15-minute animal adventure films are shown throughout the day to educate, entertain, and reinforce zoological facts that are learned throughout the park trek.

RESTAURANT

White Rhino: features a healthy homemade soup and salad bar, deli sandwiches, burgers, fresh desserts, ice cream, and daily specialties. Open for dinner during the summer, breakfast and lunch year-round.

SNACK BAR

Cookies, hot dogs, soft drinks.

CATERING

Contact the office at (503) 679-6761.

SOUVENIR SHOP

Casbah Gift Shop: T-shirts, toys, books, jewelry, fine art objects, posters, park mementos.

HELPFUL TIP ON MAKING YOUR VISIT MORE ENJOYABLE

To see the animals at their most active, visit in the early morning or in the evening and on the coolest days.

WASHINGTON

SPLASH-DOWN

Splash-Down is a water theme park located five miles east of downtown Spokane, Washington. About 400 visitors every day enjoy the 3½-acre attraction that features water slides for both adults and children. The park also has a baseball diamond, tennis courts, and basketball and volleyball courts.

ADDRESS AND TELEPHONE

Splash-Down
East 12727 Piper Road
Spokane, WA 99207

(509) 924-3079

LOCATION

Splash-Down is located five miles east of downtown Spokane. Take I-90 to the Pines exit.

OPERATING SEASONS AND HOURS

Open daily from Memorial Day to Labor Day. Hours: 10 A.M. to 7 P.M., except noon to 7 P.M. on Sunday.

ADMISSION FEES

Adults: $7.95. Children ages 4 to 11: $6.95. Children under 3: free. Seniors 60 and over: $4.

TRANSPORTATION AND ACCOMMODATIONS WITHIN THE PARK

None.

GUEST SERVICES

Restrooms, telephones, information booth, changing rooms, towel rental, lockers. Visa and MasterCard accepted.

RIDES

Slides: soar down four 400-foot slides.

KIDDIE RIDES

Mini-Slides: four tyke-sized slides and three wading pools.
Merry-Go-Round

ATTRACTIONS AND GAMES

Tennis Courts
Baseball Diamond
Video Room
Volleyball
Basketball Court
Horseshoes
Two Hot Spas
Picnic Area with Barbecue Grills

RESTAURANTS

None.

SNACK BAR

Burgers, hot dogs, pizza, corn dogs, nachos, fries, ice cream, soft drinks.

CATERING

Contact (509) 924-3079.

SOUVENIR SHOP

Swimsuits, shorts, T-shirts, park souvenirs, candy, suntan lotion, sunglasses.

WILD 'N WET WATER PARK

Spread across 10 acres of the Pacific Northwest, Wild 'N Wet Water Park hosts 40,000 visitors annually. The park features four large twisting flumes, a river ride, ramp slide, kiddie play area, and a hot tub with room for 100 bathers. Visitors can also enjoy the picnic area and volleyball court, or just soak up the sun.

ADDRESS AND TELEPHONE

Wild 'N Wet Water Park
4874 Birch Bay–Lynden Road
Blaine, WA 98230

(206) 371-7500

LOCATION

Wild 'N Wet is located in northwestern Washington, near the Canadian border. Take Interstate 5 north to exit 270, then turn left onto Birch Bay–Lynden Road. Go four miles to the end of Birch Bay–Lynden Road; the park is on the right.

OPERATING SEASONS AND HOURS

Open weekends from mid-May to mid-June. Open daily from mid-June to Labor Day. Hours: 10:30 A.M. to 7:30 P.M.

ADMISSION FEES

Adults: $7.95. Children ages 3 to 6 and seniors 55 and over: $4.75. Children 2 and under: free.

TRANSPORTATION AND ACCOMMODATIONS WITHIN THE PARK

None.

GUEST SERVICES

Restrooms, telephones, showers, first aid, lost and found, locker rental. Visa and MasterCard accepted.

RIDES

Ramp Slide: shoot down a speedy slide, then plunge into four feet of water.
River Ride: float down this river in an inner tube.

Twister Slides: soar down four twisting slides into a shallow splashdown pool.

KIDDIE RIDES

Kiddie Area: three slides lead to a 20-inch-deep splashdown pool.

RESTAURANTS

None.

SNACK BARS

Concession Stand: fish and chips, ice cream, fries, corn dogs, burgers, hot dogs.
Larry's Dining & Lounge: seafood and beef, pasta, full bar.

CATERING

Not available.

SOUVENIR SHOPS

Clothing, watches, baseball cards, postcards, park mementos, Washington souvenirs.

HINT FOR TRAVELING WITH CHILDREN, ELDERLY, HANDICAPPED

Park rides are not wheelchair accessible.

CANADA

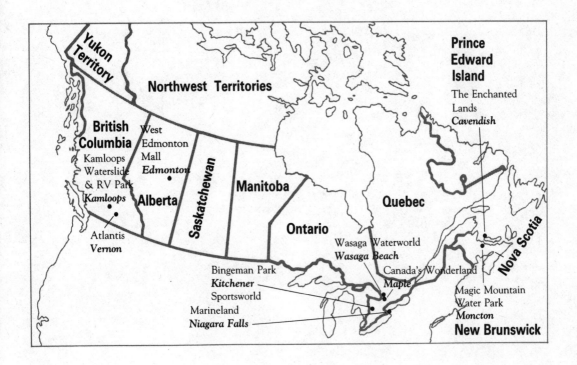

Yukon Territory

Northwest Territories

British Columbia
Kamloops Waterslide & RV Park
Kamloops

Atlantis
Vernon

West Edmonton Mall
Edmonton

Alberta

Saskatchewan

Manitoba

Ontario

Bingeman Park
Kitchener
Sportsworld
Marineland
Niagara Falls

Wasaga Waterworld
Wasaga Beach

Canada's Wonderland
Maple

Quebec

Prince Edward Island
The Enchanted Lands
Cavendish

Nova Scotia

Magic Mountain Water Park
Moncton
New Brunswick

ALBERTA

WEST EDMONTON MALL

West Edmonton Mall, located in the west end of the city of Edmonton, is the world's largest shopping and entertainment complex. In addition to the stores and services, the mall contains five major amusement areas—all indoors! The Fantasyland Amusement Park is the world's largest indoor amusement park; World Waterpark is the world's largest indoor waterpark; Deep Sea Adventure takes you on an underwater world adventure; Pebble Beach Golf Course is an 18-hole miniature golf course; and the Ice Palace is an NHL-sized skating rink where the champion Edmonton Oilers often practice. More than 20 million guests visit West Edmonton Mall every year.

ADDRESS AND TELEPHONE

West Edmonton Mall
#2872, 8770-170 Street
Edmonton, Alberta
Canada T5T 3J7

1-800-661-8890

LOCATION

West Edmonton Mall is located in the west end of the city of Edmonton.

OPERATING SEASONS AND HOURS

Open daily year-round. Hours vary with the season. Check with the park before arrival.

ADMISSION FEES

Fantasyland Theme Park: Adults: $18.95. Children under 46 inches: $15.95. Seniors 65 and over: $7.95.

World Waterpark: Adults: $18.95. Children ages 3 to 10: $15.95. Children 2 and under: free. Seniors 65 and over: $7.95.

Deep Sea Adventure: General: $11.50. Children 2 and under: free.

Pebble Beach Golf Course: General: $7.50.

The Ice Palace: General: $4.25. Children 2 and under: free. Seniors: $2.25.

Prices are in Canadian dollars.

TRANSPORTATION AND ACCOMMODATIONS WITHIN THE PARK

Fantasyland Hotel & Resort: offers 355 rooms, 230 guest rooms, and 125 "themed" rooms. Call for reservations: 1-800-661-6454.

GUEST SERVICES

Restrooms, telephones, first aid, lockers, lost and found, baby strollers, wheelchairs, day care, scooter rentals, free parking, currency exchange, coat check. Private showers, towels, and raft rentals at World Waterpark. Visa, MasterCard, and American Express cards accepted.

RIDES

At Fantasyland:
Autosled: a high-speed, quick-turning ride high above Fantasyland.
Balloon Race: balloon cars move you around on the miniature Ferris wheel.
Carousel: classic pony carousel.
Disco Dynamo: take a high-speed ride on the circular track.
Drop of Doom: 13-story free-fall ride.
Dynatron Ride: a unique experience.
Fantasyland Express: take a train ride around the park.
Flying Galleon: swings riders from side to side.
Harbour Cruisers: paddleboat ride.
Mindbender: this 14-story triple-loop coaster is the largest indoor roller coaster in the world.
Misguided Motor Cars: bumper cars.
Perilous Pendulum: this ship moves riders from side to side, higher and higher, until it completes a full loop, upside down.
Stupendous Orbitron: moves riders around in multiple directions.
Swing of the Century: swing high through the air.

At World Waterpark:
Blue Bullet: the fastest surface of all the slides, blue in color.
Cannonball Run: totally enclosed slide that plunges into 10 feet of water.
Corkscrew: two totally enclosed slides.
Geronimo's Jump: three short slides into deep water from which riders can do flips, dives, and more.
Howler: two slides that twist, turn, and drop through tunnels.
Nessie's Revenge: two side-by-side speed slides.

Raging Rapids Tube Ride: guests ride under six waterfalls in inner tubes.
Sky Screamer: two 85-foot-high water slides.
Twister: two 750-foot-long water slides.
White Lightning: two sled slides.

KIDDIE RIDES

At Fantasyland:
Aerocars: move up and around on this gondola ride.
Bumper Cars: kiddie bumper cars.
Kiddie Bumper Boats: bumper boats on water.
Kiddie Convoy: kids choose their favorite vehicle to ride in.
Motojump: miniature dirt bikes to ride on.
35th Aero Squadron: move up and down and through the air in World War II–style planes.

ATTRACTIONS AND GAMES

At Fantasyland:
The Firing Line: shooting gallery to test your shooting skills.
Aladdin's Amusement Palace: video arcade.
Games of Chance: approximately 30 games of skill and chance are located throughout the park.
Lazer Maze: life-sized walk through video game.
Fantasy World: a maze of stairs, slides, and play areas, just for the little ones.

At World Waterpark:
Blue Thunder: largest indoor wave pool in the world.
Hot Tubs: three of them.
Volleyball/Badminton Court
Kiddie Play Pool: just for the youngest guests with slides and climbing areas.
Lessons: kayaking, swimming, lifesaving.
Ping Pong Tables

Deep Sea Adventure: climb aboard one of four authentic submarines outfitted with complete instrumentation—including sonar equipment, underwater cameras, and TV monitors—and cruise past a replica of the Great Barrier Reef, complete with more than 200 species of exotic fish and marine life.

Santa Maria: see a life-sized re-creation of Christopher Columbus's flagship, handcarved and handpainted.

Bourbon Street: the sultry glitz and glamour of New Orleans is re-created and serves as a backdrop for 10 fine restaurants and spots for late-night fun seekers.

Europa Boulevard: a European-style street with exclusive shopping.

Caesar's Bingo: take a chance with Lady Luck.

Palace Casino: a 9,540-square-foot casino featuring roulette wheels, blackjack, and more.

Pebble Beach Golf Course: this par-46, 18-hole miniature golf course is laden with challenging sand and water traps.

Ice Palace: enjoy a spin on the NHL-sized rink frequently used for practice sessions by the Edmonton Oilers hockey team.

SHOWS

Dolphin Centre: four Atlantic bottlenose dolphins, including Marvy Mallphin the Mascot, do zany tricks.

SPECIAL ANNUAL EVENTS

Edmonton Oilers Hockey Team: team practices and autograph sessions, in the fall.

Safe and Happy Halloween: October 31.

Santa's Arrival: in December.

RESTAURANTS

At World Waterpark:
The Observation Deck
The Tropical Grove

SNACK BARS

There is a food court adjacent to Fantasyland.

CATERING

Contact (403) 444-5300.

SOUVENIR SHOPS

Retail stores throughout the mall sell souvenirs.

PRINCE EDWARD ISLAND

THE ENCHANTED LANDS

The centerpiece of The Enchanted Lands theme park is The Enchanted Castle, which presents children's favorite storybook characters. Visitors view the characters, who include Alice in Wonderland, Cinderella, Pinocchio, and Humpty Dumpty, in 15 animated scenes. Located on two acres on Prince Edward Island, the park's other featured attractions are a life-sized reconstruction of King Tut's Tomb and Treasures, an exceptional 18-hole miniature golf course, which is complete with a waterfall and which has been called the finest in eastern Canada, and a large playground. Annual attendance totals approximately 15,000 visitors.

ADDRESS AND TELEPHONE

The Enchanted Lands
R. R. 2, Hunter River
Cavendish, Prince Edward Island
Canada C0A 1N0

(902) 963-2889 or (902) 963-2431

LOCATION

The Enchanted Lands is located along Highway 6, just west of the intersection of Highway 6 and Highway 13, east of Cavendish.

OPERATING SEASONS AND HOURS

Open from mid-June to Labor Day. Hours: 9 A.M. to 9 P.M.

ADMISSION FEES

Adults: $3.50. Children ages 5 to 15: $2.25. Children under 5: $1.25 (for The Enchanted Castle and King Tut's Tomb: free). Seniors: $3. Families: $11.00. Prices are in Canadian dollars.

TRANSPORTATION AND ACCOMMODATIONS WITHIN THE PARK

None.

GUEST SERVICES

Restrooms, picnic area, wheelchair accessibility. Visa card accepted.

RIDES

None.

ATTRACTIONS AND GAMES

The Enchanted Castle: see your favorite storybook characters in action. Over 50 animated characters are featured in 15 scenes: Alice in Wonderland, Mother Goose, Cinderella, Three Little Pigs, Old Lady in the Shoe, Pinocchio, Little Red Riding Hood, Old MacDonald's Farm, Humpty Dumpty, Wizard of Oz, and more.

King Tut's Tomb & Treasures: visit this life-sized reconstruction of the boy king's tomb, complete in every detail. As you walk through, special effects take you on a magical journey. Through audiovisual programs learn about the tomb's discovery as well as hieroglyphics, pyramid construction, mummification, and other aspects of ancient Egyptian history.

Playground: an area with play equipment and free picnic grounds.

River of Adventure: a beautiful 18-hole miniature golf course.

SHOWS

Three Singing Bears Mayhem Band: singing bears entertain in The Enchanted Castle. Other shows and entertainment are found at The Enchanted Castle and King Tut's Tomb.

RESTAURANTS

None.

SNACK BAR

Refreshments are available.

CATERING

Not available.

SOUVENIR SHOPS

Enchanted Castle Gift Shop: focuses on children's toys, gifts, and clothing. Also has adult clothing, gifts, and Enchanted Castle souvenirs.

King Tut's Tomb & Treasures: offers Egyptian items, handmade high-quality gifts, and park mementos.

NEW BRUNSWICK

MAGIC MOUNTAIN WATER PARK

Located in the hub of Atlantic Canada, Magic Mountain Water Park is a 12-acre family-oriented water theme park. After picking up entry passes at a replica of a Mississippi paddle steamer, the 130,000 annual visitors can choose from a wide assortment of water activities, including the 40-mile-per-hour Kamikaze speed slide and the Lazy River tube ride. Children can play in Puddle Jumper's playground on an array of gentle minislides. The park also includes two 18-hole miniature golf courses.

ADDRESS AND TELEPHONE

Magic Mountain Water Park
P. O. Box 2820
Station "A"
Moncton, New Brunswick
Canada E1C 8T8

(506) 857-9283

LOCATION

Located in Moncton, Magic Mountain Water Park can be reached via the Trans-Canada Highway 2. Exit at Magnetic Hill (exit 388).

OPERATING SEASONS AND HOURS

Open daily from mid-June to Labor Day. Hours: 10 A.M. to 8 P.M. Closing times may vary at the beginning and end of the season, so check with the park upon arrival.

ADMISSION FEES

Full-day pass: Adults: $16. Children ages 4 to 11 and seniors 65 and over: $11.75.
Half-day pass (enter after 3:30 P.M.): Adults: $9.50. Children ages 4 to 11 and seniors 65 and over: $8.
Family pass for four people of any ages: $49.25. (Prices are in Canadian dollars.)

TRANSPORTATION AND ACCOMMODATIONS WITHIN THE PARK

None.

GUEST SERVICES

Restrooms, telephones, information booth, first aid, lost and found, lockers, changing rooms, picnic area. Visa, MasterCard, and American Express cards accepted.

RIDES

Bullet: superfast water speed slide.
Double Trouble: have two times the fun on this giant water slide.
Kamikaze: reach speeds up to 40 miles per hour and feel the sensation of free-falling.
Lazy River: pushed by a gentle current, you float along on an inner tube and circle around the Riverboat.
Loop De Loop: slide and twist on this ride.
The Rapids: shoot down this slide in a water tube.
Twister: twist and turn before landing in a temperature-controlled pool.

KIDDIE RIDES

Puddle Jumpers: a kiddie playground with such minislides as Little Squirt and Topsy Turvy.

ATTRACTIONS AND GAMES

Wave Pool: enjoy a full half-acre of "ocean in motion" complete with surging four-foot waves.
Riverboat: replica of a Mississippi paddle wheeler.
Whirlpool: relax and unwind in this 100-degree spa.
Magic Game Room: over 30 arcade games.
Pier 36: two 18-hole fantasy miniature golf courses.

RESTAURANT

Riverboat Restaurant: chicken, fish, roast beef, sandwiches, hot dogs, burgers, drinks.

SNACK BARS

Snack Bar 1: hot dogs, burgers, fries, pizza, drinks.
Snack Bar 2: ice cream, chips, slush, popcorn, cotton candy, drinks.
Vendors located throughout the park serve hot dogs and ice cream.

CATERING

Contact the Promotion Department at (506) 857-9283.

SOUVENIR SHOPS

La Boutique: Magic Mountain souvenirs, T-shirts, sweatshirts, sunglasses, swimwear, towels.
Beach Hut: park mementos, T-shirts, sweatshirts, towels, sunglasses.

HINT FOR TRAVELING WITH CHILDREN, ELDERLY, HANDICAPPED

Magic Mountain Water Park is wheelchair accessible.

ONTARIO

BINGEMAN PARK

Spread out over 220 acres, Bingeman Park is both a conference center and a water theme park. The water park area features a wave pool, several slides, and a children's play area. The park also offers two miniature golf courses, a driving range, bumper boats, go-carts, an indoor roller skating rink, batting cages, and a large camping area.

ADDRESS AND TELEPHONE

Bingeman Park
1380 Victoria Street North
Kitchener, Ontario
Canada N2B 3E2

(519) 744-1555

LOCATION

Bingeman Park is northeast of Kitchener on Highway 7.

OPERATING SEASONS AND HOURS

The water park is open weekends in May, then daily from June to Labor Day. Hours: 10 A.M. to dusk. (Non-water park activities are open weekdays in May; check with the park for specifics.)

The conference center is open daily year-round.

ADMISSION FEES

All-Day Pass: $16.95. Waterpark Pass: $10.95. All activities are also individually priced. (Prices are in Canadian dollars.)

TRANSPORTATION AND ACCOMMODATIONS WITHIN THE PARK

More than 650 campsites.

GUEST SERVICES

Restrooms, telephones, information booths, first aid, lockers, lost and found. Visa and MasterCard accepted.

RIDES

Bumper Boats: a seaworthy version of bumper cars.
Go-Karts: ride a cart.

Waterslides: try the two speed slides and the two curved flumes.

ATTRACTIONS AND GAMES

Wave Pool: experience four different styles of waves.
Chipper's Playhouse: young children's activity area with net climbs, ball crawls, and more.
Driving Range
Roller Skating: an indoor rink.
Batting Cages
Pitching Games
Miniature Golf: test these two 18-hole minicourses.

SPECIAL ANNUAL EVENT

Oktoberfest: Bavarian dancers, Bavarian foods, games of chance, and games of skill in October.

RESTAURANT

The Berkley Room: smorgasbord featuring meats, chicken, salads, Bavarian specialties.

SNACK BARS

Cream Supreme: ice cream.
Scoops: ice cream.
The Patio: sausage, burgers, beer.

CATERING

Contact Kitchener Caterers at (519) 576-4250.

SOUVENIR SHOP

T-shirts, mugs, sweatshirts, candy, park mementos.

CANADA'S WONDERLAND

Canada's Wonderland is among the biggest and most action-packed theme parks in all of Canada. Set on 370 specially landscaped acres, the park offers eight themed areas including the all new 10-acre SplashWorks water play area with 16 wild water slides, a lazy river, and a children's play area; and two areas just for children, Hanna-Barbera Land and Smurf Forest. The park features eight roller coasters as well as several restaurants, boutiques, and games. Visitors can also choose among many live entertainment concerts and shows, including a spectacular multimedia laser show and a variety of special musical performances.

ADDRESS AND TELEPHONE

Canada's Wonderland
9580 Jane Street
P. O. Box 624
Maple, Ontario
Canada L6A 1S6

(416) 832-2205

LOCATION

The park is located just outside Toronto, immediately off Highway 400 about 10 miles north of Highway 401. Take the Rutherford Road exit if heading north; exit on Major MacKenzie Drive if coming south. The park can also be reached by mass transit. Take the Wonderland Express "Go" Bus from Yorkdale or York Mills Subway Station.

OPERATING SEASONS AND HOURS

Open selected weekends in September and early October. Hours: 10 A.M. to 8 P.M. Open daily from the end of May to Labor Day. Opens at 10 A.M. Closing times vary, so check with the park upon arrival.

ADMISSION FEES

Adults: $23.95. Children ages 3 to 6: $11.95. Children 2 and under: free. Seniors 60 and over: $11.95. (Prices are in Canadian dollars.)

TRANSPORTATION AND ACCOMMODATIONS WITHIN THE PARK

None.

GUEST SERVICES

Restrooms, telephones, first aid, lost and found, locker rental, stroller rental, wheelchairs. Visa, MasterCard, and American Express cards accepted.

RIDES

The Bat: Ontario's first and only backward-looping coaster.
Bayern Curve: speed down this exhilarating bobsled run.
Carousel: a beauty for one and all.
Dragon Fyre: hold on to your hat for this double-loop, double-helix coaster.
Great Whale of China: feel the sensation of bumpy waves.
Jet Scream: hang suspended, then free-fall from a 10-story height.
Klockwerks: take the spin of your life.
Krachenwagen: bump your buddies.
The Mighty Canadian Minebuster: challenge the biggest, fastest, longest coaster in Canada.
Quixote's Kettles: twist and turn in picaresque fashion.
Racing Rivers: experience Pharaoh's Falls and the Watersnake on these four water slides.
Shiva's Fury: twirl up and around on this eight-armed ride.
Sky Rider: Canada's only stand-up looping roller coaster.
Sol Loco: rise up in the air and spin around.
SplashWorks: a water play area with 16 wild water slides, a lazy river, and a children's play area.

Swing of the Century: soar up and around in your own swing.
Thunder Run: take an adventurous ride through Wonder Mountain.
Timberwolf Falls: plunge over a waterfall that's five stories high.
Viking's Rage: soar in an 80-feet arc over a bay.
Vortex: Canada's only suspended roller coaster.
White Water Canyon: the park's wettest and wildest water raft ride.
Wilde Beast: a fast, looping wooden coaster.
Wilde Knight Mares: a turning, spinning adventure.
Zumba Flume: ride a log down a rush of water.

KIDDIE RIDES

Aerofield: little planes.
Balloon Race: miniature hot air balloons.
Bedrock Dock: remote-control boats.
Boulder Bumpers: little cars bump away.
Flintstone Flyboys: prehistoric pterodactyls fly around.
Ghoster Coaster: coaster fun for the family.
Hanna-Barberry-Go-Round: tiny tyke merry-go-round.
Happy Landing: a swan ride.
Hot Rock Raceway: little roadsters race.
Lazy's Snail Trail: happy snails to sit in.
Scooby Choo: all aboard these train cars.
Scoobyville Rocketport: mini rocket ships for kids.
Wonder Tour: a drive in old-fashioned cars.

ATTRACTIONS AND GAMES

Crystal Palace Arcade: favorite video games.
Live Cartoon Characters: Hanna-Barbera characters meet and greet visitors.
Street Entertainers: jugglers, storytellers, and strolling minstrels perform for visitors all day long.
Games of Skill: located throughout the park. Special games for small children are also featured.

SHOWS

Various shows and concerts are performed throughout the season. Check with the park for its performance schedule and show times.

SPECIAL ANNUAL EVENTS

Italian Celebrations: entertainment direct from Italy, authentic cuisine, contests, and more. In May and September.
Fireworks: throughout the season. Check the park for schedules.
Sports Heroes Days: autograph sessions with favorite hockey, football, and baseball stars. Check the park for schedules.

RESTAURANTS

Oriental Gardens: chicken and steak teriyaki.
All's Well Hall: ribs, burgers, chicken nuggets, fries.
Pasta House: lasagna, pastas, Caesar salads.

SNACK BARS

Dutch Treats: chicken nuggets, fish and chips, foot-long corn dogs.
Taco Stand
Fried Veggies
Sundae Stand
Chicken Werks: chicken fingers, fries.
Hot Dog Stand: foot-long hot dogs, caramel corn.
Ye Savoury Faire: burgers, fries.
Friar's Sundaes: waffle cones.
Corn Dogs
The Cooler Bar: fruit drinks.
Cookie Cafe: pastries, ice cream cookie sandwiches, donuts, milk, coffee.
Eis Haus: ice cream cones.
Barney's Burgers
Pebbles' Hot Dogs
Scrappy Doo's Chicken Fingers
Clumsey's: Smurfy blue ice cream.
Dandy Candy Stand: cotton candy.
Scooby's Ice Cream
Alphorn: funnel cakes.

La Tasca: chicken wings, deli sandwiches, nachos, pastries.
La Cantina: burritos, burgers, salads.
Ristorante: pizza, salad.
Popcorn Stand

CATERING

Contact Group Sales at (416) 832-7000, ext. 392.

SOUVENIR SHOPS

International Bazaar: clothing, jewelry, and more.
Ali Poof: themed photos.
Super Star Video Studio: record your own music video.
Capture Vision T-Shirts
The Marketplace: sweets and treats.
The Belfry: souvenirs of the Bat roller coaster ride.
Startyme Photo: souvenir snapshots.
Wood Cutter: custom-cut key rings and letters.
Canyon Trading Company: souvenirs, sweatshirts, towels.
Der Huten Hut: hats, souvenirs, film.
Toy Store: Hanna-Barbera merchandise.
The Hotel: kid's clothing and park memorabilia.
Shaggy's Snap Shot Stand: snap your photo with favorite cartoon characters.
Geschenke: fashionwear, jewelry, giftware, crystal, film.
Legetoj: kids' clothing, toys.
M & M's Candy Factory: candy, fudge.
El Rastro: sports items, NFL wear, tobacco, film.
Something en Sombreros: hats
La Casa del Regalo: park memorabilia, novelty items.
Camice: sweatshirts, T-shirts, hats.
The Painted Shirt: airbrush-painted T-shirts.
Main Gate Souvenir Shop: park souvenirs, film, and more.
International Keychain Photo: your photo on a keychain, mug, or mirror.

HINTS FOR TRAVELING WITH CHILDREN, ELDERLY, HANDICAPPED

Facilities are available for nursing mothers at first-aid and mothers' nursing station. A limited number of strollers are available. A detailed guide of accessibility for physically challenged guests is available at the front gate guest services. Handicapped parking is provided near the front gate; vehicles must have appropriate licenses or placards.

MARINELAND

Next to Niagara Falls, Marineland is considered one of Niagara's most popular attractions. The park combines marine life shows and animal areas with a variety of rides, entertainment, and eateries. Visitor favorites include the marine show, featuring killer whales, dolphins, and sea lions, and wildlife displays where guests can pet and feed deer, and see buffaloes and other wildlife. Among the newest park rides are Space Avenger, where visitors command their own spaceships, and Sky Hawk, where guests ride 112 feet skyward for a spectacular park view.

ADDRESS AND TELEPHONE

Marineland
7657 Portage Road
Niagara Falls, Ontario
Canada L2E 6X8

(416) 356-9565

LOCATION

From QEW southbound, take McLeod Road exit and follow McLeod Road east to Marineland. From QEW northbound, take McLeod Road east to the park.

OPERATING SEASONS AND HOURS

Open daily except Christmas Day, Boxing Day, New Year's Day, and Fridays in winter. Hours: 10 A.M. to 6 P.M. except 9 A.M. to 6 P.M. in the summer. Hours may vary seasonally, so check with the park before arriving.

ADMISSION FEES

Adults: $18.95. Children ages 4 to 9 and seniors 60 and over: $15.95. Children 3 and under: free. Prices are in Canadian dollars.
   Admission fees may vary slightly with the season, so check with the park upon arrival.

TRANSPORTATION AND ACCOMMODATIONS WITHIN THE PARK

None.

GUEST SERVICES

Restrooms, telephones, first aid, lost and found, locker rental, stroller and wheelchair rental.

RIDES

Dragon Mountain: reach maximum speeds of 50 miles per hour on this 5,500-foot-long steel coaster that spreads over 30 acres of land and includes 1,000 feet of tunnels.
Flying Dragon: swing in this thrill ride.
Hurricane Cove: experience high-speed fun.
Sky Hawk: climb a tower 112 feet to the top while experiencing a floating sensation.
Space Avenger: you're in command of your own spaceship as you soar, dive, and turn.
Wave Swinger: spin in the air.

KIDDIE RIDES

Tivoli Coaster: pint-sized.
Tivoli Ferris Wheel: a kid-tickling favorite.
Viking Boat Carousel: Viking boats that ride in a circle are fun for the whole family.

ATTRACTIONS

Fish Feeding Lake: feed the fish.
Buffalo Herd: a display of more than 100 bison.
Deer Park: more than 500 deer to pet and feed.
Bear Country: more than 70 black bears to watch and feed.
Bird Exhibits: display of exotic birds.
Elk Herd

SHOWS

King Waldorf's Show: a full-scale marine show featuring killer whales, dolphins, and sea lions.
Aquarium Theatre Show: a marine multispecies show with harbor seals as the main attraction.

RESTAURANTS

Hungry Lion: hot dogs, burgers, salads, desserts, drinks.
Hungry Bear: burgers, hot dogs, chicken dinners, desserts, drinks.

SNACK BARS

Hungry Squirrel: popcorn, peanuts, soft drinks.
Wagons located throughout the park serve ice cream, popcorn, hot dogs, soft drinks.

CATERING

Contact Suzanne Boutin-Irwin at (416) 356-2142.

SOUVENIR SHOPS

Whale Shop: souvenirs, gifts, seashells, Canadian products.
Dolphin Shop: Marineland and Canadian-crafted gifts and mementos.

Sea Lion Shop: souvenirs, gifts.

HINT FOR TRAVELING WITH CHILDREN, ELDERLY, HANDICAPPED

There is a special area for disabled guests to view the marine show. Check with attendants.

SPORTSWORLD

Sportsworld offers 30 acres of sports-oriented attractions in one theme park. It includes a water park featuring the Kamikaze five-flume water slide and giant wave pool, two 18-hole miniature golf courses, bumper cars and boats, a go-cart track, large indoor driving range, and baseball batting cages.

ADDRESS AND TELEPHONE

Sportsworld
100 Sportsworld Drive
Kitchener, Ontario
Canada N2G 3W6

(519) 653-4442

LOCATION

About 60 miles west of Toronto, Sportsworld is in Kitchener at the junction of highways 8 and 401, across from Lulu's Roadhouse.

OPERATING SEASONS AND HOURS

Open daily year-round. Hours: 10 A.M. to 10 P.M. Outdoor activities, such as the water park, are open from June through September only. The water park closes at dusk.

ADMISSION FEES

Admission to the grounds is free. All activities are on a pay-as-you-play basis.

TRANSPORTATION AND ACCOMMODATIONS WITHIN THE PARK

None.

GUEST SERVICES

Restrooms, telephones, information booth, diaper-changing stations (in most restrooms), first aid, lockers, picnic facilities, Royal Bank cash counter, free parking.

RIDES

Big Dipper: shoot down this speedy dry slide in a sack.
Bumper Boats: splashing, bumping fun.
Bumper Cars: landlubber's version of the above.
Go-Karts: this ¾-mile course is complete with an overpass and underpass, and the new go-carts are faster and more powerful than ever.
Kamikaze: soar down a five-flume water slide.
Old Mill Tube Slide: a delightful slide down and then a plunge into water.
Train: journey on this scaled-down train.

KIDDIE RIDE

Kiddie Cars: kids "drive" their own Model Ts.

ATTRACTIONS AND GAMES

Wave Pool: ride the waves.
Kiddie Play Pool: a low-level pool where kids can romp.
Video Arcade: more than 100 video, pinball, and redemption games.
Golf Dome: reported to be North America's largest indoor driving range; it's seven stories high and 350 feet deep.
Indoor Baseball Batting Cages: watch your ball travel as far as 300 feet.
The Old Mill: a miniature golf course with re-creations of barn raising and

plowsharing, and a small-scale replica of a hydropower project.
The Covered Bridge: a miniature golf course featuring a replica of Ontario's last remaining covered bridge.
Cruise Nights: a display of pre-1969 cars every Wednesday night from 6 to 10 P.M. May through September only.

SHOWS

Super Saturdays: free live entertainment every Saturday from May through September.

RESTAURANTS

Rafters: traditional Waterloo County fare, featuring ribs, schnitzels, pig tail.
Rafter's Patio: nachos, chicken fingers, chicken wings, salads.
Rafters II: hot dogs, burgers, fries, overlooking the wave pool.

SNACK BARS

Ice Cream Shoppe
Vending machines available.

CATERING

Contact (519) 653-4442.

SOUVENIR SHOPS

Candy, park mementos, apparel.

WASAGA WATERWORLD

Wasaga Waterworld is a 12-acre water theme park with activities and rides for the entire family. Approximately 50,000 guests each year visit the park to splash in the large, heated wave pool, experience the speed thrills of water slides, and relax in the thermal whirlpool. There is also Kiddie Waterworld, a playland with its own activity pool for kids. The park is equipped with lights for operation after dark.

ADDRESS AND TELEPHONE

Wasaga Waterworld
P. O. Box 230
Wasaga Beach, Ontario
Canada L0L 2P0

(705) 429-4400

LOCATION

Wasaga Waterworld is located in Wasaga Beach on Highway 92.

OPERATING SEASONS AND HOURS

Open daily from the end of June to Labor Day. Hours: 10 A.M. to 11 P.M. from the end of June to mid-August and 10 A.M. to 7 P.M. from mid-August to Labor Day.

ADMISSION FEES

Adults: $9.50. Children ages 4 to 12: $7.50. Children 3 and under: free. Prices are in Canadian dollars.

TRANSPORTATION AND ACCOMMODATIONS WITHIN THE PARK

None.

GUEST SERVICES

Restrooms, telephones, changing rooms, first aid, lockers, lost and found. Visa and MasterCard accepted.

RIDES

Paddleboats: take a wet and bouncy ride on these paddle crafts.
Speed Slides: take up the racing challenge on twin speed slides.
Water Slides: bank the curve of huge water slides.

ATTRACTIONS AND GAMES

Giant Wave Pool: imagine the thrill of riding the big surf in Malibu in this giant, heated wave pool.
Kiddie Waterworld: a playland for young children featuring a separate kiddie wading pool and fun activities.
Thermal Whirlpool: treat your body to a relaxing massage.
Video Arcade

RESTAURANTS

None.

SNACK BAR

Snidely's: burgers, hot dogs, fries, onion rings, ice cream, soft drinks.

CATERING

Not available.

SOUVENIR SHOP

Spanky's Emporium: park souvenirs, toys, swimwear, shirts, hats.

BRITISH COLUMBIA

ATLANTIS

Taking in the spectacular view of Swan Lake is one of the most thrilling activities at Atlantis, a water theme park located in British Columbia, Canada. The 10-acre park also offers a variety of water slides, including Double Trouble with its 360-degree turns and The River Riot, a white water rafting ride. For children there's Puddle Jumpers Playground with novice runs, ramp slides, and kiddie play area.

ADDRESS AND TELEPHONE

Atlantis
R. R. #5, Site 15, Comp. 4
Vernon, British Columbia
Canada V1T 6L8

(604) 549-4121

LOCATION

Atlantis is located three miles north of Vernon on Highway 97.

OPERATING SEASONS AND HOURS

Open daily from mid-June to early September. Opens at 10 A.M. Closing times vary, so check with the park upon arrival.

ADMISSION FEES

Check with the park.

TRANSPORTATION AND ACCOMMODATIONS WITHIN THE PARK

None.

GUEST SERVICES

Restrooms, information booth, first aid, picnic area. Visa and MasterCard accepted.

RIDES

Double Trouble: twist your way through double 360-degree turns to the landing pools.

The River Riot: tube your way down 300 feet of foaming, turbulent water.

Zoom Flumes: get ready to soar on six slides that combine tunnels and turns.

KIDDIE RIDES

Kiddie Flumes: a special treat for tots.
Bouncing Bobbers: kids slide down into lots of balls.

ATTRACTIONS AND GAMES

Puddle Jumpers Playground: novice runs, ramp slides, and kiddie play area.
Hot Tub: take in the view of Swan Lake and the Okanagan Valley while you enjoy a relaxing soak.
Miniature Golf
Volleyball
Horseshoe Pit
Video Arcade

RESTAURANTS

None.

SNACK BARS

Concession: burgers, hot dogs, chicken, fish, subs.
Ice Cream Parlor

CATERING

Not available.

SOUVENIR SHOP

Summer sportswear, park souvenirs, candy, film.

KAMLOOPS WATERSLIDE & RV PARK

Kamloops Waterslide & RV Park, a self-described "oasis in the desert," is located between Calgary and Vancouver, next to Kamloops Wildlife Park, in the British Columbia interior. Its feature attraction is its 2,000-plus feet of adult water slides punctuated by dips, curves, and speedy straightaways. For visitors who desire a calmer vacation break there are hot tubs and a complete 18-hole miniature golf course. The highly rated adjacent RV park offers 85 sites with full hookups.

ADDRESS AND TELEPHONE

Kamloops Waterslide & RV Park
R. R. #2, Site 17, Comp. 7
Kamloops, British Columbia
Canada V2C 2J3

(604) 573-3789 or (604) 573-4242 off-season

LOCATION

Kamloops is located along the Trans-Canada Highway between Calgary and Vancouver, next to Kamloops Wildlife Park.

OPERATING SEASONS AND HOURS

Kamloops Waterslide is open weekends from mid-May to mid-June. Open daily from mid-June to Labor Day. Opens at 10 A.M. Closing times vary, so check with the park upon arrival.
    The RV park is open from April to October.

ADMISSION FEES

Adults: $10.25. Children ages 4 to 6 and seniors: $7. Children 3 and under: free. Prices are in Canadian dollars.

TRANSPORTATION AND ACCOMMODATIONS WITHIN THE PARK

RV Park: full hookups, hot showers, laundromat, barbecue pits, bus service to town, pay phones, sanitation dump, convenience store, fruit stand, children's playground, 10 percent discount at Kamloops Waterslide Park.

GUEST SERVICES

Restrooms, telephones, first aid, lockers, wheelchairs. Visa and MasterCard accepted.

RIDES

Speed Slides: two straightaway fast slides.
Twisters: an action-packed ride that loops, twists, and turns.

KIDDIE RIDES

Kiddie Waterslides: two pint-sized slides for youngsters.

ATTRACTIONS AND GAMES

Wading Pool: for tots and their parents.
Picnic Area

Video Arcade
Miniature Golf
Horseshoe Pit
Volleyball Court

RESTAURANTS

None.

SNACK BARS

Concessions stands located throughout the park sell hot dogs, candy, ice cream, chips, sandwiches, soft drinks.

CATERING

Not available.

SOUVENIR SHOP

T-shirts, hats, magazines, sweatshirts, Kamloops mementos.

SPECIAL-INTEREST GUIDES

ROLLER COASTER RECORDS

Tallest Roller Coaster from the Ground Up: "Magnum XL-200" at Cedar Point, Sandusky, OH. It is a steel roller coaster that is 205 feet tall.

Tallest Wooden Roller Coaster: "The Mean Streak" at Cedar Point, Sandusky, OH. It is 161 feet 11.8 inches tall.

Tallest Looping Roller Coaster: "The Viper" at Six Flags Magic Mountain, Valencia, CA. It is 188 feet tall.

Tallest Indoor Roller Coaster: "The Mind Bender" at Fantasyland in the West Edmonton Mall, Edmonton, AB, Canada. It is 136 feet 2 inches tall.

Longest Roller Coaster: "The Beast" at Kings Island, Kings Island, OH. It is a wooden roller coaster that is 7,400 feet long.

Fastest Roller Coaster: "Steel Phantom" at Kennywood Park, West Mifflin, PA. It is a steel roller coaster that travels at more than 80 miles per hour.

Longest Drop on a Roller Coaster: "Steel Phantom" at Kennywood Park, West Mifflin, PA. It is a steel roller coaster with a drop of 225 feet.

Steepest-Angled Drop on a Roller Coaster: two-way tie: "Magnum XL-200" at Cedar Point, Sandusky, OH, and "Excalibur" at Valleyfair!, Shakopee, MN. Both have a 60-degree-angle drop.

Roller Coaster That Turns Riders Upside Down the Greatest Number of Times: three-way tie: "Shock Wave" in Six Flags Great America, Gurnee, IL, "Great American Scream Machine" at Six Flags Great Adventure, Jackson NJ, and "The Viper" at Six Flags Magic Mountain, Valencia, CA. They all turn riders upside down seven times.

(All statistics are for North America.) Information courtesy of *American Coaster Enthusiasts*.

WONDERFUL WATER PARKS

Largest Wave Pool: "Typhoon Lagoon" at Walt Disney World, Lake Buena Vista, FL. It covers 2½ acres.

Longest Elevated Water Slide: "Pepsi Aquablast" at Dorney Park and Wildwater Kingdom, Allentown, PA. It is 70 feet long and 66 feet high.

Longest Inner Tube Ride: "Cliffhanger Tube Chute" at Schlitterbahn, New Braunfels, TX. It is 1.5 miles long.

State with the Most Waterparks: Ohio.

Information courtesy of *World Waterpark Association*.

LARGEST PARKS*

Busch Gardens, The Old Country, Williamsburg, VA	360 acres
Canada's Wonderland, Maple, ON, Canada	370 acres
Cedar Point, Sandusky, OH	364 acres
Idlewild Park, Ligonier, PA	410 acres
Lion Country Safari, West Palm Beach, FL	500 acres
Point Mallard Park, Decatur, AL	750 acres
Six Flags Great Adventure, Jackson, NJ	2,000 acres
Universal Studios Florida, Orlando, FL	444 acres
Universal Studios Hollywood, Universal City, CA	420 acres
Waimea Falls Park, Haleiwa, HI	1,800 acres
Walt Disney World, Lake Buena Vista, FL	28,000 acres
Wildlife Safari, Winston, OR	600 acres

*Over 350 acres.

TYPES OF THEME PARKS

Multitheme Parks
Action Park, Vernon, NJ
Adventureland Park, Des Moines, IA
AstroWorld, Houston, TX
Bingeman Park, Kitchener, ON, Canada
Canada's Wonderland, Maple, ON, Canada
Canobie Lake Park, Salem, NH
Carowinds, Charlotte, NC
Cedar Point, Sandusky, OH
Clark's Trading Post, Lincoln, NH
Darien Lake Theme Park, Darien Center, NY
Disneyland, Anaheim, CA
Dorney Park, Allentown, PA
Dutch Wonderland, East Lancaster, PA

Elitch Gardens, Denver, CO
Fantasy Island Theme Park, Grand Island, NY
Geauga Lake, Aurora, OH
Great America, Santa Clara, CA
The Great Escape, Lake George, NY
Hersheypark, Hershey, PA
Idlewild Park, Ligonier, PA
Kennywood Park, West Mifflin, PA
Kings Dominion, Doswell, Va
Kings Island, Kings Island, OH
Knott's Berry Farm, Buena Park, CA
Lagoon Amusement Park, Farmington, UT
Miracle Strip Amusement Park, Panama City, FL
Ocean Breeze Fun Park, Virginia Beach, VA
Seabreeze Amusement Park, Rochester, NY
Six Flags Great Adventure, Jackson, NJ
Six Flags Great America, Gurnee, IL
Six Flags Magic Mountain, Valencia, CA
Six Flags Over Georgia, Atlanta, GA
Six Flags Over Mid-America, Eureka, MO
Six Flags Over Texas, Arlington, TX
Valleyfair! Family Amusement Park, Shakopee, MN
Walt Disney World, Lake Buena Vista, FL
Weeki Wachee Spring, Brooksville, FL
West Edmonton Mall, Edmonton, AB, Canada
Worlds of Fun, Kansas City, MO

Water Theme Parks
Adventure Island, Tampa, FL
Atlantis, Vernon, BC, Canada
Attitash Alpine Slide & Waterslides, Bartlett, NH
The Beach Waterpark, Mason, OH
Big Sky Waterslide, Columbia Falls, MT
Big Splash Water Park, Tulsa, OK
Emerald Pointe, Greensboro, NC
Family Land, Wisconsin Dells, WI
Island of Big Surf, Tempe, AZ
Kamloops Waterslide, Kamloops, BC, Canada
Magic Mountain Water Park, Moncton, NB, Canada
Oakwood Lake Resort, Manteca, CA
Oasis Waterpark, Palm Springs, CA
Point Mallard Park, Decatur, AL
Raging Waters, San Dimas, CA
Schlitterbahn, New Braunfels, TX
Sengme Oaks Water Park, Valley Center, CA
Shawnee Place Play & Water Park, Shawnee on Delaware, PA

Splash-Down, Spokane, WA
Wasaga Waterworld, Wasaga Beach, ON, Canada
Water Country USA, Williamsburg, VA
Water Mania, Kissimmee, FL
Water World, Dothan, AL
Water Town USA, Shreveport, LA
Wet 'n Wild, Las Vegas, NV
Wet'n Wild, Garland, TX
Wet'n Wild, Orlando, FL
Whale's Tale Water Park, Lincoln, NH
White Water, Marietta, GA
Wild 'N Wet Water Park, Blaine, WA
Wild River Country, North Little Rock, AR
Wild Rivers Water Park, Laguna Hills, CA
Wild Waters, Boise, ID
Wild Waters, Coeur d'Alene, ID
Windsor Waterworks & Slides, Windsor,CA

Water Theme Parks Within Larger Parks
Barracuda Bay at Darien Lake Theme Park, Darien Center, NY
Boardwalk Shores at Geauga Lake, Aurora, OH
Buccaneer Bay at Weeki Wachee Spring, Brooksville, FL
H₂OHHH Zone at Idlewild Park, Ligonier, PA
Lagoon A Beach at Lagoon Amusement Park, Farmington, UT
Oceans of Fun at Worlds of Fun, Kansas City, MO
Racing Rapids Action Park at The Three Worlds of Santa's Village, Dundee, IL
Raging Rivers at Seabreeze Amusement Park, Rochester, NY
Riptide Reef at Carowinds, Charlotte, NC
Shipwreck Island at Miracle Strip, Panama City, FL
Soak City at Cedar Point, Sandusky, OH
Typhoon Lagoon at Walt Disney World, Lake Buena Vista, FL
Water Works at Kings Island, Kings Island, OH
Wild Water Rapids at Ocean Breeze Fun Park, Virginia Beach, VA
Wild Waters at Silver Springs, Silver Springs, FL
Wildwater Kingdom at Dorney Park, Allentown, PA

Holiday/Santa Theme Parks
Holiday World, Santa Claus, IN

Santa's Land, Cherokee, NC
Santa's Village, Jefferson, NH
The Three Worlds of Santa's Village,
    Dundee, IL

Imaginary Characters Theme Parks
(Animated/Cartoon/Storybook)
Children's Fairyland, Oakland, CA
Deer Acres Fantasy Park, Pinconning, MI
Dogpatch USA, Dogpatch, AR
The Enchanted Lands, Cavendish, PEI
Pixie Woods, Stockton, CA
Sesame Place, Langhorne, PA
Story Land, Glen, NH
    Many parks have themed sections featuring
imaginary characters as well.

Movies Theme Parks
MGM Studios Theme Park at Walt Disney
    World, Lake Buena Vista, FL
Old Tucson Studios, Tucson, AZ
Universal Studios Florida, Orlando, FL
Universal Studios Hollywood, Universal
    City, CA

Musical Theme Park
Dollywood, Pigeon Forge, TN
Opryland, Nashville, TN

Marine Life Theme Parks
Marineland, Marineland, FL
Marineland, Niagara Falls, ON, Canada
Sea Life Park Hawaii, Waimanalo, HI
Sea World of Florida, Orlando, FL
Sea World of Ohio, Aurora, OH
Sea World of San Diego, San Diego, CA
Sea World of Texas, San Antonio, TX

Historic-Theme Parks
Alaskaland Pioneer Theme Park, Fairbanks,
    AK
Busch Gardens, The Old Country,
    Williamsburg, VA
Libertyland, Memphis, TN
Silver Dollar City, Branson, MO

Western-Theme Parks
Frontier City, Oklahoma City, OK
Frontier Western Theme Park, Berlin, MD
Ghost Town in the Sky, Maggie Valley, NC
Ponderosa Ranch, Incline Village, NV
Rawhide, Scottsdale, AZ
Tweetsie Railroad, Blowing Rock, NC

Animal/Safari/Jungle Theme Parks
Busch Gardens, Tampa, Tampa, FL
Deer Forest, Coloma, MI
Jungle Larry's Zoological Park, Naples, FL
Lion Country Safari, West Palm Beach, FL
Marine World Africa USA, Vallejo, CA
Silver Springs, Silver Springs, FL
Wildlife Safari, Winston, OR

Nature Theme Parks
Aquarena Springs, San Marcos, TX
Waimea Falls Park, Haleiwa, HI

Sports Theme Park
Sportsworld, Kitchener, ON, Canada

ANTIQUE WOODEN CAROUSELS

Authentic antique wooden carousels can be
found at the following parks in this book. (The
date indicates the year the carousel was built.)
Astroworld, Houston, Texas (1895)
Busch Gardens, The Old Country,
    Williamsburg, Virginia (1919)
Canada's Wonderland, Maple, Ontario,
    Canada (1928)
Canobie Lake Park, Salem, New Hampshire
    (1903)
Carowinds, Charlotte, North Carolina
    (1923)
Cedar Point, Sandusky, Ohio (five: 1905,
    1953, 1925, 1912, 1921)
Disneyland, Anaheim, California (date
    unknown)
Dollywood, Pigeon Forge, Tennessee (1924)
Dorney Park, Allentown, Pennsylvania
    (1901)
Elitch Gardens, Denver, Colorado (1920–28)
Geauga Lake, Aurora, Ohio (two: 1918, year
    unknown)
Great America, Santa Clara, California
    (1918)
Hersheypark, Hershey, Pennsylvania (1919)
Idlewild Park, Ligonier, Pennsylvania (1931)
Kennywood Park, West Mifflin,
    Pennsylvania (1926)
Kings Dominion, Doswell, Virginia (1917)
Kings Island, Kings Island, Ohio (1926)
Knott's Berry Farm, Buena Park, California
    (two: 1902, 1860)
Lagoon Amusement Park, Farmington, Utah
    (1900)

Libertyland, Memphis, Tennessee (1909)

Seabreeze Amusement Park, Rochester, New York (1915)

Silver Dollar City, Branson, Missouri (1984)

Six Flags Great Adventure, Jackson, New Jersey (1881–90)

Six Flags Great America, Gurnee, Illinois (1920–22)

Six Flags Magic Mountain, Valencia, California (1912)

Six Flags Over Georgia, Atlanta, Georgia (1908)

Six Flags Over Mid-America, Eureka, Missouri (1915)

Six Flags Over Texas, Arlington, Texas (1926)

Storyland, Glen, New Hampshire (1900)

Valleyfair! Family Amusement Park, Shakopee, Minnesota (1925)

Walt Disney World, Lake Buena Vista, Florida (1917)

Information courtesy of the *National Carousel Association.*

INDEX

Join AAA today and let our travel professionals take the complications out of vacations.

We can help you with:

- Complete travel agency services, including expert travel planning and all travel reservations
- Passport photos and International Driving Permits
- Fee-free American Express® Travelers Cheques
- Discounts on Avis and Hertz car rentals
- Hotel reservations
- Rail tickets
- Individual and escorted tours

- Travel insurance
- Tour Operator Default Protection Plan
- TripAssist, including 24-hour emergency access to legal, medical, and travel-related services worldwide
- AND Emergency Road Service abroad — AAA maintains reciprocal agreements with auto clubs in 20 countries on five continents around the world

To join AAA today just call
1-800-336-4357

☐ **YES!** I want to learn how a Triple-A membership can take the complications out of vacations. Please send me FREE information at no obligation.

NAME _____

ADDRESS _____

_____

CITY _____ STATE _____ ZIP _____

PHONE _____
(Membership is available only to residents of the USA and Canada.)   TP-91

Discover the benefits of membership BEFORE you take your next trip.

Complete the postage-paid reply card TODAY.